Child Care and Education

Penny Tassoni

Heinemann

Heinemann Educational Publishers,
Halley Court, Jordan Hill, Oxford OX2 8EJ
A division of Reed Educational & Professional Publishing Ltd

Heinemann is a registered trademark of Reed Educational & Professional Publishing Limited

OXFORD   MELBOURNE   AUCKLAND
JOHANNESBURG   BLANTYRE   GABORONE
IBADAN   PORTSMOUTH NH (USA)   CHICAGO

First published 1998
2002 2001 2000 99 98
10 9 8 7 6 5 4 3 2 1

A catalogue record for this book is available from the British Library on request.

ISBN 0 435 40153 X

Pages designed by Artistix

Cover photograph by Gareth Bodum

Cover design by Sarah Garbett

Typeset and illustrated by 𝍂 Tek-Art, Croydon, Surrey

Printed and bound in Great Britain by The Bath Press, Bath

Acknowledgements

I would like to thank all my colleagues in the Health and Social Care Department at Bexhill College for their support this year, especially Harriet Eldridge for her help with Chapters 3, 6 and 13; Elizabeth Etherton and Karen Hucker for their help with the chapter on food and nutrition and Linda Johnson for finding time to look at Chapter 9.

I am also grateful to the managers of these nurseries for answering my queries and allowing me to reproduce items in the book: Jean Tindall, Maplehurst Nursery; Alison Lawrence, Claverham Day Nursery; Elaine Piper, The Gables Nursery; and Janet Hopkins, Beaky's Nursery.

I would also like to thank Sarah Allen for her help with Chapter 1; Christine Banks, Training Officer for Hastings and Ruther NHS Trust for cheerfully going through Chapter 3; Peter Edmonds for updating my information for Chapter 12; Meg Marshall, CACHE Co-ordinator at West Kent college and External Verifier for CACHE for giving me valuable feedback on Chapter 2.

Particular thanks are due to Gill Hesletine, Chantry Infant School, Bexhill for her moral support and ability to kick start my sometimes fuddled brain!

A huge thank you must also go to Mary James, my commissioning editor, who not only talked me into this project, but thankfully has guided me through it with abundant cheerfulness and patience.

Finally I must apologise to all my friends and family members who have been neglected by me during the writing of this book.

Picture Acknowledgements

The author and publishers are grateful to the following for permission to reproduce photographs and other material:
British Standards Institute
Bubbles Photo Library/Jennie Woodcock
Bubbles Photo Library/Peter Sylent
Bubbles/Ian West
Bubbles/Loisjoy Thurston
Trevor Clifford
Collections/Anthea Sieveking
Collections/Sandra Lousada
Haddon Davies
Sally & Richard Greenhill
KIDSCAPE
Mckenzie Heritage Picture Archive/Embeke Waseme
Mckenzie Heritage Picture Archive/Jeni Mckenzie
The British Toy and Hobby Association
Tony Stone Images

Dedication

This book could not have been written without the support of the 'Tassoni team' – Jean-Michel, Anne-Marie, Marie-Lise and Jess the cat – and so it is dedicated to them.

Contents

Equality of Opportunity

The phrase 'equality of opportunity' is widely used, but what does it really mean? Perhaps equality of opportunity is more about fairness than anything else. It is about making sure that everyone has a fair and equal chance in life. Children begin to learn about values from the moment they are born. It is therefore very important for this 'fairness' to start in early years settings. It is here where children need to feel valued and learn to respect one another. The promotion of equal opportunities is therefore the responsibility of every adult who works with children.

This chapter looks at some of the issues involved with equal opportunities. It also looks at the ways in which early years workers can promote equal opportunities.

Attitudes and values

Building relationships with children and others – for example, parents and co-workers – in the workplace is an essential part of an early years worker's role. Good relationships are based on trust and respect. Although this is easy to say or write, it can often be hard to respect those who do not share your values. It is important, therefore, to look first at our own values and attitudes.

We are not born with a set of values and attitudes, but start to develop them when we are children. At first our values come mainly from our parents. As we get older, we begin to develop our own values. Values and attitudes affect the choices people make in their lives. We often choose friends who have similar values to our own and we may prefer to work among people who share our values. Sometimes, though, being surrounded by people with similar attitudes can mean we forget that there are people who feel differently.

As early years workers, it is important to consider our attitudes towards some of the issues relating to the care of children. If we have strong feelings about some issues, they may change the way we react to others.

Think about it

Here are some issues where opinions can differ:

Teenage mothers should be encouraged to give their babies up for adoption.
Abortion should be freely available.
Gay men should be allowed to adopt children.
Women should be allowed to fight as soldiers.
People with learning difficulties – for example, a mental age of eight – should be sterilised.

1   What do you honestly think about these issues?

2   Choose one topic to discuss with your friends. Do you share the same views?

3   How easy is it to change other people's views? (You might like to try!)

Now consider your attitudes about the following issues that relate to children

- Should mothers work while having young children?

- Do you think that men can be as good at caring for children as women?

- Is it ever right to smack a child?

- Should parents of children who break the law be punished?

- How can our values and attitudes affect the way we build relationships?

Sometimes, although our values and attitudes may be invisible to us, they can be seen by other people. For example, if you are not comfortable with some people – perhaps because you disagree with what they are saying – your face and body may show it. You might cross your arms, look away or not smile as much as you usually do. These are all signals that you do not share the same values and people will pick these signals up. It will then be difficult to establish a good relationship with them as they will sense that you feel uncomfortable with them.

No one likes the feeling of being judged or not being accepted. As early years workers we must learn to make sure that we are sending positive signals. By doing this we can ensure children and their parents feel welcome and comfortable – regardless of who they are and what values and attitudes they hold. If children and parents do not feel that early years workers accept them as they are, there will be tensions in the relationships between them.

Look at this example.

Case Study

Mary is working as a nanny. She cares for a three-month-old baby, but although she has not said anything to her employer, she does not agree with mothers leaving their babies. She thinks that women who have babies should look after them.

Sarah is Mary's employer. She has decided to return to work because she loves her job and knows that she would not be happy at home. She has chosen Mary because she is well qualified and she thinks that her baby is in good hands.

When Sarah gets in from work, Mary finds it difficult to ask her if she has had a good day and often says things such as 'The baby noticed her feet today. What a shame you missed it!' Over the past few weeks they have talked to each other less and less.

Questions

1 *How might the lack of communication affect Mary's relationship with her employer?*
2 *How might the lack of communication affect the baby?*
3 *Is it possible for Mary to feel this way about working mothers and still do a good job?*

Children can sense values and attitudes

Children can quickly pick up the signs given out and they can sense if there is tension between adults. This means that we must ensure our own values do not stop us from giving our best to all children and to their parents. Look at this example of a family that is not being valued.

Case Study

Kerry comes from a travelling family. The family have been in town for three weeks and Kerry is going to nursery. Staff at the nursery have not yet had a proper conversation with her parents. When she starts talking about her caravan, the staff do not really listen. They think that children should not be moved around all the time.

Questions

1   *Why do the staff at the nursery treat Kerry's parents differently?*
2   *How may this affect Kerry?*

Stereotypes

Sometimes our ideas of what people are like are based on stereotypes. A stereotype is a fixed image of a group of people. The stereotype of a French man may be someone wearing a beret and smelling of garlic.

Stereotypes are not helpful. They can make us think that we know what a group of people – say football supporters, blondes, or teachers – are like and this may change our attitude towards someone who belongs to a stereotyped group. Stereotypes are often learnt indirectly – for example, through watching the television or reading newspapers and magazines. When we meet someone from a stereotyped group we often realise that the images are not accurate. This is why it is important to meet and get to know people before making judgements about them.

Think about it

Mrs Smith is a child minder and she is going to look after a little Asian girl. She is surprised to see that the girl's mother is wearing a pair of jeans and that she speaks English. She says afterwards to her friend, 'You would never know that she was Asian, she looked so normal.'

1   What did she mean by 'normal'?

2   What stereotype image did Mrs Smith have of this child's mother?

3   If you were the child's mother and had overheard this remark, how might you feel?

Prejudice and discrimination

In an ideal society we would not have stereotypes and we would get to know someone before making up our minds about them. Having a bad opinion of someone before getting to know them is called **prejudice**. People have all sorts of prejudices – for example, some people don't like men with beards, others don't like teachers! Prejudice becomes more serious when it turns into action – for example, refusing to talk to someone with a beard. This is called **discrimination**.

At present in this country, groups of people are being unfairly treated because of other people's prejudices. Discrimination in this country is often based on:

- age
- race
- gender
- sexual orientation
- health and social class.

Look at the ways in which people could find themselves discriminated against when looking for work (opposite).

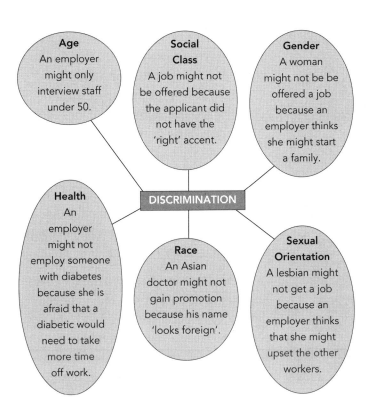

Discrimination affects people's lives in different ways depending on the reason for the discrimination. A disabled person might not be allowed into a restaurant because there is no room for a wheelchair, or a black teenager might be stopped by the police more often than a white teenager. An employer might not give an interview to a 60-year-old man because of his age, even if he is more experienced and skilled than other applicants. Look at the examples of discrimination to the left.

Think about it

Maureen is a teacher. She wanted to be a deputy head. She went to four interviews where she was the only female, but was not offered the job even though, sometimes, she had more experience than the men. She has now stopped applying for jobs.

Rajeet has just left school. He has been trying to get a job in an office. He has had no interviews, but his white friend who left school at the same time has had an interview for each job he has applied for, even though they had the same exam results.

Malcolm is a computer operator. He needs a wheelchair to get around. He has been offered a job in an out-of-town business park. The firm has a minibus, but he cannot get on it with his wheelchair. He cannot afford to take a taxi every day and so he turned down the job.

1   Why might these people feel discriminated against?
2   How might this affect their lives?

How discrimination can affect society

Discrimination is not only unfair for the individual, but it is also damaging for society because:

■   We do not always have the best people doing some jobs because talented people can go unrecognised.

Collections/Anthea Sieveking

Good role models are important for children

■ Groups of people feel that they are not part of the system. They feel that no one who understands their values is in power. For example, there are not many black judges or many Asians in the police force.

Children can also be discriminated against. This is particularly unfair as they need to feel valued in order to fulfil their potential and eventually take their place in society.

In some communities a pattern of low achievement is formed. The children do not have good role models to follow. Black children may not see black teachers or doctors. Because of this, they may start to believe that black people cannot do this type of work.

Legal issues

Over the past twenty years, laws have been passed to protect some groups of people from discrimination. The laws are meant to prevent people being discriminated against on the basis of their gender, race or marital status – married or single.

In practice, it is often hard for the victim to prove beyond reasonable doubt that there has been discrimination.

Opposite is a table that shows some of the recent laws that are meant to protect people from discrimination.

Children and discrimination

The children we care for will be the next generation of adults, and by teaching them to value and respect each other we may be able to make society fairer. There are many reasons why some children may not feel valued. See page 8.

Laws which protect against discrimination

Sex Discrimination Acts (1975 and 1986)	The 1975 Act was later followed by the 1986 Act. These acts make it illegal to discriminate against someone on the grounds of gender – e.g. not giving a job to someone because she is a woman. The law also protects people from sexual harassment. The 1975 act also set up the Equal Opportunities Commission which sends out information about discrimination and can carry out investigations into alleged sexual discrimination.
Race Relations Act (1976)	This act makes it illegal to discriminate on the grounds of race, colour, nationality and ethnic origin in housing, education, employment, entertainment and provision of services and goods. The act also set up the Commission for Racial Equality which carries out research, sends out information and can carry out investigations into cases of alleged racial discrimination.
Education Act (1980)	Local authorities have a duty to make sure that no child is discriminated against 'on the basis of her or his "handicap"' This act provides that children with special needs – e.g. having a physical or mental disability – should be integrated into mainstream schools wherever possible.
Equal Pay Act (1984)	Under this act, equal pay must be given for work of equal value. This act is designed mainly to help women who are often discriminated against in employment.
Disabled Persons Act (1986)	This act requires local authorities to provide sufficient resources for disabled people and their carers, so that they may lead as independent a life as possible. It is not always effective because local authorities do not always have enough money to pay for the needs of the disabled people.
Children Act (1989)	This act states that the needs of children are the most important when making decisions. It asks local authorities to consider a child's race, culture, religion and languages when making decisions. The guidelines to the act say that all childcare services – e.g. nurseries – should promote self-esteem and racial identity.

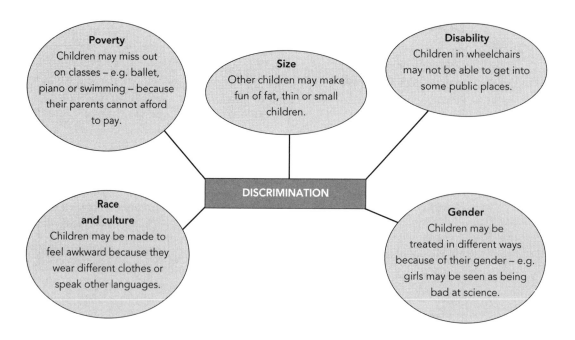

Ways in which discrimination can affect disabled children and their families

Disabled children and their families often find that they are discriminated against in several ways:

- Parents may not be given enough support in caring for their children. They may have to stop work because they are the main care givers. This means that the family may have to rely on state benefits.

- Disabled children do not always achieve their potential because schools do not have enough resources or staff.

- Services to disabled children and their families are often cut when local authorities need to save money.

- Parents often have to fight to get the best treatment or resources for their children. Some parents find it difficult to cope with this constant battle. This may affect the support their children receive.

- Disabled children are often treated differently when they are in public places. Access in shops may be difficult and members of the public may stare. Some restaurants have been known to refuse to serve disabled children because they are afraid that the child will upset other customers.

- Other children in the family may not receive as much attention because their parents need to care for the disabled child. This can affect the other children's development.

Case Study

Laura is five years old. She has a degenerative muscular disease that means she is now in a wheelchair. Her local authority has said that she cannot carry on attending her primary school, because there is no wheelchair access into classrooms. The local authority wants her to attend another school that is seven miles away. Laura's parents feel that she has suffered twice – once through her illness and again through not being allowed to be with her friends.

Questions

1 *Do you agree with Laura's parents?*
2 *How might other children benefit from being with Laura?*

What is equality of opportunity in child care?

As professional early years workers we have a duty to make sure that children are valued and that they are not discriminated against either by adults or by other children. In order to promote equal opportunities it is important to think about what this actually means when working with children.

> Equality of opportunity means making sure that children in our care are seen as being individual and special. This does *not* mean treating all the children the same. Some children may need more adult help or special equipment to carry out an activity. Equality of opportunity means making sure that children are equally valued and are given the same opportunities to fulfil their potential.

Knowledge into Action

■ *Harry is four years old and has a visual impairment. This means that he is given more adult support during the sessions. For example, he often sits near an adult at story time and an adult often stays alongside him when he is outside.*

One of the other parents feels that this is unfair to the other children as they do not receive the same treatment. He has come to complain about this.

In pairs act out a role play of the conversation between the father and the teacher.

1 *Explain why Harry needs more adult help.*
2 *Explain why it is not possible for every child to get this amount of extra care.*

Codes of practice and equal opportunities policies

To promote equality of opportunity in early years settings, codes of practice and equal opportunities policies need to be written. These help everyone involved think about what is meant by equal opportunities and about their role in promoting this equality. Employers can ask employees to sign a code so that everyone in a workplace understands the values of that particular setting. Some local authorities make sure that nurseries, playgroups and other early years settings have codes and policies before they allow them to be registered.

MAPLEHURST NURSERY

HEALTH AND SAFETY POLICY

Accidents
All the equipment provided has been designed with safety as a priority but children do fall and hurt themselves. Staff are aware of the capabilities of the children and will not allow the children to be placed at risk.

In the event of a minor accident, the child concerned will be comforted and cared for with medical attention if necessary. Please let us know if your child is allergic to sticking plasters etc.

All accidents will be noted in the accident book, the Parent/Guardian will then be asked to sign and date the book.

If a more serious accident occurs or we are concerned about your child, you will be contacted immediately and the child will be taken to the "Conquest Hospital"

Fire Drill:
Fire Drills will be held at least once a term where possible. Please see separate Fire Drill procedure. All parents and staff should familiarise themselves with the procedures.

Outings
You will be asked to sign a consent form each time your child goes on an outing. As well as organised outings. It will be part of the nursery routine to take children to the library, local park, swimming etc. and if you are happy to do this, you will be asked to sign a general consent form to cover this. The staff ratio for outings depends on where we are going, the mode of travel etc. but on trips beyond the school grounds it will be 1:2 children.

Health
Health information on the children is kept on index cards in the nursery office.

Sickness
If your child has a temperature, is suffering from sickness or diarrhoea, or is obviously unwell please do not bring him or her into nursery until your doctor says he/she is well again, or for 24 hours after the last bout of sickness or diarrhoea.

Colds
As it is impossible to prevent children from catching colds, especially in winter, a child with a slight cold who seems happy and isn't running a temperature may come into the nursery. At any sign of more serious illness (coughing or sore throat,) he/she must be withdrawn immediately to safeguard her/his health and that of the other children.

MAPLEHURST NURSERY

EQUAL OPPORTUNITIES POLICY

Equal Opportunities within our nursery are positively encouraged. The provision of care and activities provided in our nursery reflect this regardless of Race, Colour, Nationality or Religion.

Different Abilities Our staff actively encourage each child to achieve at their own level and each their own potential. Praise is freely given and without comparison.

- **Physical** To provide equipment and activities which allows for a wide range of abilities and ages.

- **Social /Emotional** Emotional development through play. To help establish Self Discipline, Self Control and to help any child gain in confidence.

- **Gender** Both boys and girls should be encouraged to participate in all activities.

- **Awareness** We try to develop the children's awareness of their environment and of the other children and staff in the nursery. e.g. - Children with hearing disabilities, Children wearing glasses, Children with physical disabilities.

- **Activities:** Jigsaw Puzzles .... Dressing / Roleplay .... Television ... Woodwork .... Sporting activities ... Musical movement .... Home-Corner

Health and safety and equal opportunities policies

Portfolio activity

Ask your supervisor if there is an equal opportunities code or policy in your workplace.

1 *Write down what the code covers.*
2 *How is the code reviewed?*

When policies are written they help everyone to focus on what is going on in a setting. It is important that they are reviewed regularly because otherwise issues can be forgotten. Policies need to consider how discrimination can be prevented by asking these questions:

- Do all the children have equal access to equipment or are any groups of children prevented from using it because of a disability or because other children are dominant?

- Is name-calling or any form of bullying happening in the playground?

- Are children who do not have well-off parents made to feel different by staff or other children?

- Are children ever labelled by staff (even in private) as 'thick' or 'a brat', etc?

- Are all parents treated with the same respect and friendliness?

- Are children taught to respect and help each other?

- Are children aware that there are many different cultures, religions and languages in the world?

The effects of racism, sexism and other forms of discrimination on children's development

Understanding the effects of discrimination and bullying is important if we are to take our role of promoting equality of opportunity seriously.

- The effects of discrimination are lifelong.

- Children may not be able to fulfil their potential.

- Low self-esteem means that children can find it harder to form relationships.

- Children may lack the confidence to try new activities.

- Children may feel ashamed of their culture or race.

- Children may feel guilty and think that they deserve poor treatment.

It could be useful for early years workers to think about their own experiences of childhood and make sure that these are not holding them back from caring for others.

Look at this example:

Case Study

As a child Yasmine was not encouraged to be noisy and shout when playing. She remembers being told to go to her room if she was making too much noise. Yasmine now works in a nursery. She often finds herself telling the children to be quiet.

Questions

1   *How might Yasmine's early experiences be affecting her work?*
2   *Does it matter if Yasmine gets cross with children when they are playing?*

Praise and encouragement are extremely important to children and sometimes adults can find it harder to give this praise if they were not praised as children themselves. Praise makes children feel good about themselves and gives them more confidence. We should remember to praise children not only for their achievements but also for their efforts. Sometimes a little praise can make a big difference to a child – and to an adult too!

Portfolio activity

Making children feel valued and supported is an essential part of promoting equal opportunities.

1   *Think of a situation when you have praised children or made them feel special.*
2   *Write about this situation.*
3   *Write down what you said or did.*

Challenging racism, sexism and other forms of discrimination

To be able to challenge any form of discrimination, you first need to be able to recognise that it is happening. Discrimination can be direct or indirect. An example of direct discrimination is when children may stop playing with another child because he is black. Indirect discrimination means that it is hidden. This type of discrimination is harder to detect, but is just as damaging. For example, an Asian child in a nursery might be encouraged to make Easter cards but never to celebrate festivals from her own religion.

Direct discrimination – challenging remarks

Children who make remarks that are offensive may well be echoing remarks they have heard, or saying something that they do not realise is offensive, such as:

'I don't like Shina's hair' or 'Jack's stupid, he can't write his name yet.'

It is important that we do not ignore offensive remarks. Depending on what is said and how old the child is, we can do the following:

- Ask the children what they mean and where they heard it.

- Tell the children that what they have said is not appropriate.

- Explain why it is not appropriate and that it may be hurtful.

- Correct any information that is misleading – e.g. 'Black people are hard to tell apart'.

- Support the other child or children by letting them know that we care about them.

- Consider whether the workplace is sending out discriminatory messages.

- Look at resources and activities to make children more aware of the different groups of people in our society.

Knowledge into Action

In pairs, choose one of these scenarios and work out a role play to show other members of your group how you would handle this situation.

1   *You overhear a four-year-old calling another child a spastic.*
2   *A parent comes into the nursery. She wants you to stop her child from playing with another child who comes from a family of travellers. She says that she doesn't want her child to pick up 'bad habits'.*
3   *A member of staff asks if you could send a group of boys to help them put away the PE equipment. You are working with both boys and girls at the time.*

Direct discrimination – challenging bullying

Bullying is never a bit of harmless fun. All types of bullying are harmful, from teasing to acts of violence. Children who are being bullied are being discriminated against and they have the right to be protected. This message is gradually becoming understood by early years professionals. A few years ago, children who were being bullied were often left to struggle on by themselves. Their cries for help were often met with responses such as 'you need to stand up for yourself' or 'you need to fight your own battles'.

As an early years worker, you have a duty to protect and help children who are being bullied. If you suspect that a child is being bullied, you should talk to your supervisor so that strategies such as closer supervision can be developed to prevent further bullying. Information about resources and strategies to prevent bullying can be obtained from KIDSCAPE (see address at end of chapter).

SIGNS AND SYMPTOMS:
(from Stop Bullying! KIDSCAPE)

A child may indicate by signs or behaviour that he or she is being bullied. Adults should be aware that these are possible signs and that they should investigate if a child:

- is frightened of walking to or from school
- is unwilling to go to school
- begins to do poorly in school work
- becomes withdrawn, starts stammering
- regularly has books or clothes destroyed
- becomes distressed, stops eating
- cries easily

- becomes disruptive or aggressive
- has possessions go 'missing'
- has dinner or other monies continually 'lost'
- starts stealing money (to pay bully)
- is frightened to say what's wrong
- attempts suicide or runs away
- has nightmares.

These signs and behaviours could indicate other problems, but bullying should be considered a possibility and should be investigated.

Indirect discrimination – looking at resources

Challenging all forms of discrimination often means looking hard at the resources and images that we have in the setting. We need to decide if any of them are sending out hidden messages that might reinforce stereotypes and prejudices.

Books

- Books need to be checked for stereotypes. Images of people should be positive. For example, a book that has an image of black children not wearing any shoes is negative and children may think that all black children are poor.

Posters and wall displays

▪ Are children able to see positive images of people around them, especially children with disabilities?

▪ When we put up a wall display does it show that we live in a multicultural country?

Activities and equipment

▪ Are activities planned that actively promote an awareness of other cultures and religions?

▪ Are any other religious festivals celebrated apart from the Christian ones – e.g. Easter and Christmas?

▪ Are materials and equipment such as jigsaw puzzles and board games showing a range of positive images?

Case Study

The Tinie Tot nursery is in an area which is mainly white, middle class and professional. At a staff meeting the team is planning themes for next term. You ask if it would be a good idea to celebrate a festival such as Diwali or Hanukkah.

The supervisor looks surprised and says, 'There is no point doing that here, and the children don't need to do any of that. Anyway the parents won't like it. They send their children here to learn things, not to waste their time!'

Questions

1 What does this tell you about the supervisor's values?
2 Do you think that she is being racist?
3 What arguments could you put forward to show the team that an awareness of other religions is important?

Promoting a positive environment for children

There are many benefits to providing all children with an environment that is positive and encouraging. This means making sure that it provides for children with special needs as well as being multicultural and respecting other languages.

▪ Children can learn that everyone is different and special.

▪ Children see a wider view of life. They learn that there is more then one way to prepare food, talk or pray.

▪ Children gain learning opportunities through different tastes, ways of painting, and through hearing different types of music. This helps them to be more creative.

We are preparing children to be able to form relationships with others through respecting others' lifestyles and values.

There are three main ways that we can create an environment that promotes equal opportunities:

1 value all children and their families

2 be good role models

3 provide varied play activities, resources and images.

Valuing children and their families

Involve all parents and families. They may wish to help in the early years setting or be able to provide information, resources and books that can help us – for example, objects for the home corner, dressing up clothes. Where families have more than one language they may be able to lend books, songs and even come in to teach all the children some words.

Display positive images of groups of people who are often discriminated against. Children who wear glasses need to see that other children also wear glasses, and that they are not the odd ones out. A good range of books, posters and other images are important. All children need to feel proud of who they are so providing positive images is particularly important where children are likely to feel different – for example, children who have asthma, live in a caravan or don't have the same colour skin.

Case Study

Zainab is four years old. She is the only black child in the nursery. The nursery staff feel that they should not make any 'fuss' about this difference. One day the children are asked to draw themselves. Zainab draws herself with white skin.

In groups, discuss the following questions.

Questions

1 *Should the member of staff ask Zainab to change the picture?*
2 *Why might Zainab draw herself in the same way as the other children?*
3 *How can the nursery make sure that Zainab feels as valued as the other children?*

Good role models

Children also need to see good role models. Children learn more from how they see us act, than from what we say.

We must make sure that our language is not prejudiced. This means not saying things like 'I don't expect girls to behave like that.'

Positive images of people who may be discriminated against

- Children need to see us co-operating and being pleasant with everyone we come into contact with – this may be parents, other workers and visitors. This also means that we must be careful that we do not make any assumptions – Tiffany's mother may not be a Mrs, or the person who has come to collect Tom may not be his grandad but his dad.

- Children also need to see adults being open minded and interested in the world around them. We could show them beautiful objects from different countries or clothes that are worn in other cultures.

Planning play activities

Children also need to have the opportunity to play and learn in an environment that makes them feel valued whilst encouraging them to respect others. Providing play resources that allow children to express themselves and explore the differences between them is important. There are many ways of doing this.

Activities that allow self expression help children to talk about themselves and their feelings. They may draw happy pictures or sad pictures or they may need to have some activities where they can be angry or quiet – e.g. by playing with dough, sand or water.

Homecorners can help children realise that there are other ways of setting up a home. Different cooking utensils can be used, and a range of dressing-up clothes can be provided. Where children do not have direct experience of using some equipment in their own home, it can be helpful for an adult to play alongside the children. For example, this would prevent objects such as chopsticks being used as spoons because children do not know what they are for. Children can also benefit by playing with dolls of different colours, providing they are attractive and accurate.

Materials that show different ways of communicating help children to learn about others. Examples of braille and books written in languages other than English can be brought into the early years setting. There are also some very good videos that can be used to teach children to sing and sign nursery rhymes.

Displays and interest tables can add to the learning environment. Interesting objects, fabrics and artwork can help children to appreciate the interesting world in which we live. Activities can be based on objects – e.g. if an item is made of papier-mâché or batik, children could have a try at making something using the same technique.

Celebrations are always enjoyed by children. Festivals from many religions and cultures can be celebrated. They make good learning opportunities as children can make some of the food, enjoy dressing up and listen to music.

Portfolio activity

Ask your supervisor if you can plan an activity that will make children more aware of another culture or religion. For example, you could try a cooking activity, create a display, use musical instruments or prepare the home play area.

1 *Write a plan of the activity and carry it out.*
2 *How did the children respond?*
3 *What did you learn from doing this activity?*

Obtaining information and resources

There are many organisations that provide information, ideas and resources to promote equality of opportunity. It is also worth remembering that there are often local organisations that are happy to send out information or even provide a speaker – for example, children's charities, local churches, synagogues etc. Public libraries and telephone books are often useful sources of contact numbers for these local organisations.

There are two national organisations that were set up to check that the laws on discrimination relating to race and gender are effective. They also provide information on equal opportunities for work settings.

Commission for Racial Equality
Elliot House
10–12 Allington Street
London SW1 5EH

Equal Opportunities Commission
Overseas House
Quay Street
Manchester M3 3HN

KIDSCAPE
152 Buckingham Palace Road
London SW1W 9TR

Good practice – equal opportunities

✓ Be a good role model. Think about your own values, attitudes and prejudices and make sure that you are not discriminating against children or their families.

✓ Make sure that activities always take into consideration the needs of all the children.

✓ Check that the images of disability, race and culture in books are positive. Some books may include negative images.

✓ Look for ways of valuing all children. This is the starting point for helping children to be tolerant and respectful of others.

✓ Be careful that you do not have a 'tourist' approach to race and culture. Images of other countries should show everyday life – e.g. children in school, families eating.

✓ Think of equal opportunities as a way of expanding all children's learning opportunities – food, music, language and knowledge.

Unit test

Quick quiz

1 Early years and educational workers should put equality of opportunity into practice by:
   a treating all children the same
   b encouraging children to help those with disabilities
   c making sure that they value and help every child
   d encouraging boys to play in the home corner.

2 The parents of a black child ask that their child should not play with any Asian children. This would contravene the:
   a 1989 Children Act
   b 1976 Race Relations Act
   c 1974 Health and Safety at Work Act
   d 1980 Education Act.

3 A multicultural approach is needed in:
   a schools with mainly black children
   b schools with Muslim and Sikh children
   c all schools regardless of the culture and religion of children
   d schools in large cities.

4 Books showing positive images of disability are important because:
   a children enjoy seeing attractive people
   b children learn that disabled people can take on a variety of roles
   c children can see that everyone is different
   d children can learn that everyone is the same.

5 Equal opportunity policies need to be reviewed:
   a to check that they are effective
   b to show parents that they are discussed
   c to make sure that people read them
   d to keep up with the changes in the law.

6 Cooking equipment reflecting a range of cultures is needed in the homecorner:
   a to help the children practise their skills
   b to help children to play for longer
   c to help children understand that there are different ways of preparing food
   d to help the boys become more interested in cooking.

7 A girl starts making racist comments. The early years and educational worker should:
   a immediately contact her parents
   b make the child say she is sorry
   c explain to her why these comments are hurtful
   d find out where she heard the comment before.

8 Which of these acts set up the Equal Opportunities Commission?
   a 1976 Race Relations Act
   b 1975 Sex Discrimination Act
   c 1989 Children Act
   d 1980 Education Act

9 Gender stereotypes can be avoided when books show:
   a boys and girls joining in all activities
   b girls playing with cars
   c boys using dressing-up clothes
   d boys and girls playing together in the home corner.

10 Which people in a nursery should read the setting's equal opportunities policy?
   a the manager
   b the manager and the deputy manager
   c the parents
   d everyone working in the setting

Short answer questions

1 Name three ways in which the early years workers in a playgroup can promote equal opportunities.

2 Give two reasons why discrimination is damaging for society.

3 Name three groups in society which are often discriminated against.

4 Why is it important for children to celebrate festivals from different religions?

5 Why can stereotypes be misleading?

The Care and Education Environment

Do you remember your first day at a new school, college or job? Can you remember feeling nervous and worrying about how you would cope? Most probably there is a young child feeling the same way at this very moment – perhaps tossing and turning in bed or holding tightly on to a parent's hand!

As early years workers we want children to feel happy and secure and this means that we need to be able to create a positive environment for them. To do this we must make sure that not only is it a safe and attractive environment but also a caring, reassuring and stimulating one. Every aspect of the child's experience is included in the meaning of the term 'environment'.

This chapter looks at how we can create an environment for children that meets their needs.

Bubbles Photo Library/Peter Sylent

Types of setting where children are cared for

Children can be cared for in a variety of settings. Some children go to playgroups every morning, whereas others are in daycare nurseries every day. Every setting will have its own atmosphere and ways of meeting children's and parents' needs. Some parents may need to have their children looked after for long periods of time – perhaps in their own home – whereas other parents may need just a few hours, for example two sessions a week in a playgroup. As early years workers we have a choice of many different types of settings in which we can look after children.

Ways in which children are cared for

Childminders	A childminder looks after other people's children in the childminder's own home. This might include looking after older children after school as well as children under five during the day.
Nannies	A nanny looks after children in their own home.
Day nurseries	A day nursery is open all year round and children under five can stay all day.
Workplace nurseries	A workplace nursery is organised by an employer and the places are often subsidised. This means that the employee does not pay the full cost.
Crèches	Crèches look after children under eight for short periods of time. For example, they are found in new shopping centres allowing parents to shop for a few hours.
Playgroups	Playgroups are non-profit-making groups that are designed to give children under five an opportunity to play. Sessions are often two to three hours long.
Nurseries or kindergartens	Nurseries and kindergartens offer sessions in mornings and afternoons that allow children under five to learn and play.
Nurseries within schools	Some infant or primary schools have a nursery attached. The nurseries take children from three to four years of age. No charge is made to the parents.
Infant and primary schools	Infant and primary schools take children from the age of five. The normal school day is about six hours long.
After-school clubs	After-school clubs look after children over the age of five after school has finished during term time. They are often used by working parents.
Holiday play schemes	Holiday play schemes look after children over the age of five during school holidays. They are often used by working parents.

Most settings in which children are cared for have to be registered and inspected by the local authority's Social Services department. The 1989 Children Act states that settings that care for children under the age of eight, for periods over two hours, have to be registered and inspected by the local authority.

Case Study

Tracy has just moved into your area and has two children aged three and six years old. She would like to return to work part time in the mornings. She has found a job which starts at 9.30am and finishes at 12.15pm.

Questions

1   Find out what childcare is available in your area that would meet Tracy's needs.
2   How much would this cost a week?
3   Write a short report – no more than one side of A4 – giving Tracy details of your findings.

Creating a pleasant and caring environment

When we care for children we try to create a good environment for them. This means making sure it is safe, hygienic and that the equipment and activities that are provided are suitable for the needs of the children being cared for. A caring environment, though, is more than just meeting the basic needs of children – it also involves making sure that children feel valued and that their experiences in the setting are pleasant ones. A happy environment also has a good atmosphere between staff and parents. Atmosphere is invisible but very important. To create such an environment, early years workers also need to be able to work with parents and other team members.

The essentials of being a good early years worker

Some people think that a good early years worker is someone who gets on well with children. Unfortunately it is not enough just to like children to be a good

Providing a reassuring environment

Making the environment safe

One of the roles of an early years worker is to make sure that the environment is safe for children to be in. This means carrying out checks to make sure that there are no potential hazards; supervising children; and making sure that equipment and materials are right for their age. (Keeping children safe is so important that the next chapter looks at it in more detail.)

Keeping the environment tidy and hygienic

Children need to be in environments that are tidy and hygienic. We need to take responsibility for tidying away equipment so that accidents are prevented and the setting is kept clean. Materials and equipment need to be put away in their correct places. Keeping the environment hygienic is also a major responsibility when working with children. Although most large early years settings employ a cleaner, it is still the duty of the early years worker to keep equipment clean, wipe up spills and clean surfaces. This may not always be a pleasant task for example, if a child has been sick, but it is still an essential one. We also need to act as good role models by washing our own hands, wearing aprons and being tidy and clean in appearance.

Working with parents

Establishing a good relationship with parents is another major role of early years workers. A good relationship with parents can help children to settle in more quickly and help us to understand the needs of the children. To build a good relationship with parents and carers we need to respect their wishes and values and show that we value their support and help. (Valuing and working with parents is covered in more detail in Chapter 10, pages 212–213.)

Confidentiality

Whilst caring for children we may learn information about them and their families that is confidential. We may see medical records, financial information or hear reports about children. Breaching confidentiality is considered to be serious as it means that the trust of the setting and/or the parents has been broken. If you are unsure whether information is confidential it is a good idea to ask your supervisor or manager.

Meeting children's needs

Being able to meet children's needs is not the same as getting on well with children. An early years worker needs to be able to understand which activities will help children to develop as well as being able to support children in a range of situations for example, when they feel ill, are finding it difficult to settle or are upset and angry. We also need to be able to identify children's needs for example, see when they are ill and also recognise day-to-day needs for example, needing to go the toilet or wanting to go on the slide.

Being a good team member

There are many jobs that involve being able to work as part of a team. A good team creates a happy environment around it and this can be sensed by children and parents. To be a good team member we need to respect the other members and be ready to support them. This sometimes means lending a hand or putting away something that we did not use. It also means understanding the lines of responsibility within a setting for example, parents may need to be referred to a senior team member if they wish to discuss their child.

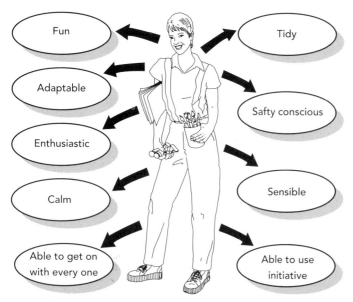

Fun

Tidy

Adaptable

Safty conscious

Enthusiastic

Calm

Sensible

Able to get on with every one

Able to use initiative

A good early years worker

early years worker. There are many other roles and responsibilities that need to be considered.

A good early years worker has a combination of skills. We could see these skills as pieces making up a jigsaw. Each is needed for the picture of a good early years worker to be complete.

Providing a reassuring environment

Many children come into early years settings feeling nervous and afraid. They may be leaving their parents for the first time or they may have had a holiday and not been in the setting for some time. As early years workers we need to be able to reassure them and make them feel settled. (If you wish to read more about helping children to separate from their parents and carers turn to page 202 in Chapter 9.)

Knowledge into Action

Here is a checklist of ways in which we can make children feel welcome.

Use this list to monitor your performance during one day in your workplace.

1   Do you greet children with a smile and a hello when they come into the setting or when you arrive?

2   Do you say hello to any parents that you meet?

3   Do you bend down to the children's level when you are talking with them?

4   Do you listen to what they are saying and show them that you are listening?

5   Do you respond immediately if you see a child who seems unsure or who is alone?

6   Do you sit and play with a child or group of children?

7   Do you respond quickly to children who need help – for example, when they want to go to the toilet or need someone to fasten an apron for them?

8   Do you praise children?

9   Do you laugh and smile with children?

10 At the end of the day do you make sure that you tell children that you are looking forward to seeing them again?

One of the key elements in providing a reassuring environment for children is a warm and welcoming atmosphere.

Helping children to feel that they belong

There are a number of things we can do to help children feel they belong. We can label their coat pegs or drawers so that they know that some space in a setting is specially for them. Settings can also have displays that show children's photographs, names and how old they are. Young children can have their own beakers and mugs, whereas older children could have special tasks to do which will make them feel important – for example, tidying the book corner or giving out pencils.

Homecorners are also ways of making children feel that they belong. This is especially important for children who come from homes where the culture and language are different from those of other children in the setting. This means that they should see things that looks familiar to them. If you are unsure about what you need to put in the homecorner, you could ask the parents for help. They might be able to show you the cooking utensils that they use at home or bring in some fabric or books that are more familiar to the child.

Comfort objects

Many children have comfort objects that they need to make them feel secure. It is surprising what children can get attached to! You may find that some children have scraps of blankets, teddies or even cushions.

In earlier times children were not encouraged to have such objects, but now it is known that they can help children enormously for several reasons:

- They are a link with home.

- Children associate them with being happy or secure.

- They can help children to relax and therefore get to sleep more easily.

It is considered good practice to talk to parents about when children might need their comforters and to make sure that children have access to them. This can help children to settle down more quickly if they are changing environments.

Daily routine for toddlers: 1½–2½ yrs

8.00 Welcome to the nursery – free play
8.45 Stories
9.00 Free play
9.50 Garden
9.50 Snack time and singing/music time
10.20 Messy activities
11.15 Tidy up and wind down ready for lunch
11.40 Lunch

After lunch the full-day children lie down for a sleep while the part-time children go out to play in the garden until they are met by parents/guardians. The children sleep for as long as they wish. If they wake before the others they play quietly.

1.00 New arrivals – free play
1.45 Stories

The afternoon session will then follow the same format as the morning including different activities.

4.30 Tea time

After tea the children go out into the garden or play in their rooms until they are collected by 6.00pm.

✱ Nappies are checked and changed every two hours starting at 9.15 and when necessary between times. Children who are potty training will be taken to the toilet regularly throughout the day and if they ask. ✱

Why routines can help children

A regular routine often helps young children to feel secure and comfortable. After a few sessions children learn the routines of the early years setting. A routine could include a story before hometime or a drink and a snack just before outdoor play – these help children to predict what is going to happen next and therefore feel more settled.

Routines vary according to the needs of the children and the early years setting, but meal, snack and sleep times tend to be at the same times each day.

Routines in home settings

Where children are being cared for in their own homes or by a childminder, there is usually still a pattern to the day. Children may go to a parent and toddler group one day and swimming on another. Meal times and nap times are often around the same time every day.

Knowledge into Action

1   Find out what the day-to-day routine of your workplace is – for example, times when children are given meals and snacks, have free play, etc.

2   Consider how this routine meets the needs of the children and their parents.

3   Write down any suggestions you have for improving the routine.

Helping children to cope when there are changes to the routine

There are often times when routines need to be changed – for example, when children need to be collected by someone else or a member of staff is off sick. Some children can find a change in routine upsetting and at these times we need to reassure them. Where possible we can help children by talking through what is going to happen. It often helps when adults seem very positive about any change as this makes children feel that there is no need to worry. It is a good idea to encourage children to ask questions about what is going to happen because the questions that they ask often relate to their fears. Look at this example.

A child is going to be collected by another person after nursery:

Early years worker	Your mummy told me that Sarah is going to collect you today.
Child	When will she come for me?
Early years worker	At hometime, after we have had our story.
Child	Will she know where to come?
Early years worker	Yes, because mummy and I have told her and I am going to look out for her and stay with you until she comes.

Think about it

You are working as a classroom assistant and today the infant children are going to have their playtime with the older children because work is being carried out on the drainage systems in their playground. You are going to be on duty and have been asked to tell a group of children about this change.

1 Why would some children find this frightening?
2 What would you say to them to reassure them?
3 What could you do to make this change seem fun?

There are times when a change to the child's routine happens quite unexpectedly – for example, the fire alarm might go off or a parent may come to collect a child early because of a family crisis. Unexpected changes can be worrying for children especially if there seems to be a rush. We can help children by talking to them at the same time as dressing or carrying them. Children need to know what is happening and how it will affect them. Some young children may need their comforters at such times to help them cope with the change.

Portfolio activity

Think about a time recently when you needed to reassure a child or group of children because there was a change to their normal routine.

1 Write down when this situation happened and why.

2 Write down what you said and did to reassure the child or children.

3 Why do you think that this helped them?

Making the physical environment child orientated

Children are more likely to enjoy being in a setting if the physical environment around them is pleasant and attractive and meets their needs. It is helpful if children can be made to feel 'at home' – for example, being able to get out toys for themselves or being able to go to the toilet without too much help.

Bubbles Photo Library/Jennie Woodcock

A child-orientated environment

Making sure that the environment is comfortable

Where possible furniture and fittings such as sinks and toilets need to be child sized. This means that children are less likely to have accidents and are able to show independence. In purpose-built settings, toilets and other fittings are child sized, but in home settings we may need to look at ways of making the environment more child friendly. We may be able to put coat hooks at the child's height or have some drawers and cupboards where children's toys are stored and that they have easy access to.

The lighting and heating of a setting is important in making the environment comfortable. We need to make sure that the room temperature is pleasant and that children are not too hot or cold. Most early years settings are kept at between 18°C and 21°C. We must also make sure that any indoor setting is adequately ventilated – for example, by opening a window so that fresh, clean air can enter. This is important in preventing infections, as germs flourish in warm, stuffy rooms.

Natural light is thought to be the best for most settings, but some rooms may not have large enough windows. Good lighting helps prevent children and adult from straining their eyes which can lead to headaches.

Portfolio activity

Ask your supervisor if you can check the temperature and lighting of your work setting before the children arrive.

Write down how you did this and whether you took any actions as a result of carrying out these checks – for example, opened a window or turned on more lights.

Using layout to make an environment attractive

How a room or hall is laid out can make a difference to its attractiveness. Careful planning can make the most of the available space and ensure children's needs are met.

Considerations when planning a layout include:

- Fire exits and other access points should be kept clear.
- There should be enough space for children to move from one activity to another safely.
- Enough space should be allowed for the activities planned for the area.
- Specific children's needs should be considered – for example, enough room for a wheelchair.
- Activities that require water or hand-washing should be near to the sink.
- Good use should be made of available natural light – for example, the book corner could be near a window to allow children to look at books in daylight.
- The room should be as easy to clean as possible.
- The room should look inviting and attractive.
- Storage space should be used effectively and children should be able to collect equipment easily without crossing through other areas.

Layout in home settings

Most homes where children are cared for are not as large as group settings. Children can be cared for at a childminder's or in their own home. Here the layout might be affected by the other needs of a family. This means that equipment and activities are put out and then changed at different times in the day. The kitchen table may be used for a meal at lunch time and then later in the day for painting. The lounge may be used for dressing up and then for a quiet time later on. We can make a home environment more child friendly by removing any objects that could be broken or that could cause an accident – for example, vases of flowers, ornaments. As toys and equipment can be expensive, some childminders and nannies use toy libraries as a way of borrowing new equipment for the children they care for.

Layout in a baby and toddler room

Some babies and toddlers are cared for in baby rooms within day nurseries. Most nurseries keep furniture to a minimum in these rooms to allow the children to explore safely. Babies and toddlers are able to play with toys on the floor and have plenty of space in which to crawl and walk safely. Sleeping and changing areas are often separate to this room to make sure it is a hygienic area.

Think about it

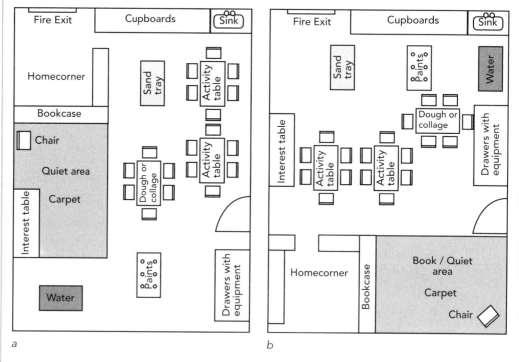

a

b

Look at both of these layouts in pairs.

1 Which of these layouts do you think would be the best for children aged between two and four years?

2 Write down your reasons for this choice.

3 Find out what the other people in your group think.

Small spaces for small people!

Children often enjoy having a space in which they can tuck themselves away. This can make them feel secure. In larger early years settings the space may need to be big enough for several children to be in it at once. This is often the home corner. In a home setting this could be under a table draped with a cloth. Although children want to feel that they are hidden away, it is still important that they can be supervised.

Quiet areas

There are often times in a day when children feel that they would like to be quiet and rest. Some children enjoy looking at books, whereas others might want to do a puzzle or quietly play with a toy. The room or hall layout may include an area that is carpeted to allow children to stretch out and relax. In a home setting, this area could be the lounge where children can curl up on a sofa.

Areas for creative play

Children enjoy painting, playing with sand and water and other activities that can be messy. Most settings need an area where children can carry out these activities safely and where any mess or spills can be mopped up without causing any damage. These areas often have floors that can be wiped easily as well as sinks nearby for hand-washing and for cleaning equipment.

Knowledge into Action

1   Make a list of the types of equipment and materials that are used for creative play in your workplace.
2   Ask your supervisor if you can set out an activity or area – for example, prepare the painting area.
3   Write down how you did this and whether the children enjoyed using the area or equipment that you had set out.

Outdoor areas

Many settings have outdoor areas for children. Sometimes these areas are quite small, but all children benefit from having some fresh air and being outdoors. Most settings have a paved area so that even when it has been raining, children can spend some time outside. We can make these areas attractive by planting bulbs and tubs of flowers with the children. Most settings with outdoor areas use them for tricycles, slides and large play apparatus. In good weather we can put out other activities – for example, sand, water and paint.

Layout for special needs

Adapting a layout for children with special needs

Children with special needs should not miss out on play and learning opportunities because they cannot physically get to them. In purpose-built settings this may not be a difficulty because doorways and ramps will probably have been planned. In other settings it may be possible to make some simple changes that can improve access – for example, moving tables to allow a child greater access. Parents and specialist workers are often the best source of advice as they tend to know what the child needs. A range of specialist equipment has been developed to allow children with special needs to play and learn alongside other children, including adjustable chairs, tables and painting easels.

Time for a change

From time to time it can be refreshing for adults to look at the room layout and move things around. This helps create a new interest in equipment and can make the environment more interesting for everyone. Sometimes a layout may need to be changed because staff realise that one area or a piece of equipment is popular and needs more space.

Portfolio activity

You have been asked to design a layout for a nursery. The room measures 10m × 15m.

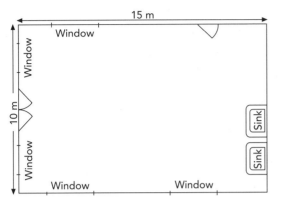

Here is a drawing of the room that shows where there are sinks and windows.

When planning your room layout you must allow enough space for a child in a wheelchair. Show how you would place furniture and equipment and where you would store materials.

Activities, equipment and materials

When children come into a room or hall, they often focus on the materials and equipment that is available. A colourful slide or an attractive homecorner can sometimes make the difference between joining in the fun or staying close to an adult.

When we put out activities and equipment we need to be aware of the amount of space that is needed and the number of children who may wish to join in. Some equipment – for example, train tracks, building blocks and tricycles – need large amounts of floor space and there may not always be enough space for all of them to be put out.

At times we may also find that we need to limit the number of children involved in an activity. A sand tray may be large enough for six children, but the risks of squabbles and accidents are likely to increase if there are eight children trying to play there.

Good practice – checking layouts

✓ Make sure that areas for children look attractive.

✓ Spend time planning activities before the children arrive at the setting.

✓ Make sure that activities look attractive and inviting.

✓ Check the lighting and temperature.

✓ Look out for potential hazards (see Chapter 3, pages 47–51 for more information).

Common tasks to prepare activities

Painting area	Get out paper, aprons and fresh, clean paint.
Homecorner	Display dressing up clothes. Lay the table, dress the dolls and make the bed.
Jigsaws	Put a few attractive ones out. Make sure all the pieces are there. Start off a floor puzzle.
Sand tray	Rake the sand and arrange the equipment attractively – for example, by colour.
Water play	Get aprons ready. Put some items in the water. The water could be coloured with food colouring.
Dough	Put out some brightly coloured dough. Arrange tools in an attractive way.

Portfolio activity

Here is a checklist for choosing equipment and activities for children.

1 *In pairs add to this checklist for choosing activities.*

2 *Ask your supervisor if you can choose two different types of equipment/materials to put out.*

3 *Write down how you did this and why you chose what you did.*

> **Checklist**
> Is there enough room for the activity?
> How many children can use it?
> Is it suitable for the age and stage of the children?

Being adaptable

As early years workers we have to be very adaptable. We may find that we have planned to use a piece of equipment only to discover that someone else has already asked for it! This means that we have to smile and quickly think of something else to do.

The weather can also influence our choice of activities. On days when children have been unable to go outside, we might decide to provide activities that encourage physical activity. We could move furniture back to create more space and play some simple games or put some music on to allow children to dance. On a warm sunny day, the garden or paved area could be used to allow children to play outside.

Think about it

Can you think of some activities for children to do outdoors on these days?

* Windy autumn day
* Warm spring day
* Snowy winter day

Creating interest in activities and equipment

It is a good idea to rotate activities and equipment so that children do not lose interest in them – for example, one day the dough is not put out and plasticine is used instead or building bricks are put out on one day and the train track on another. Changing the activities and equipment in this way is especially important when children are in the same early years setting several days a week.

Where too much equipment is set out children find it harder to choose what to play with. In this situation there is a danger of a lot of it ending up on the floor which can in turn cause accidents. Look at this example.

Case Study

Sarah is working as a nanny. The children have so many toys that they find it difficult to keep their playroom tidy. They also seem bored and uninterested in doing anything. Sometimes the youngest child tips out all the toys on the floor. Sarah finds that she is constantly tidying up. Toys are not kept together so there are pieces of puzzle in the same box as the building bricks. The children have four cupboards full of toys as well as a little shop and equipment for a home corner.

Sarah has told her employer that she does not think that the children are getting the most from the toys that they have. Her employer has said that she can do whatever she thinks is necessary.

Questions

1   How can she make the playroom a better environment?
2   How can she involve the children in helping her?

How displays can make an environment attractive and stimulating

We can use displays to make the environment more attractive for everyone. Dark corners can be transformed by bright posters or framed prints. Corridors and entrance ways can be made to look more welcoming. Visitors, new parents and children are given the impression that the people who work in the setting care about their work.

Displaying children's work

Children love to see their work on display. This could include drawings and objects that they have made as well as pieces of writing. Where possible it is a good idea for displays to be put where parents can see them – for example, in a cloakroom or an entrance. This means that even if they are not able to come into the setting – for example, because they are in a hurry – they can still see what their child has been doing. This can make them feel both proud and reassured.

All children gain enormous benefits from seeing their work on display. It can help them to feel valued and part of the setting as well as giving them confidence. We can encourage children to look at each other's work and ask them what they like about it. This is a way of helping them to value others' efforts and achievements.

Process not perfection

We need to be careful that when children's work is displayed we do not fall into the trap of putting out only work that is perfect. Where space is limited we can keep a list of children's names to check that every child has some work displayed. Children need to understand that although the end product is important, the process and their effort are always what count. This is an important message for children because they can sometimes lose their confidence if they think that they have, in some way, failed.

Using displays as a way of promoting equal opportunity

Displays can be used to break down stereotypes and to encourage children to learn more about others. Visual images can be very strong. We can use posters and other pictures that show positive images – for example, children wearing glasses playing happily, boys and girls playing alongside each other and adults who have different skin tones working together. Positive images of women, black people and people with disabilities are particularly needed. We can help children to learn about different cultures by putting together an interest table with musical instruments, articles of clothing, books and photographs from other cultures. We may also be able to arrange for a speaker to come in and talk to the children about the items. This might help children to understand that although there are differences between people and the way they live, there is not one correct way.

Interest tables

As we saw in Chapter 1, the idea of interest tables is to allow children to touch and see objects of interest. Interest tables can link to a theme – for example, shells, toys, clothes we wear.

Safety is always a consideration when choosing items for an interest table, as young children may put objects in their mouths or drop items on the floor. We also need to put the interest tables in a place which is not too busy as items can get knocked over.

In a home environment it might not be possible to use a table, so the shelf of a bookcase or an area on a low piece of furniture could be used instead.

Preparing an interest table

Interest tables are quite easy to prepare and older children will enjoy helping you set them up.

- Cover the table or surface with fabric. Old sheets or curtains are cheap ways to cover a table. Look out for remnants of interesting fabrics in shops. In settings where children may pull at a cloth, paper could be used instead.

- Boxes can be put underneath the cloth to raise some of the objects.

- Choose objects that are solid, not too precious and that will be attractive to children.

- Try and have a range of items, including books, to make the table look interesting.

- Arrange the objects so that children can see and feel them.

- Label the items neatly.

Children often like to bring in objects from home to add to interest tables. This shows that they are enjoying the theme and is a link between home and the childcare setting. When children bring in items, it is a good idea to label them with the child's name so that they can be sent home later. Children should be encouraged to ask their parents' permission before bringing items in.

Using natural materials for interest tables

We can use interest tables to make children more aware of the wider environment. Through interest tables we can help them to think about the seasonal changes outside – for example, an interest table about autumn or spring. Children can plant bulbs and seeds and watch them grow as well as collect natural materials from outside. Plants can make settings look attractive and children often enjoy taking caring of them. Any plants that we bring into the setting need to be placed where they are not a hazard and also need to be non-poisonous.

Although we want children to be interested and to bring items in, we must be aware that some products from animals may not be hygienic or safe.

Case Study

Simon has brought in a match box containing a dead mouse that his cat has caught. He is very proud of his mouse and wants you to show it to the rest of the group.

Questions

1   What would be your first priorities in this situation?
2   How can you avoid spoiling Simon's enthusiasm but at the same time make sure that the mouse is not handled by other children?
3   Why is it important that you act calmly and avoid showing any feelings of disgust or fear in front of the children?

When we are with children we may need to gently remind them that wild flowers are not to be picked. However, items from their gardens can be brought in with their parents' permission.

Portfolio activity

1   Ask your supervisor if you can set up an interest table. It could be displaying books, natural materials or other objects – for example, musical instruments.
2   Make neat labels for your objects and display them carefully.
3   Take a photograph of the finished table.
4   Write down how the children responded to your table. Did they notice the objects? Did your interest table encourage them to talk?

Preparing wall displays

Wall displays can improve an environment by their visual impact. Some settings have purpose-built boards that are lined with hessian, whereas others may have simple notice boards. We can adapt areas in a setting for a display – for example, using a fridge or cupboard door to show items of interest. These may include posters, photographs and charts as well as children's work.

Putting up a wall display can take time and it is not always safe to do this when there are children around, although children can be involved in making items for the display. If you are not very confident start with a small area and keep to a simple idea.

Good practice – wall displays

✓ Have everything to hand before you start.

✓ Do not take down a display until you have enough time to put another one up in its place.

✓ Displays always take longer than you think. Allow enough time.

✓ Take down other team members' displays carefully.

✓ Consider whether you need to put up some backing paper or fabric to make the surface of the wall or cupboard look more attractive.

✓ Prepare labels for the items including children's names correctly spelt.

✓ Make a title for the display.

✓ Consider making frames for children's pictures to enhance their appearance.

✓ Plan out the position of the work before fixing it to a wall. You could use just one pin or some blu-tac.

✓ As you put items up, keep stepping back to check that they are straight and look effective.

✓ Make sure that you do not leave pins and staples around where children can find them.

✓ Keep a list of children's names to make sure that it is not always the same children who have their work shown.

Labelling and spelling

Labels add a finishing touch to displays. They can help children to recognise simple words and to understand that words have meanings. Children also enjoy seeing their name next to their work and will often want to show their parents and friends what they have done.

Labels need to be clear and it is good practice to use lower-case lettering, although capital letters can be used for the first letters of names. Some early years settings have particular ways of lettering – for example, they may put 'tails' on some letters. Most people find it difficult to keep their lettering straight and so it can be useful to draw some pencil guidelines.

Computers and templates are also useful ways of producing lettering.

It can be a good idea to ask someone to check your spelling as it is easy to make a simple mistake and embarrassing to have it staring out at you on a wall! It is also a good idea to check the spelling of children's names as correct spelling shows that you value the children.

Older children can be encouraged to join in with a display by making their own labels, and where children speak more than one language it might be possible to ask a parent to write some labels in the home language.

Mounting children's work

When children's work is mounted it looks as if it has been framed, which makes it look more attractive. This is not difficult to do. Choose a slightly larger piece of paper and put the piece of work on top. Check that the borders are equal and trim. Where possible it is a good idea to use a paper cutter as this gives a straight edge, otherwise a pencil and a ruler should be used to keep the edges straight.

A contrasting-coloured paper is put behind the drawing or painting

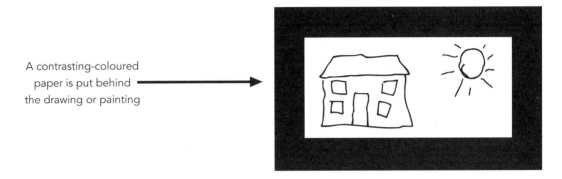

Good effects can be achieved by using contrasting colours for the paper that makes the mount.

Maintaining and changing displays

Displays need to be checked and maintained if they are to remain effective. Interest tables may need to be rearranged as children will be moving the objects around. With wall displays, items can start to fall off and young children may 'pick' at items. Once a display is no longer being noticed, it needs to be changed. Some large childcare settings have rotas for staff members so that everyone takes it in turn to change displays.

Portfolio activity

1   Ask your supervisor if you can put up a display. You might choose to mount children's work or you could put up a frieze.
2   Label your display.
3   Take a photograph of the display.
4   Write down how the children responded to the display.

Using music

Music can be used to create atmosphere in a setting. Soft music can make a setting calm and help children to settle in. Playing some favourite music can help a new child feel welcome.

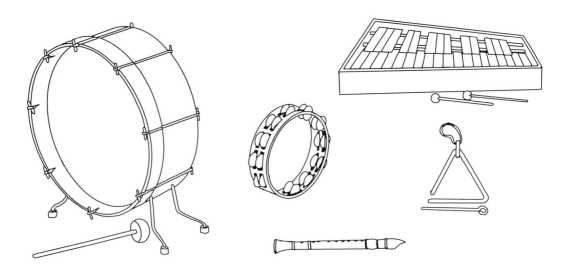

Music can be chosen to fit in with themes or the time of year. We should try to play as many types of music as possible including music from other cultures and countries. This is important because at home a child may be hearing only one sort of music. Listening to different types of music encourages children to respect other cultures and widens their knowledge and understanding of others.

Promoting equal opportunities

In Chapter 1 we looked at the ways in which discrimination can affect children. Stereotypes of gender, race and disability can mean that some children are not given the same opportunities as others. This means that we must make sure that we are actively promoting equal opportunities when planning and providing an environment for children.

Think about it

Throughout this chapter we have looked at ways of providing a reassuring, safe and stimulating environment for all children.

Look back through the chapter and write a list of the ways in which an early years worker can promote equality of opportunity – for example, when displaying work or when reassuring children.

Unit test

Quick quiz

1 Which of these is most important when planning a layout?
   a The home corner has enough equipment.
   b The fire exits are clear.
   c The quiet corner has cushions.
   d The paper cupboard can be locked.

2 Which of these qualities are most important in an early years worker?
   Ability to:
   a draw well
   b understand confidentiality
   c communicate well with parents and children
   d dress neatly and fashionably.

3 What is the most important reason for naming children's coat pegs?
   a It keeps settings tidy.
   b Children learn to read their names.
   c It makes it easier to find coats at hometime.
   d It helps children feel part of the setting.

4 When there is a change of routine, an early years worker can best help children by:
   a telling them that they need to be sensible
   b reading a story
   c explaining what is going to happen
   d asking them to play quietly.

5 Interest tables can encourage learning mainly because they:
   a help children learn to read
   b stimulate children's curiosity
   c encourage children to be tidy
   d help children be creative.

6 A suitable temperature of a nursery is:
   a 6°C
   b 18°C
   c 22°C
   d 24°C.

7 Displaying children's work is important mainly because it:
   a boosts their confidence
   b encourages other children to work harder
   c makes the walls look attractive
   d helps to make the environment hygienic.

8 The most important way comfort objects help children is by:
   a giving them something to hold
   b giving them something they can show to others
   c making them feel secure
   d being shown on interest tables.

9 Routines can help children to:
   a feel secure
   b develop social skills
   c feel independent
   d learn the time.

10 Equipment and furniture placed at children's height:
   a encourages them to share
   b prevents them from becoming bored
   c prevents them from bothering the adults
   d helps them to be independent.

Short answer questions

1 Name three ways in which children can be made to feel welcome in a setting.

2 Which act of government states that many childcare settings must be registered?

3 Give one example of how a layout can be adapted for children with special needs.

4 What is an after-school club?

5 What is meant by the term confidentiality and why is it important?

Child Safety

One of the duties and responsibilities of early years workers is to keep children safe. Children are more vulnerable to accidents than any other age group. Over a million children are taken to hospital each year. Whatever early years settings we work in we have a duty to keep children safe. As young children have no sense of danger and the consequences of their actions, we need to do the thinking for them. There have been cases where early years workers have been taken to court because they have not kept children safe. Keeping children safe is an important area and covers accident prevention, hygiene routines and other issues such as abuse. It is also important that early years workers know what to do in the event of an emergency. This chapter is divided into three sections:

1   *Preventing accidents*

2   *Emergency procedures and First Aid*

3   *Child protection*

The **Health and Safety Act of 1974** is a good starting point when looking at our duties in keeping children safe. This act is designed to protect everyone in any early years setting. Under this act:

- Employees must use the safety equipment provided – e.g. an early years worker must use safety equipment provided like disposable gloves or stairgates.

- Employees must make sure that their actions do not harm others – e.g. leaving a hot drink in the reach of children would endanger a child.

- Employees also have a **duty** to report hazards and to follow the safety policy of the early years setting.

Knowledge into Action

Every employer must have a qualifed First Aider at work.

1   *Find out who this is in your workplace.*
2   *Find out about the Health and Safety policy and First Aid practices of your setting.*

1 Preventing accidents

Promoting a safe environment

We can make sure that children's environments are safe by carrying out checks and by being generally observant. Every environment has different risks. A family home may have a kitchen that is also used as a living area, a nursery with many children may have to ensure the entrance and exit points are kept clear. In school settings the playground is likely to be an area that is hazardous because of the number of children at play.

The most common injuries to children are:

- burns and scalds

- injuries caused by falls

- choking and suffocation

- poisoning

- cuts.

The following diagram shows hazards that commonly cause the above type of accidents in indoor settings.

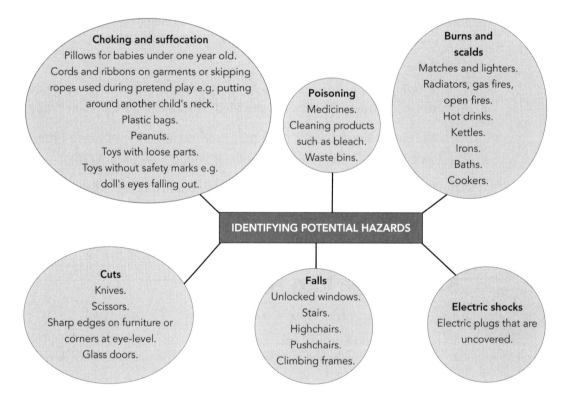

Choking and suffocation
Pillows for babies under one year old.
Cords and ribbons on garments or skipping ropes used during pretend play e.g. putting around another child's neck.
Plastic bags.
Peanuts.
Toys with loose parts.
Toys without safety marks e.g. doll's eyes falling out.

Poisoning
Medicines.
Cleaning products such as bleach.
Waste bins.

Burns and scalds
Matches and lighters.
Radiators, gas fires, open fires.
Hot drinks.
Kettles.
Irons.
Baths.
Cookers.

IDENTIFYING POTENTIAL HAZARDS

Cuts
Knives.
Scissors.
Sharp edges on furniture or corners at eye-level.
Glass doors.

Falls
Unlocked windows.
Stairs.
Highchairs.
Pushchairs.
Climbing frames.

Electric shocks
Electric plugs that are uncovered.

Some of these common hazards can be avoided by using safety equipment – for example, harnesses on highchairs, stairgates or cooker guards. There is a wide range of safety equipment available and early years workers have a duty to use it. Accidents often happen when adults:

- do not use the equipment properly

- think that it will be all right just this once.

Safety equipment

Equipment	Purpose
Reins and harnesses	To prevent children from falling out of highchairs and from running into the road.
Safety gates	To stop children from climbing stairs and from going into certain rooms – e.g. toilets and kitchens.
Play pen	To have a safe area for children in a certain room – e.g. a kitchen.
Smoke alarm	To detect smoke and raise the alarm.
Fire blanket	To smother flames – they are kept in kitchens to throw over a pan that has caught fire.
Catches for windows and cupboards	To prevent children from opening windows and cupboards.
Saucepan guard	To prevent children from tipping pans from cookers on to them.
Electric plug sockets	To prevent children from putting their fingers into sockets
Plastic film	To cover glass and make it safer – e.g. glass windows in the home environment.
Plastic corner covers	To put on furniture with sharp edges.

Think about it

Look at these two pictures and consider how the hazards should be managed.

Checking equipment and toys can also prevent accidents. Equipment can become worn or unstable so buying secondhand equipment that will be used by many children is not advisable. It is particularly important that regular checks are made on any piece of equipment that:

- has moving parts

- is taking children's weight.

For example, slides need to be checked for stability and tricycles need to be checked for steering.

Most equipment wears out eventually.

The chart below shows how the main materials used in making equipment may wear.

Wear and tear of equipment

Type of material	Look out for	Examples of equipment
Plastic	cracking, fading colours, sharp edges	chairs, sit and ride, seats on tricycles
Metal	signs of rust, flaking paint, metal fatigue	climbing frames, tricycles, see-saws, pushchairs, highchairs, swings
Wooden	rough edges, splinters, flaking paint	chairs, bookcases, wooden blocks, jigsaw puzzles

Cleaning toys and equipment is often a good way of checking that they are safe, while at the same time preventing the spread of any infection. Manufacturers' instructions must be followed when washing toys and other equipment such as baby mats or rattles.

Equipment that is used for feeding needs to be cleaned each time it is used, whereas outdoor equipment can be cleaned every month. Any toys that are regularly handled – for example, duplo bricks – should be washed at least once a week. Some toys can be washed while other equipment needs to be wiped over with a weak solution of disinfectant. Using a mild solution of disinfectant kills bacteria.

Portfolio activity

Ask your supervisor if you can check and clean an item of equipment.

1   *Write about how you checked this item.*
2   *What were you looking for?*
3   *How did you clean this item?*

Toys and play materials

Accidents can be prevented by making sure that toys and materials are suitable for the children using them. All new toys and equipment should have a safety mark on them. Toys without marks can be dangerous. They may have parts with sharp edges or they may fall apart.

Accidents happen when children choke on small pieces or use equipment that is designed for older children – for example, a three-year-old trying to get on a skateboard. This is why manufacturers' instructions must be followed. By law manufacturers must state if a product could be dangerous for younger children. If you are unsure about a toy it is better to remove it and talk to supervisors or parents.

Case Study

You are working as a nanny for two children aged two and three years. Their grandmother is staying with them for a few days. You notice that she is about to give them a toy with very small parts and you are worried that the youngest child may swallow them.

Questions
1 *Is it your responsibility to take any action?*
2 *In pairs consider how you would handle this situation. (You could do this as role play.)*

Close supervision is an essential part of avoiding accidents. Most accidents happen very quickly. The level of supervision will vary according to the age of the children and the activity that they are involved in.

Toddlers need to be supervised very carefully as their actions tend to be unpredictable – for example, they may suddenly drop or throw an object. They are also unsteady in their movements and are more likely to trip over. Children under two years are also likely to put objects into their mouths, climb up furniture and pull things down from tables or shelves. This means that if you need to leave a room, you must take them with you unless someone else is free to supervise.

Case Study

You are looking after an eight-month-old baby and a three-year-old toddler. The baby is crawling. The toddler has shown some signs of aggression towards the baby. You need to go to the toilet which is upstairs in the bathroom.

In small groups consider what you could do to make sure that both children are safe.

Supervising older children

As children become older, they are more able to understand the need for rules and to be aware of dangers. We can explain to them why, for example, they must wait for their turn on the slide. Children are also influenced by the way we act. This means that we must be good role models – children need to see us tidy up, use safety equipment and generally not take risks.

We can turn safety issues into learning opportunities for children by explaining why certain equipment is dangerous – for example, knives have sharp blades, matches can cause fires. We can invite fire officers to the early years setting or visit ambulance stations to make children more aware of safety.

Think about it

A group of children is having a lot of fun jumping on and off a wall. One child starts to push the others off as part of the game.

1 *What would you do and say to prevent this game from becoming dangerous?*
2 *How could you help the children to carry on enjoying jumping while not risking any accidents?*

Good supervision is a balance between allowing children to have fun and making sure that they are not doing anything dangerous. The following chart shows some of the common signs that suggest we should check or intervene.

When to intervene

Loud, angry voices	This is often a sign that a child is about to hit another or that an object is about to be thrown.
Squeals of laughter	This is often a sign that a game is getting out of hand and that the children are not seeing the possible dangers – e.g. jumping off equipment or daring others to do something.
Silence	This is often a sign that a child has found something that is very interesting for them – e.g. a container of bleach.

In early years settings where there are many children, it is important for all the adults to keep an eye on what the children are doing. This means that even when you, personally, are working with only one or two children, you should still be aware of the other children – they may need your support or may be doing something that could cause an accident.

Layouts also have a great impact on safety. A good layout means that children have room to move about safely and that toys and equipment can easily be tidied away. Most large settings separate activities into different areas for these reasons.

We need to make sure that floor areas are kept tidy, clean and dry to avoid accidents – for example, tripping up or slipping over. Whatever early years setting we work in, we must always make sure that access points such as front doors and fire exits are kept clear in case of fire or other emergencies. In many settings certain areas – for example, kitchens – are kept out of bounds by using safety gates.

Outdoor areas which also need to be checked for safety

Plants and animals

- Are any plants poisonous?

- Is there a risk of any animal harming children – e.g. dogs not on leads, guinea pigs or rabbits in cages where children can put their fingers?

- Is there any dog or cat **faeces** (pooh/mess) around? (Children can pick up a disease through being in contact with dog and cat faeces.)

Access and fences

- Can children wander off?

- Can strangers come into contact with children?

Hidden dangers

- Is there a risk of drowning because of water – e.g. ponds, streams, paddling pool?

- Are there any litter bins that children could reach?

- Do litter bins have lids on them?

- Are there any tools or items – e.g. clothes lines – that could cause accidents?

- Are there any steep steps that could be unsafe for toddlers?

- Is play equipment safe and clean?

Portfolio activity

Ask your supervisor if you can check an outdoor area at your workplace for safety.

1   *Write down how you did this.*
2   *Did you spot any potential hazards?*
3   *How were these hazards managed?*

Reporting hazards

There may be times when hazards need reporting to a supervisor or the person responsible for health and safety in your workplace. Where children are being cared for in their homes it will be the parent or carer who needs to be informed. Information about dangers and hazards must be passed on promptly. Where there is an immediate danger, children should be kept away from a piece of equipment or a certain area until it is safe.

Knowledge into Action

Using a computer, design a form that can be used in an early years setting to report potential hazards.

Your form should contain spaces for the following information to be entered:

Date	Area or piece of equipment	Potential Hazard
	Action taken so far	Signature of staff member

**WIZARD NURSERY
EVACUATION PROCEDURE**

Your assembly point is

DUKE STREET PLAYGROUND

What you <u>must</u> do in the case of a fire or other emergency

When the fire alarm sounds

- The senior person or authorised deputy will take charge of any evacuation and ensure that no-one is left in the area.

- Leave the building as instructed by the nearest exit and report to the person in charge of the assembly point at the place indicated above. A roll call will then be taken.

Remember

- keep calm
- use the **nearest** available exit
- do **not** use the lift
- do **not** stop to collect personal belongings
- do **not** re-enter the building for any reason until the safety officer or his or her representative gives you permission

2 Emergency procedures and First Aid

As early years workers, we must know what to do in the event of a fire or other emergency. Most early years settings have procedures to deal with the majority of emergencies. It is important that everyone working in a setting knows where all the exit points are and what their role is in an emergency. It is usual for settings to have fire notices as well as fire practices to make sure that staff are able to evacuate a building quickly. Where children are being cared for in their homes, it is still important to make sure that there is more than one exit available in the case of a fire.

What to do during an alarm or practice

As part of the fire regulations, all workplaces must carry out fire practices regularly. These are important as they give adults the chance to check that the procedures work well.

Knowledge into Action

Find out about the emergency procedures in your workplace.

1   *Who is responsible for these procedures?*
2   *Where is the meeting zone?*
3   *Are there any fire extinguishers or other emergency equipment?*
4   *Who is responsible for this equipment?*

WATER	FOAM	POWDER	CO_2	FIRE BLANKET
Wood, paper, textiles, etc.	Wood, paper, textiles, etc., petrol, oils, fats, paints etc.	Wood, paper, textiles, etc., petrol, oils, fats, paints etc., electrical hazards, vehicle protection.	Petrol, oils, fats, paints etc., electrical hazards.	For smothering fire (chip pan or deep fat fires, waste bin fires, wrapping around someone whose clothes are burning)

There are different types of fire extinguisher and it is essential that anyone using them reads the instructions carefully. Instructions are printed on the extinguisher. Always remember that your first duty in a fire is to raise the alarm and evacuate the building.

There are three parts to most emergency procedures:

1   Make sure that everyone leaves the building rapidly and calmly.

2   Group adults and staff together in a safe zone.

3   Use a register to check that everyone is present.

Remaining calm is one of the most important things that adults can do when faced with any sort of emergency. Fire alarms are designed to be loud, but to a young child they can be terrifying. We need to reassure children and explain clearly what is happening and what they need to do. A register of children's names is needed to check that all the children are out of the building and each setting will have someone who is responsible for this.

Emergency contacts

Emergency numbers or contacts are essential for all settings. Children may become ill or have an accident and if this happens, then their parents or carers should be contacted. Such information is often stored in a central place – in large work settings this might be an office, but where children are being cared for at home it might be placed by the telephone or in another agreed place.

Making sure that children are safe at the end of sessions

The end of a day or a session can be a very busy time and every early years setting will have a procedure to make sure that children are collected safely. In some settings parents or carers come indoors to collect children, while in others children wait outside to be collected. Most settings ask parents to let them know in advance if a different person is collecting a child. It is always better to check with a supervisor if you are unsure of the arrangements as in some cases children's parents may not be living together and one parent may not have access to a child.

Case Study

You are waiting for Tom's mum to come and collect him. Another mum sees that Tom has not been collected and says that she can take him home because it is on her way. You know that this mum is a good friend of Tom's mum and that she sometimes brings Tom to the nursery.

Discuss in pairs what you should do and check your answers with your tutor or supervisor.

Keeping children safe on outings

Children of all ages enjoy going on outings and even a small outing such as posting a letter can provide learning opportunities. The amount of preparation depends on the scale of the outing. In large settings an outing that requires transport should be planned at least two months ahead of the date. Insurance and parental permission as well as considering supervision arrangements will all take time to plan.

The secret of an enjoyable outing is to choose somewhere which is not too tiring for either the children or the adults. There should be plenty to see and do at the children's level. The only way to really find out what a place is like and to make sure that it is safe is to do an advance visit.

If children are being cared for at home or by a childminder, parents still need to give their consent to outings. Most parents and early years workers may have an arrangement that some types of outings are not discussed in advance – for example, walking to the local park or shops – but that early years workers ask in advance if they wish to take the children for longer trips.

Supervision
How many adults are needed to accompany children?
(Must meet local Social Services guidelines or schools policy.)
Prepare registers, allocate groups.

Permission
Parents must give written permission for children to go on trips organised by settings.
Letters should include date, timings, purpose of visit, cost, transport arrangements and details of what children should wear.

Possible costs
Entry price for children.
Entry price for adults.
Transport costs.
Insurance.
Can parents afford this cost?

PLANNING AN OUTING

Things to take
Food and drink.
Spare clothing.
First Aid kit.
Emergency contact numbers.
Registers.
Medication e.g. inhalers for asthmatic children.
Spare money for phone calls.
Suncream and sun hats.
For younger children:
Reins and harnesses.
Nappies.
Comforters.
Pushchairs.

Venue
How far is it?
What would happen if it rained?
What are the learning opportunities?
Is it value for money?
Where are the toilets?
How safe is the venue?
Advance visits are essential when organising large outings.

Transport
Walking – how far?
Public transport: trains, buses – can they be booked?
Private transport: minibuses, coaches – do they have seatbelts?
Private cars – do drivers have insurance that covers this type of outing?

Think about it

1 *Choose three places in your area where you could take children aged between two and five years.*
2 *Give reasons why you think that they would be good places to go.*

Stranger danger

• Most settings no longer put badges on children for outings.

• Young children are likely to trust and go with a stranger who seems to know their name.

Providing a hygienic environment

Hygiene is about keeping things clean. In most environments there will be bacteria and viruses present. This is what is meant by the term **germs**. Young children pick up infections easily so it is very important that early years settings are as hygienic as possible. As children get older they develop more resistance to infection.

1	Being breathed in **(Inhalation)**	Droplets of moist air contain viruses and bacteria.	
2	Being swallowed **(Ingestion)**	We take in bacteria in our food and drink as well as by licking our fingers, etc.	
3	Through a cut in the skin **(Inoculation)**	Bacteria in the air or on objects enters through the cut.	

The chart opposite shows the three ways that bacteria and viruses can get into the body.

When infections are passed on to others this is called **cross infection**. Where children are being cared for in large groups there is always a danger of cross infection as children are sharing equipment and are in close contact with each other. Colds, food poisoning and gastroenteritis can all spread through cross infection.

Ways of minimising cross infection

There are some simple measures that we can take to prevent cross infection, although it is impossible to provide a completely sterile environment.

Hand-washing

Bacteria is often spread on hands. Children share toys and put things in their mouths which often means that infection can be spread. It is, therefore, important that we make sure that children wash their hands during the day:

- before snacks, meals and drinks
- after using the toilet
- after playing outside or touching animals
- after using substances such as water, paint or dough where bacteria may be present on the hands.

As we are in contact with many children and may also be responsible for preparing and serving food, it is essential that we make sure that we wash our hands frequently. For example, after helping children to blow their noses!

There is more detailed information on food hygiene in Chapter 5 (pages 107–109).

To prevent cross infection it is important that bacteria is not spread on towels or other items that children touch. In some settings paper towels are used to make sure that no cross infection can take place. Other settings have flannels and towels that are named and only used by these children.

Paper tissues are also better than handkerchiefs because they can be thrown away whereas a handkerchief may still have bacteria on it from the last time it was used.

Babies and children under two years

This group of children is particularly vulnerable to infection and so great care must be taken when preparing food or drinks for these children. If babies are in daycare settings, then sterilisation procedures must be carried out for longer than in a home environment – probably until 12 to 15 months. This means that bowls, cutlery and beakers all need to be sterilised before they are given to children. We need to follow the manufacturers' guidelines on sterilisation procedures. Chapter 13 looks at how to sterilise equipment. Unfinished foods should be thrown away as bacteria from spoons will grow on the food even if it is kept in the fridge.

Handling and disposing of waste material

When working with children there are times when we may come into contact with body fluids – e.g. blood, urine, faeces and vomit. Many infections, including HIV and hepatitis, can be passed on through contact with these fluids so we must take the following precautions:

- Wear protective gloves when dealing with body fluids.
- Make sure that any cuts on hands are covered by plasters.
- Wash hands after disposing of waste materials and cleaning up.

Disposing of waste material

Waste material includes tissues, cloths that have been used to mop up and nappies. In large settings these should be placed in a separate covered bin which is then sent for incineration (burning). In the home environment this is not possible so any waste material should be wrapped and put in an outside bin to make sure that it cannot be handled again.

Never try to flush nappies down toilets. This can block the toilets.

General hygiene routines

On page 60 is a chart that outlines the general hygiene routines that need to be carried out.

In order to provide a high standard of hygiene, we need to carry out frequent checks in the setting. During the sessions, we should wipe up any spills and areas should be kept tidy. It is the responsibility of every member of staff to report any

Hygiene routines

Item	Why it needs to be cleaned	Method
Toys and play equipment	These are frequently handled and may be put in the mouth.	Sterilise plastic items in solution.
Feeding equipment	Spoons, bowls and other items are put in the mouth.	Sterilise all items of feeding equipment for children under two years.
Tables	Children may put items that have been on the tables in their mouths.	Wipe with a clean cloth every time they are used – a mild disinfectant should be used.
Worktops	Food may be prepared on these surfaces.	Wipe with a clean cloth – a mild disinfectant should be used.
Toilets Handbasins Sinks	Toilets and areas for hand-washing are places where bacteria grow.	Clean regularly with bleach solution. Check toilets frequently during sessions.
Bins	Items such as damp paper, food and nappies will have bacteria on them.	Empty bins frequently. Place nappies in sealed bags. Wash out bins every day.
Floors	Children will put their hands on floors when playing. Food may be dropped on the floor. Toys that have been on the floor may be put in the mouth.	Clean floors regularly – a disinfectant should be used.

areas or equipment that need attention and perhaps to carry out the necessary cleaning.

Plastic gloves should be worn for protection and cloths that are used should be thoroughly rinsed after use and regularly put in a solution containing disinfectant.

Caring for animals in a hygienic and safe way

Children enjoy having pets and animals around them. Many group settings have small animals such as hamsters, rabbits and guinea pigs, whereas in a home setting there may be cats and dogs. Unfortunately different animals are associated with a range of infections – for example, humans can pick up an infection from dog and cat faeces that is linked to the worms these animals carry. An example of this is the disease toxicarosis which can make children blind and is caused by a worm in dog faeces.

How we meet the needs of pets and at the same time keep the environment safe and hygienic depends on:

■ the age of the children

■ any allergic reaction that they may have

■ the animal itself.

Good practice – children and animals

✔ Supervise children at all times when animals are around.

✔ Make sure that children cannot touch feeding bowls and litter trays.

✔ Clean feeding bowls and litter trays away from children it is a good idea to wear gloves for your own protection.

✔ Make sure that spoons and other equipment used for caring for pets does not come into contact with children's plates and cutlery.

✔ Make sure that children get into the habit of washing their hands after touching pets.

✔ Do not encourage children to kiss pets or to put their fingers into their cages.

✔ Clean up any faeces from animals quickly using disinfectant.

✔ Help children to understand that pets are not toys and that they have their own needs and sometimes like to be left alone.

✔ Make sure that babies are not left alone in a room with either dogs or cats.

Portfolio activity

1 Record the hygiene routine of your workplace.
2 Who is responsible for making sure that these tasks are completed?
3 Ask your supervisor if you can help carry out one of the hygiene tasks.
4 Write down what you did, the materials you used and what you learnt from doing this.

Further information about how to look after pets and animals can be obtained from a local vet or the RSPCA.

Immunisation

In earlier times many children died of childhood diseases – for example, polio, diphtheria and whooping cough.

Childhood diseases are no longer such a threat for several reasons.

- Washing and toilet facilities in homes have improved.

- Housing conditions are better. There is less overcrowding and most people can afford to heat their homes.

- Most people can afford to eat and feed their children.

- Antibiotics can be used against many common illnesses – e.g. pneumonia.

- People no longer have to pay to see the doctor which means diseases are diagnosed earlier.

The other main reason that there are fewer childhood diseases in this country is childhood immunisation. Injections or drops are given to children that encourage the body to make antibodies. The antibodies can fight the infection later if needed. Although in some countries immunisation is required before children can enter school, in this country parents do not have to have their children immunised and some choose not to do so for many reasons – for example, on religious or medical grounds.

The most recent addition to the immunisation programme has been an injection against a form of meningitis. This is often referred to as the Hib vaccine.

Age	Disease
8 weeks 12 weeks 16 weeks	Diphtheria, whooping cough, tetanus – a combined injection Polio – taken by mouth Hib – injected *This is often called the 'triple'*
12–18 months	Measles, mumps and rubella – a combined injection. *Known as the MMR.*
4–5 years	Whooping cough, tetanus – a combined injection Polio – taken by mouth

The chart above shows a typical immunisation programme.

Think about it

From time to time, there are reports in the newspapers that suggest that certain vaccines are unsafe. For example, press articles recently suggested that the MMR vaccine may cause autism in children. Some medical professionals feel very strongly that these type of articles are damaging as they cause parents to panic. They also feel that parents are not often given the whole truth as articles can be biased or sensationalised.

Discuss the following issues in pairs.

1 *Do you think that newspapers should run 'health scare' stories?*
2 *Do you know of parents who have decided not to have their children immunised?*
3 *Do you think that immunisations should be compulsory as in some other countries?*

First Aid

It is *essential* that adults working with children have some First Aid training. Taking a practical course in First Aid can save lives. This section gives a summary of First Aid procedures, but cannot replace the experience and knowledge that a First Aid course will give you.

There are procedures for dealing with accidents so that the correct action is taken.

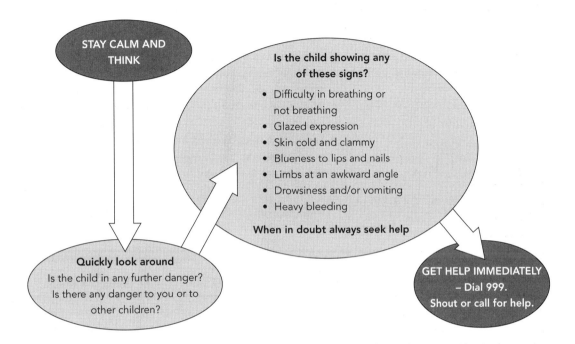

STAY CALM AND THINK

Is the child showing any of these signs?

- Difficulty in breathing or not breathing
- Glazed expression
- Skin cold and clammy
- Blueness to lips and nails
- Limbs at an awkward angle
- Drowsiness and/or vomiting
- Heavy bleeding

When in doubt always seek help

Quickly look around
Is the child in any further danger?
Is there any danger to you or to other children?

GET HELP IMMEDIATELY
– Dial 999.
Shout or call for help.

Getting emergency help

If there is an emergency situation, you may need to dial 999. The operators will guide you by asking you some questions. This information helps them to send out the appropriate help.

1   Your name and the telephone number from where you are calling.

2   The location of the accident. (Think carefully and give as much information as possible so that the ambulance can find you.)

3   What has happened. (This helps the ambulance crew know what they need to do when they arrive.)

4   What you have done so far to treat the injury.

If the child is seriously injured the operator may give you some advice while the ambulance is on its way.

Dealing with a child who is unconscious

If you think a child is unconscious, you must shout for help.

Note: To be able to follow these points more effectively, it is important for early years workers to follow a practical First Aid course.

First Aid

General points	Poisoning	Cuts and wounds
• Call or shout for help. • Stop any treatment and follow **ABC** if a child stops breathing or • Do not give food or drink to children who have had a major accident. • Remain calm and reassuring.	(Children may not look well, begin vomiting or you may see what has been taken.) • Ask the child what they have eaten or drunk if this is possible. • Watch for signs of losing consciousness. • Do not make the child vomit or give any drinks. • Take the suspected poison with you to the hospital so that they can give the appropriate treatment.	• Direct pressure needs to be applied to the wound with a clean pad. If it is a large wound try to press the edges together. • Do not remove anything from a deep wound as you may cause more bleeding. • Tie a bandage around the pad – firmly but not too tightly. • If blood comes through apply another pad and bandage over the top. • Keep applying pressure for about 15 minutes. • Lie the child down and raise the injured part so that it is higher than the heart.
Fractures, dislocations and sprains	**Choking**	**Burns and scalds**

• It is not always easy to spot that a child has a fracture although signs may include:
  • loss of movement and power
  • swelling
  • awkward angle of limb.
• Keep the child still and get a first aider to come and help you.
• If a leg is thought to be broken, tie bandages around both legs above and below the fracture to keep the leg still.
• Use a scarf or bandage to make a sling to keep an arm still.
	• Hold the child so that their head is downwards. This can be over your knees.
	• Slap firmly five times between the shoulder blades.
	• Repeat if necessary.
		• Cool down the affected area immediately using cold water or any harmless liquid – milk – if you are not near water.
		• Do this for at least 10 minutes.
		• Keep talking to the child and explain what you are doing.
		• Do not remove clothes that have stuck to the skin or put on creams of any kind.
		• Cover the area with a clean cloth – e.g. a teacloth (do not use anything fluffy like a towel).

Think about it

Gary is five years old. He fell over in the playground and bumped his knee and his head. Cotton wool squeezed in cold water was put on his head and a plaster was applied to his knee. He said he felt better and he was sent back to his classroom.

He now complains of feeling sick. His teacher is concerned that he is just trying to get out of doing his work.

1   *Why could Gary be telling the truth when he says that he feels sick?*
2   *What action should be taken in the setting?*
3   *Why is it important that everyone in a setting knows when a child has had a minor accident?*

Put 2 fingers under the child's chin and 1 hand on the forehead.

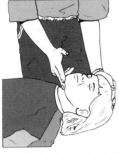

Gently tilt the head well back. Straighten limbs. Tuck the hand nearest you under the child's thigh – keep the arm straight and palm upwards.

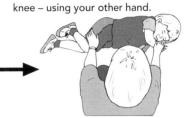

Bring the other arm across the child's chest. Place the hand against the child's cheek – with palm outwards.
Pull up the child's far leg, just above the knee – using your other hand.

Pull on the far leg and roll the child towards you still pressing the hand against the cheek – until the child is lying on her side.

To stop the child rolling too far, use your knees as support. Bend the upper leg so that it is at a right angle from the body.

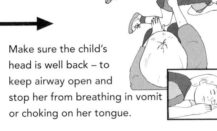

Make sure the child's head is well back – to keep airway open and stop her from breathing in vomit or choking on her tongue.

Make sure the lower arm is free and lying next to the back – palm facing up.

The recovery position

Injury	Treatment	Check for
Bump to the head – e.g. falling over or running into another child	Apply cotton wool squeezed in cold water. If the bump is bad apply wrapped crushed ice.	Drowsiness, vomiting or headaches – these could indicate concussion.
Nose bleed	Tip the head forward. Pinch the soft part of the nose just below the bridge. Wrapped crushed ice can be put onto the nose if needed.	Seek medical attention if the bleeding continues for more than half an hour or if it is mixed with clear fluid
Grazed skin	Rinse the wound with clean water. Allow to heal in the air.	
Bruises and trapped fingers	Apply cotton wool squeezed in cold water or wrapped crushed ice.	Run a hand gently over the limb to check that nothing feels lumpy which might be a sign of a fracture.
Vomiting	Do not leave the child. Reassure them. Offer a sip of water to take away the sour taste.	If vomiting occurs after a bump to the head, medical attention is needed as this is a sign of concussion.
Insect stings	Reassure the child. Try to remove the sting by scraping it out with a finger nail. Do not squeeze the sting. Use a wrapped ice pack to reduce the swelling.	Urgent medical help is needed if the sting is in the mouth or if the child starts to look ill. Some children are allergic to stings.

Assessing minor injuries

Once we are sure that children are in no serious danger, we need to assess the injuries.

It is a good idea to encourage children to stay lying down or sitting up – unless they are in immediate danger – while you look at their injuries and talk to them. With some small bumps and knocks, a cuddle and some adult attention is all that is needed to help children feel better.

The First Aid box

Every early years setting should have at least one First Aid box that is kept in a convenient place – out of reach of children but easily accessible to adults. If children are being cared for at home, it is important that you know where the First Aid box is kept.

First Aid boxes need to be checked regularly as some items may need replacing or be past their Use By date. If you notice that items need replacing you must report this to the supervisor. Never borrow items such as scissors out of kits. They may be needed for an emergency.

The contents of First Aid boxes tend to vary according to the needs and policies of the setting. In large workplaces, First Aid boxes are often green with a white cross. They must meet the requirements of the Health and Safety at Work Act.

A first aid box should be a strong container impervious to dust and damp, clearly labelled with a white cross on a green background, and easily available at all times.
The following contents are recommended by the Health & Safety Executive.

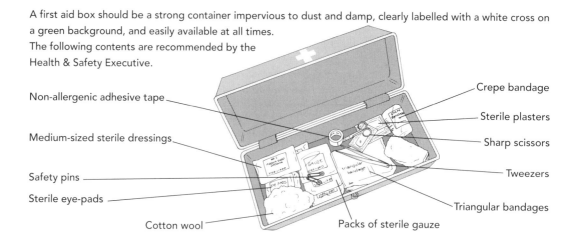

Non-allergenic adhesive tape

Medium-sized sterile dressings

Safety pins

Sterile eye-pads

Cotton wool

Crepe bandage

Sterile plasters

Sharp scissors

Tweezers

Triangular bandages

Packs of sterile gauze

Knowledge into Action

Ask your supervisor if you can look at the First Aid box in your workplace.

1 Write down a list of what is in it.
2 Find out what all the items are used for.

Informing parents

All accidents, major or minor, need to be reported to parents. Sometimes a minor injury may be more serious than it looks. This is often the case with bumps to the head where children may complain of feeling unwell after a few hours.

Many settings will tell parents about minor injuries when the child is collected. When parents are not able to collect their children most settings send a slip home with the following details.

- What happened and at what time.

- The treatment that was given.

- Who gave the treatment.

If children have a major injury, parents and carers need to be contacted at once. It is important that they know exactly what is happening to their child – for example, if the child is going to hospital they need to know which one. Parents and carers also need to know who is with their child and, if possible, they should be involved in making decisions about the treatment. For example, they may prefer for the child to be taken to the family doctor.

Parents are likely to be upset when they hear their child is injured and we can help by showing that the emergency is being handled calmly. There may be ways in which we can help further – for example, by offering to make sure that an older child is collected from school.

ACCIDENT REPORT

Full name of casualty *Jamie Gray*
(Child or adult)
Date and time of accident *1.25   29/4/97*
Where it happened *In the garden*
What happened *Jamie got a splinter in his little finger of left hand.*

What injuries occurred *A splinter*
Treatment given *Splinter taken out washed under tap.*
Medical aid sought

Name of person dealing with accident *Kathryn Dixon*
Name of witnesses *Jean Tindal*

Parents signature *W. Gray*

For some accidents you may want to draw a sketch, as you would after a traffic accident, to indicate:-
The layout of equipment in area where accident occurred.
The position of adults and children.
Please use the back of the duplicate sheet so you keep it for your records.

WHITE COPY: To Parent/Carer   YELLOW COPY: Group File

Recording accidents

By law, all accidents, major or minor, must be recorded in workplaces. Workplaces have accident books where the following information needs recording:

- What happened.

- Where the accident took place.

- The time of the accident.

- What treatment was given.

- Signature of the person reporting the accident.

It is a good idea for settings to look at the accident book and consider if any accidents are happening at particular times or in particular areas. This may mean that there needs to be more supervision or a change in the layout.

Think about it

You are supervising a group of children playing with a ball. Two children run into each other. One falls down. Both children are crying. One has a bumped head and the other has grazed knees.

1 In pairs, discuss what you should do.
2 Work out an action plan for treating the children.
3 What signs should you be looking out for when children have bumped their heads?
4 Would this incident need to go into an accident book?

Portfolio activity

Ask your supervisor if you can help another member of staff to give First Aid treatment for a minor injury.

1 *Write down what the nature of the injury was and how the child was treated.*
2 *If you reassured or helped to give First Aid, write down your role.*
3 *What did you learn from this activity?*

3 Child protection

As much as we would like to think that all the children we care for are happy and safe, it is a fact that some children are abused. This means that children may not be treated in a safe and proper manner – for example, being burnt by cigarettes or being left to get their own food. Abuse can take place in children's homes or even in early years settings and can be by relatives or friends of the family as well as by acquaintances and strangers. It is hard for most people to understand, but parents who abuse their children often still love them and children may find it hard to tell someone that they are being abused. To protect children from abuse, we must be able to recognise its signs and symptoms.

Abuse is often grouped into four categories:

▪ physical

▪ emotional

▪ sexual

▪ neglect

and children may suffer from more than one of these.

Physical abuse

Although the law allows parents to use 'reasonable chastisement' – for example, a slap on the hand – it is not legal for anyone to bite, burn, shake or in any other way injure a child. This is physical abuse.

Signs of physical abuse include:
• bite marks
• bruising on areas of the body that are not associated with normal accidents such as falling over – e.g. marks on thighs
• bruising or marks that forms a pattern – e.g. hand- or belt-shaped
• burns and scalds.

Other signs that children are being abused could include:

- aggressiveness towards other children

- reluctance or difficulty in explaining how they received bruises or injuries

- unwillingness to change for swimming or games.

When children come into the early years setting with a bump or a bruise, we should always ask in a friendly way how the accident happened. Most children are keen to explain exactly how they hurt themselves and are delighted to show off the plaster or the mark. There may be cause for concern if a child becomes tearful or does not want to talk about what has happened.

Emotional abuse

Children need unconditional love and can be emotionally harmed by taunts, threats and being made to feel guilty. Parents who abuse their children emotionally are likely to be insecure and need reassurance that their child loves them. This form of abuse has only been recognised in the past few years. It is often hard to be sure if children's behaviour is linked to emotional abuse but signs include:

- low self esteem and confidence

- attention seeking and clinginess

- telling lies

- stammering or stuttering

- tantrums at an age that is not usual i.e. beyond five years

- tearfulness.

Sexual abuse

The media has played a strong role in making us recognise that some children are sexually abused. Most sexual abuse is carried out by someone that the child knows and trusts. Sexual abuse is any action that gives an adult sexual satisfaction and can include kissing and fondling through to rape. Most cases that come to our attention involve men abusing children although it is not uncommon for women to abuse as well. Many children are told that what they are experiencing is normal or that it is just a secret and this can make children unsure about whether they should tell someone.

Physical signs of sexual abuse may include:

- wetting or soiling themselves

- pain on urinating

- bedwetting

- bruises and unexplained scratches or marks

- loss of appetite

- itchiness of genital areas.

Sometimes it is the behaviour of children that leads early years workers to suspect sexual abuse. Most children are interested in their bodies, but children who are being abused have more knowledge than is usual for their age. This knowledge may be reflected in their drawings and in their play as well as their behaviour towards adults.

Other behavioural signs may include:

- regression – e.g. wanting to be fed or wear nappies

- withdrawn and solitary behaviour

- low self-esteem and confidence.

Neglect

Neglect is the term used when children's needs are not being met. They may not be adequately clothed, fed or washed. There are sometimes cases where children are left in their cots while their parents are out. Sometimes children are neglected because their parents are not coping with the responsibility of having children or are having separate problems of their own. Sometimes children are neglected because their parents do not understand their needs. They may not know how important it is to talk to a baby or that children need to be stimulated.

Signs of neglect include:

- often hungry

- dirty or badly fitting clothes

- tiredness (this is sometimes due to lack of food as well as sleep)

- poor personal hygiene – dirty hair, skin and bad breath

- constant colds or infections such as sore throats

- underweight and not thriving

- late in arriving to sessions and many unexplained absences

- bumps and bruises from accidents (due to a lack of safety awareness and supervision).

What to do if you suspect that a child is being abused

The Children Act (1989) makes it clear that adults caring for children have to put a child's welfare first. This means that if you are concerned about a child, you need to pass on this concern. Although we must put the child first, we must be sure that we are not jumping to any conclusions. We need to be aware that some of the signs of abuse such as tantrums or attention seeking are also shown by many children who are unsettled – for example, by a new baby in the family. Children who are being abused are more likely to show signs for longer periods – for example, often having bruises that are not explained or nearly always being hungry and unwashed.

Every setting that cares for children will have a procedure to follow if abuse is suspected. In most procedures concerns about children are passed on to a supervisor. The supervisor may decide to contact the child protection team or Social Services in the area.

If you are caring for children in their own homes, you can contact either the NSPCC or Social Services, both of which have a 24-hour helpline.

Case Study

Darren is often late in the mornings. He often seems untidy and has been known to take other children's snacks at break time. Today he comes in with his older brother. He has a bruise on his forehead. You ask him if it still hurts and how he did it. He looks at his older brother who says that he fell out of the window.

Questions
1 Why would you have some concerns about Darren?
2 What would you do next?
3 Why is it important that your concerns about Darren are dealt with?

What to do if a child tells you that he or she are being abused

Sometimes children tell early years workers that they are being abused. This may happen during an ordinary conversation or a child may say that he or she wants to tell you something. It is important that adults know how to handle this situation as children need to feel that they are believed and that they are not doing anything wrong.

Good practice – helping abused children

▨ Reassure the child that you believe them and that you want to help them.

▨ Listen carefully to what the child is saying. You will need to write it down afterwards.

▨ Do not ask the child questions. Where a criminal act has taken place, the police may find it hard to prosecute if there is any doubt that a child has been influenced by what an adult has said to them.

▨ Do not promise the child that you can keep this a secret. This is unfair on the child because you are not able to do so. Say to the child that you need to talk to other people so that they can help.

▨ Reassure the child that they are not to blame for what has happened to them.

▨ Report what has been said to a supervisor immediately and write down the times and what was said in as much detail as possible. You will also need to write down any incident that led up to the disclosure.

Confidentiality

Confidentiality is always important, but in cases where child abuse is suspected, it is essential. Any written notes need to be passed on to a supervisor and stored away and any conversation or information that you have heard must be kept confidential. Passing on information which is confidential could harm the very children who need protecting.

Unit test

Quick quiz

1   An early years worker in a nursery is concerned about a child with a burn mark on the chest. The child does not want to say how it happened. The early years worker should:
    a   ask the parents how the burn happened
    b   tell the manager of the setting
    c   phone social services
    d   wait and see if the child comes in again with marks.

2   A child falls over and has a graze on the leg.
    The early years worker should **first**:
    a   fill in the accident book
    b   find out why the child tripped over
    c   wash the graze under cold water
    d   put a plaster on.

3   During a fire alarm an early years worker should **first**:
    a   shut the windows
    b   take a register and count the children
    c   find out where the fire is
    d   reassure the children.

4   Immunisation can prevent:
    a   chicken pox
    b   eczema
    c   measles
    d   tonsillitis.

5   Nurseries keep a record of the child's details including phone numbers
    so that they:
    a   know who to contact in an emergency
    b   can send out letters
    c   can teach children their addresses
    d   can find out whether children have any brothers or sisters.

Short answer questions

1   Give two of the ways in which bacteria and viruses get into our bodies.

2   How could the following cause cross infections?
    a   Tasting food with child's spoon.
    b   Picking up a dummy from the floor and giving it back to a child.
    c   Using the same spoon for feeding twins.
    d   Letting a child finish eating a piece of toast whilst sitting on the potty.

3   As an employee what duties do you have under the Health and Safety at Work
    Act (1974)?

4   If a child may have been poisoned what should be taken to the hospital?

5   Why must children always wash their hands after playing with animals?

Physical Care and Development

Making sure that children's physical needs are met is likely to be part of your day-to-day work. These needs include exercise and activities to promote physical development as well as cleanliness, sleep, rest and clothing.

This chapter starts by looking at how children develop and your role in promoting this development. The second half of the chapter looks at the physical needs of the body and your role in meeting these.

Stages of physical development

Whatever early years setting we choose to work in, it is important to understand the ways in which children physically grow and develop. Early years workers may work with children who are beginning to walk, starting to ride a bicycle or learning to dress themselves and supporting their development will be a major part of their role.

Understanding the difference between growth and development

There is a difference between growth and development. Growth means that children gain in height and weight, whereas development means that that they are gaining control of their bodies. Although most children's growth and development are matched, there are some children who may grow without developing control of their bodies – for example, because of a disability. Checking that children are growing and developing well is therefore important so that any problems can be detected as early as possible. Most checks are carried out by health visitors, doctors and school nurses, although sometimes it is early years workers and parents who notice that children are not developing well. This is why early years workers need to have some understanding of physical development.

Measuring growth

Children's height and weight are measured and plotted on standard charts. These charts are called percentile charts, although many people call them 'centile' charts. There are separate charts for boys and girls because boys tend to be larger than girls.

Health professionals, such as health visitors and doctors, measure children's height and weight. These measurements are then plotted on a percentile chart. As children grow and are measured, a pattern of growth can be seen.

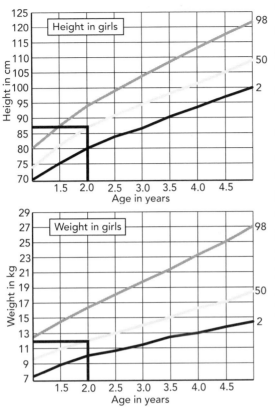

The charts to the left show the weight and height of a two-year-old girl. This girl would be considered to be of average weight as the mark is on the 50th centile. This means that 50 per cent of two-year-old girls weigh this much.

There are two main factors that can affect growth. The size of parents and other family members usually has a strong influence on the height of children. The quality and quantity of food that children eat also affects growth patterns. As a nation our diets have improved greatly in the last sixty years and this is why most people today are larger than their great-grandparents!

(There is more information about food and how it affects children's physical growth in Chapter 5, pages 101 and 109.)

Think about it

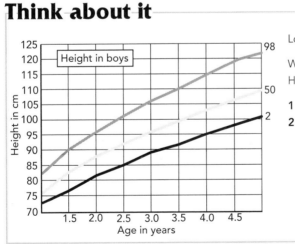

Look at the height chart opposite.

William is a three-year-old boy. He measures 95 cm.

1 *Plot where he is on the percentile chart.*
2 *Is he taller or shorter than most boys of his age?*

Measuring development

To gain complete control of the body, children need to master two different types of movements: large movements, such as walking and running and smaller movements, such as turning a page in a book and throwing a ball. The large movements are called gross motor skills and the smaller movements, fine motor skills.

Fine motor skills are split into gross manipulative skills and fine manipulative skills. Gross manipulative skills use a single limb only, but are more controlled than gross motor skills. Fine manipulative movements are more precise – for example, threading beads. Fine manipulative skills are mentioned frequently in this chapter as they are particularly important in the physical development of children. These skills allow children to become increasingly independent – for example, by using these movements they are able to play with toys and feed themselves.

Think about it

1 *Look at these tasks and decide if they are fine manipulative or gross motor skills.*

Kicking a football   Writing a letter   Threading beads
Skipping   Pedalling a tricycle   Doing a jigsaw puzzle

2 *Check your answers with a friend or tutor.*
3 *Write a list of three things that you have done today that have used your fine manipulative skills.*

What is 'normal'?

Development is harder to measure than growth because it is a gradual process and children gain control of their bodies at different rates – for example, some children may walk at nine months, whereas others may not walk until they are nearly two years old.

The wide variation between children means that it is impossible to say that by a certain age all children will have mastered a movement or skill. It is important to remember this when working with children so that activities or equipment are matched to meet individual children's needs.

To measure children's development most health professionals look at what skills children have mastered. These skills can be broadly linked to age and are often called milestones, the idea being that children have reached a certain point in their development – for example, most children can kick, throw and bounce a ball by the age of five. Although this chapter looks at physical development from 12 months, it is important that early years workers have an understanding of development before this age. (More details on development in babies can be found in Chapter 13, pages 270–277.)

Before 12 months

In the first year of life, babies develop very quickly. At birth they have no voluntary control over their bodies, but have survival reflexes such as the swallowing reflex and the rooting reflex (looking for the nipple). Over the next few months, these reflexes are replaced by voluntary movements.

- By two months, babies can lift their heads and hold them for a few minutes.

- By four months, babies can roll from side to side and push themselves up with their arms when lying on their fronts.

- By six months, babies can grasp objects and sit unsupported for a few seconds.

- By nine months, babies are trying to crawl or bottom shuffle. They can sit unsupported and reach out for objects.

Building up a picture of development

CHILD HEALTH SURVEILLANCE – 18 MONTHS

Examiner Name: ....Date: ....
Doctor/HV (please delete)

Child's Name: ....DOB: .... Sex: M/F

Parental Concerns:

....

....

....

ASSESSMENT
R = Reported   O = Observed

Locomotor and Posture

Walks well, feet slightly apart
Runs
Pushes and pulls large toys
Climbs stairs/onto furniture
Squats to pick up toy

Hearing and Language

Attends to spoken words
Uses 6 recognisable words
Obeys simple commands
  e.g. shut the door
Shows own or dolls hair, shoes etc
Points to desired object

Vision and Fine Movements

Fine pincer grip
Builds tower 3 cubes
Holds crayon and scribbles
Turns pages, several at time
Squint?
Any evidence of abnormal
  vision

Social Behaviour and Play

Holds spoon and gets food to
  mouth
Eye contact
Takes off shoes, socks, hat
Plays alone but likes to be near
  adult
Imitates every-day activities
  e.g. washing up, hoovering

Examination

Height
Weight
Observe gait

Results

Satisfactory/unsatisfactory
Recall in ....wks/mths
Referred to ....

Examiner's Comments

....

....

....

Checking children's development is a major part of health professionals' roles. It is usually done by health visitors. Timings for developmental checks vary from area to area, but checks are usually carried out around the following ages:

- 6–8 weeks

- 6–9 months

- 18–24 months

- 36–48 months

- on school entry.

A slow rate of development may sometimes indicate that a child has a particular need – for example, they are not hearing well. The routine checks by health visitors can mean that possible difficulties are diagnosed early.

The wide variation in children's development means that an individual approach is taken when assessing children. Checklists are often used so that a picture of development can be built up from one visit to another. Health professionals are particularly looking out for children who do not seem to be showing any signs of reaching their next milestone – for example, a child who can stand up by holding onto furniture but who, over a period of a few months, is not walking.

Age	Fine manipulative skills	Gross manipulative skills	The carer's role	Toys and equipment
12 months	• Picks up objects with thumb and forefinger • Picks up and holds toys such as rattles • Points to objects • Holds cup with help • Puts small objects in a container	• Mobile – either crawling, rolling or shuffling (Some children may be walking) • Sits up unsupported for long periods • Walks with assistance • Tries to crawl up stairs	To support this stage of development, carers need to supervise carefully and give plenty of praise and encouragement. We need to spend time playing alongside the child – e.g. making a tower of bricks for them to knock down or putting a cuddly toy in their truck to push along.	• stacking beakers • large balls • push and pull toys • bricks
15 months	• Holds and drinks from cup using two hands • Builds tower of two blocks • Makes marks with crayons • Tries to turn pages in books	• Crawls down stairs feet first • Walks independently • Seats self in small chair	Carers need to supervise children of this age very carefully, as they are keen to explore and may start to climb. Children enjoy discovering new toys especially if they make sounds. We can help children by showing them how to use toys and by playing alongside them. Children of this age can often follow simple instructions – e.g. they may collect their hat and put it on. These early self-help skills need to be encouraged and praised so that children gain in confidence.	• picture books • bricks • shape sorters • toys that make music • large crayons
18 months	• Strings four large beads • Turns door knobs and handles • Pulls off shoes	• Bends down from waist to pick up toys • Squats down to look at toys • Rolls and throws a ball • Walks down stairs with adult help • Pushes and pulls toys whilst walking	The main role of the adult is to allow children the time and space to play. Children are likely to spend more time playing alone and may play quite repetitively – e.g. putting objects into and taking them out of boxes. As children gain in self-help skills – e.g. taking off shoes and coats – they need to be praised and allowed time to complete the task.	• prams • rocking horses or chairs • threading toys • bricks • toys to ride on

Age	Fine manipulative skills	Gross manipulative skills	The carer's role	Toys and equipment
2 years	• Use a spoon to feed themselves • Zips and unzips large zippers • Places five rings on a stick • Puts on shoes • Draws circles and dots • Builds a tower of five to six bricks • Begins to use a preferred hand	• Kicks a ball that is not moving • Climbs on furniture • Puts together and pulls apart snap-together toys • Walks up and down stairs confidently	Children of this age are enjoying exploring their environment and are beginning to have favourite toys and activities. Going to play parks and using swings and rocking equipment are a particular treat. Children's self-help skills are developing although there may be times when children become frustrated – e.g. an arm of a coat may be twisted and they cannot get their hand through. Praise and encouragement need to be offered and we need to look at ways of making children feel independent.	• ride and sit on toys • push and pull toys • shape sorters • bricks • crayons • dough • picture books
3 years	• Turns pages in a book one by one • Holds crayon and can draw a face • Uses a spoon without spilling • Washes and dries hands with help • Puts on and takes off coat	• Walks and runs forwards • Walks on tiptoes • Throws large ball • Kicks ball forward • Jumps from low steps • Pedals and steers a tricycle	Children of this age are starting to enjoy playing together and enjoy new challenges. Adults need to provide stimulating activities that allow children to develop fine movements – e.g. painting, cooking – as well as opportunities to engage in pretend play.	• large outdoor apparatus • puzzles • paints and crayons • dough • sand and water • tricycles • prams • dressing-up clothes
4 Years	• Buttons and unbuttons own clothing • Cuts out simple shapes • Draws a person with head, trunk and legs • Puts together 12-piece puzzle	• Walks on a line • Aims and throws ball • Bounces and catches large ball • Runs, changing direction • Hops on one foot • Pedals and steers a tricycle confidently	Children at this age are gaining in confidence and are able to become more independent. We can encourage them to wipe up spills, pour drinks and tidy away. This will help prepare them for school. Most children of this age enjoy being busy and playing co-operatively.	• balls • climbing frames • slides • materials for creative activities • crayons • glue • scissors • puzzles • construction toys • books

Continued

Age	Fine manipulative skills	Gross manipulative skills	The carer's role	Toys and equipment
5 years	• Forms letters, writes own name • Draws recognisable pictures of trees, houses, people and animals • Colours in pictures neatly • Dresses and undresses easily • Completes 20-piece jigsaw puzzles • Cuts out shapes using scissors quite accurately • Draws around a template	• Skips with a rope • Runs quickly and is able to avoid obstacles • Is able to use a variety of large equipment – e.g. swings, slides • Throws large ball to partner and catches it • Hits ball with bat or stick	Children are starting to enjoy playing games with rules – e.g. snakes and ladders, chase etc. Adults can help by introducing new games into their play – e.g. hide-and-seek – as well as encouraging children to make up their own games. Adult support and encouragement is needed as there may be times when arguments break out! We should also be encouraging children to be as independent as possible – e.g. folding their clothes when changing, hanging up their coats.	• hoops • balls • roller-skates • bicycles with stabilisers • large equipment • creative materials – e.g. paints, crayons, card and paper • construction toys • board games
6–7 years	• Is able to sew simple stitches • Cuts out shapes accurately and neatly • Handwriting is evenly spaced and may be joined • Drawings are detailed and representative • Makes a simple sandwich • Ties and unties laces	• Rides a bicycle without stabilisers • Runs • Chases and dodges others • Hops, skips and jumps confidently • Kicks a ball with direction • Balances on a beam or wall	Children of this age are independent and able to do many day-to-day tasks – e.g. tidying away, laying the table. They are gaining in confidence and enjoy trying out new activities – e.g. making models, origami, cooking. They are starting to have preferences and their own hobbies – e.g. some children will be learning to swim whilst others may go to karate or dance lessons. By eight years some children may need to be encouraged to join in some types of physical activities. This is often due to self-consciousness – e.g. they feel that they are not as good as other children.	• bicycles • skateboards • roller-skates • balls • bats and rackets • kits – e.g. modelling kits, origami • jigsaw puzzles • board games

Portfolio activity

The aim of this activity is to compare the gross motor skills of a child in your workplace with the list on pages 78–80.

1 *Ask your supervisor if you can observe a child in your workplace. You will need to find out their age in years and months.*
2 *Make a list of the gross motor skills that most children of this age have mastered.*
3 *Tick off which skills the child you have chosen is able to do.*
4 *Write down what you have learnt from doing this tick chart.*
5 *Is the child at the same stage of development?*

Your role in supporting children's physical development

One of the key ways of helping children to develop physically is to provide opportunities for physical activity and exercise.

Everyone needs some physical activity in order to keep the body functioning well. When we are looking at a routine for children we must always make sure that it contains some time for physical activity, even if this means just going out in the fresh air for a short walk. Physical exercise helps the body in many ways and as children's bodies are growing and developing, it is especially important that they are given opportunities to enjoy physical activity.

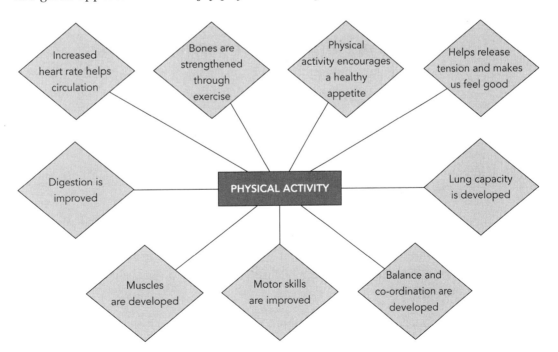

Think about it

1 *Have you been in an early years setting where children have been unable to go outside and run around because of bad weather?*
2 *Did this affect their mood and concentration and if so, how?*

Other benefits for children

Although physical activity can help children to develop physically, there are also many other hidden benefits. Children can gain in confidence and independence. You may hear children say 'Look at me, I can climb to the top of the slide all by myself!'

Many activities that involve physical activity also help children to socialise and work together. Older children may play organised games such as chase, whilst younger children may pretend that the climbing frame is a ship or a house.

Knowledge into Action

1   Look at the routine of your workplace.
2   Are there times in the day when children can have some exercise?
3   Observe a child at one of these times. Look to see what this child is doing and consider how the activities are helping physical development.

Providing opportunities for physical activity

In order to gain many of the skills associated with physical development, it is important that early years workers provide appropriate activities and environments for children both indoors and outdoors. Children must have equal access to these activities and they must be safe and appropriate for the level of the children.

Opportunities for all

Early years workers may at times need to consider whether all the children in a setting have equal access to activities and equipment. For example, as children become more aware of their gender, it is common for them to reject certain activities – for example, girls may not want to use a football or boys may not wish to skip.

To overcome this, you will need to think about some strategies – for example, by being a good role model and making sure that your comments encourage all children to use equipment. You could also set aside time for a particular group of children if they never seem to use a certain piece of equipment. For example, younger children may not feel that they can use the climbing frame because the older children always use it at break times. Look at how this could be managed by an early years worker.

Adult: You look like you're all having fun.

Child: We're seeing if we can climb up and down at the same time.

Adult: Jo and Simon want to climb to, but as they're younger they may need someone sensible to help them. What do you think?

Child: Me and Rob will look after them, won't we Rob?

Adult: That would be great.

Most children do have a sense of fairness and they can be encouraged to share equipment especially when we ask what they think. This means that because the solution often comes from them, they are more likely to accept it.

Case Study

Look at this example and consider in pairs how you would handle this situation.

You are supervising children playing outdoors in a pre-school setting. You notice that Jack and Daisy who are two and a half years old and have just started at this setting are not being allowed to have a turn on the tricycles. The children on the tricycles who are nearly five years old, keep telling the younger children that they have not finished their turn yet.

Questions

1 *Why is it important for the older children to let the others have a turn?*

2 *How would you intervene in this situation without making the older children feel that they are in trouble?*

Safety and physical activity

We need to be sure that children are safe when carrying out physical activities. This means there must be enough space for the activities we are planning. Many bumps and bruises are the result of children running into each other.

Equipment also needs to be checked carefully for safety and cleanliness before it is used.

Good practice – safety and physical activity

Check the following aspects of safety.

✔ Is there enough room between pieces of equipment for children to move safely?

✔ Is the equipment the right size for the age and level of the children?

✔ If outdoors, has the area been checked for safety – e.g. broken glass, animal faeces? (See Chapter 3, pages 53–54)

✔ Is the equipment clean?

✔ Is the equipment safe? (Think about rust and stability.)

✔ Is there enough equipment for the number of children using it?

Good supervision is essential when children are engaged in physical activity. Accidents can happen very quickly and children can get over excited.

Good practice – supervision

✔ Make sure that you can see all the children.

✔ Keep moving around.

✔ Check that children are not getting over excited.

✔ Look out for children who are not using the equipment correctly – e.g. standing on swings.

✔ Look out for children who are becoming tired and encourage them to rest.

✔ Help children to exercise and join in by praising them.

Portfolio activity

In your workplace ask your supervisor if you can supervise children playing outside using equipment. You should refer to the safety checklist (page 83) and stages of development (pages 78–80) to make sure that equipment is safe and suitable.

1. *Write about how you made sure that the equipment was safe and suitable for this age group.*
2. *Write about how you supervised their play, ensuring children were playing safely and all children were able to benefit from being outside.*

Choosing activities and equipment

There are various factors to consider when thinking about providing activities or equipment. These include:

▪ Making sure that the activity is not too difficult for children so that they do not become frustrated or bored.

▪ Varying the activities from day to day. Children enjoy using different equipment and trying out new activities. This means that one day you may not put the bikes out but instead put out hoops and beanbags.

Opportunities for physical activity indoors

There are times when it is not possible for children to go outside to exercise. This means that we need to look at ways of providing physical activity indoors. In most settings this will mean that vigorous physical activity is not possible due to lack of space. In some settings, it may be possible to move the furniture back to allow more room – although permission should be asked for first.

Ideas for indoor activities include:

- music and dance
- drama
- traditional circle games – e.g. 'The farmer's in his den'
- party games – e.g. 'musical bumps'
- throwing and catching soft items – e.g. bean bags, soft balls.

Opportunities for physical activity outdoors

Where possible, children should spend some of their day outdoors, even if it is just for a few minutes. In cold weather children can be wrapped up warmly and can enjoy running around.

The type of equipment for children to use outside will vary from setting to setting depending on the amount of space and resources available. Equipment can be borrowed from toy libraries or children can be taken to a local play area.

The following table shows how different physical activities can benefit children.

Activity	Possible equipment	Benefits
Walking and running	Benches, hoops and cones can provide an obstacle course.	Develops leg muscles, stamina and builds awareness of environment.
Throwing, catching and kicking	Bean bags, hoops, soft balls, different size balls	Develops hand-eye co-ordination and arm, leg and hand muscles.
Hopping and jumping	Trampolines, beams and benches	Develops general co-ordination, strengthens leg muscles, promotes balance and improves stamina.
Riding tricycles, bikes	Tricycles with and without pedals, bikes	Develops leg muscles, hand-eye co-ordination, balance and sense of speed.
Swimming	Floats, armbands, rubber rings	Develops the body overall and improves co-ordination and stamina.
Skipping	Skipping ropes, hoops	Develops sense of rhythm and co-ordination, builds stamina and develops leg muscles.
Climbing	Climbing frames, walls, suitable trees	Develops arm and leg muscles and promotes confidence and spatial awareness.

Supporting children with special needs

Equipment can be adapted to allow children to join in – for example, a child with a visual impairment may need a bell inside a bean bag in order to be able to catch it. Specialist equipment can often be borrowed from charities or toy libraries. We may need to ask parents or other professionals if we should be working on any particular aspect of development as some children may be involved in a programme of physiotherapy.

Portfolio activity

Ask your supervisor if you can plan an activity that will encourage children's physical development.

1   *Write your plan down. It should include: the aim of the activity; what the children will gain from the activity and the equipment that is needed. You should also add what your role is in preparing and supervising this activity.*
2   *Carry out this activity.*
3   *Write about how the children responded to this activity and what you learnt from carrying it out.*

Providing physical care

Most early years workers need to provide some physical care for children during their day-to-day work. This means looking after children so that they have enough sleep and are clean, properly fed and clothed.

Why sleep is important

New-born babies spend most of their time asleep whilst young children need considerably more sleep than adults. Sleep seems to be essential for the human body. The body uses the time we are asleep to rest muscles, repair cells and refresh itself. Children also need sleep because during this time the body releases a hormone that helps them to grow. Sleep is also needed by the brain – although scientists are still working out what exactly the brain does in this time. Lack of sleep can affect our mood, memory and ability to concentrate.

Recognising that children are tired

You will need to learn how to recognise when children are tired and need sleep or rest. Some children need more sleep than others of the same age and so first you must find out about a child's routine and sleep habits.

Common signs that children are tired include:

- rubbing eyes
- twiddling hair

- sucking thumb

- needing comforter

- lacking interest in what is going on around them

- mood changes – e.g. tearfulness, unco-operativenes

- rings around eyes.

How to help children sleep

Most young children have a sleep routine, although they vary enormously from child to child. This may mean that a three-year-old may have a nap after lunch for an hour or a child of 18 months may have a short nap in the morning and another before tea. The wishes of parents are always important in establishing a sleep routine. Some parents may prefer for their child to have a sleep in the late afternoon so that they can spend some time with them after work, whilst other parents may find that a late afternoon nap can mean that they cannot get their child to sleep at night. Finding out about children's sleeping habits by working with parents can help us to meet children's needs.

You will need to know:

- When they go to bed or have a daytime nap.

- How long they tend to sleep for.

- If they have a comfort object.

- If they are used to having a light on or the door wide open.

When children are being cared for in large settings, they may at first find it difficult to get to sleep. They may not be used to the environment and may be unused to sleeping in a room with other children. In some settings, adults stay next to the child until they have fallen asleep and carry on doing this until the child is used to the new routine.

Good practice – helping children to sleep

✔ Make sure that the time before the nap or bedtime is quiet and relaxing. Looking at books or singing nursery rhymes can often help.

✔ Make sure that children understand that it is soon time to sleep.

✔ Check that children have been to the toilet.

✔ Darken the room by drawing curtains or blinds.

✔ Reassure children that they are not being left alone and that someone they know will be there when they wake up.

Some children do not need a nap in the day but do need to rest. Activities for resting children may include listening to story tapes, doing jigsaws, reading a book or playing a quiet board game.

Case Study

You are working with two children: Melissa, aged two and Sam, aged four. Melissa has a nap after lunch, but will not fall asleep if she can hear Sam playing. The house is quite small and Sam does not really understand why he needs to be quiet.

Questions
1   *What activities could you give Sam that will allow him to play quietly?*
2   *How could you help Melissa to sleep?*
3   *How would you make sure that Sam was safe whilst you put Melissa to bed?*

(You might like to work on this in pairs.)

Bowel and bladder control

Gaining control of bowel and bladder movement – i.e. moving from wearing nappies to using the toilet – is a gradual process. At first urine and faeces are a reflex action over which babies and very young children have no control. As children get older, they develop more muscle control and awareness of their bodies which means they are more able to feel the bowel or bladder movement and have time to get to a potty. There is a wide variation between children in the age at which they gain bladder and bowel control. Some children are out of nappies during the day at 18 months whereas other children may not gain the control and awareness until they are three years old. Generally children become dry and clean during the day before staying dry at night. Most children are able to stay dry at night by the age of five, although some children may still wet their beds for much longer.

The links between gaining control and other areas of development

Although bowel and bladder movements are essentially physical, there are links to other language and emotional development.

Language development

Children need some communication skills, so that they can signal to an adult that they need a potty or a toilet. Some children with special needs may be taught a sign to show that this is what they want.

Emotional development

Where children are under stress or feel insecure, bladder and bowel control may not develop. It is also common for some children who are normally clean and dry to begin to wet and soil themselves again. This is called regression and is often temporary – for example, after the birth of a sibling, a toddler who was dry might have many accidents or an older child might start wetting the bed because they are unhappy at school.

Other reasons why children may have difficulty in gaining control include:

- damage to the nervous system – the brain does not receive messages

- being on medication.

Helping children move out of nappies or 'toilet training'

In earlier times it was common for babies to be put on the potty as it was thought that children could be taught how to gain control. Nowadays it is recognised that control comes gradually, although the phrase 'potty training' is still used.

In many ways the role of the adult is to support rather than train children although there are often signs that children are gaining control and awareness.

- Nappies are drier for longer periods.

- Children point to nappies when they are dirty or wet.

- Children try to remove their nappies.

- More interest is shown in potties and toilets.

The decision to help children out of nappies is one that needs to come from parents, although we may be able to let them know that their child is showing signs of awareness and control. A parent may ask us to try putting their child on a potty at certain times of the day or they may decide to wait until after the birth of a sibling before seeing if the child is ready.

It is important to share information with parents during the period of 'potty training'. Words that are used at home with the child need to be exchanged – for example, a family word for the potty. This is especially important where children speak a different language at home to the one used in the setting. It is also useful to know what equipment children are used to using at home – for example, some children may only use a toilet with an inner seat.

Some children are very quick to learn how to use a potty or a toilet, whereas other children are slower and may miss the security of feeling a nappy on them. Adults need to be patient and take a relaxed attitude. This is important because when children are worried they become unable to relax the muscles needed to make the bowel or bladder movement.

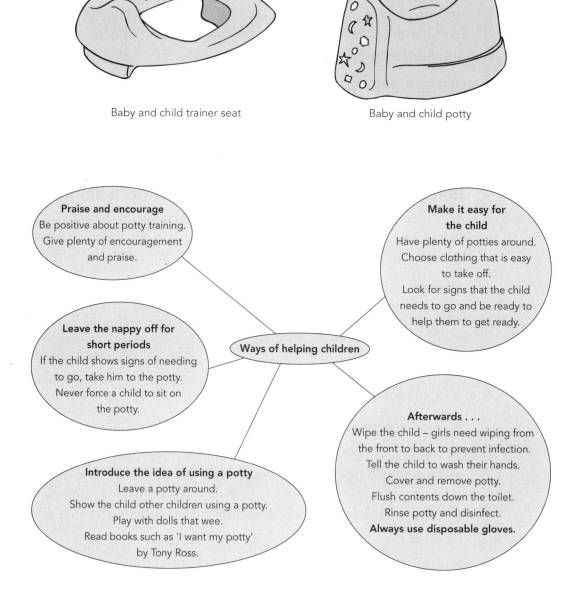

Baby and child trainer seat

Baby and child potty

Praise and encourage
Be positive about potty training. Give plenty of encouragement and praise.

Make it easy for the child
Have plenty of potties around. Choose clothing that is easy to take off. Look for signs that the child needs to go and be ready to help them to get ready.

Leave the nappy off for short periods
If the child shows signs of needing to go, take him to the potty. Never force a child to sit on the potty.

Ways of helping children

Afterwards . . .
Wipe the child – girls need wiping from the front to back to prevent infection. Tell the child to wash their hands. Cover and remove potty. Flush contents down the toilet. Rinse potty and disinfect. **Always use disposable gloves.**

Introduce the idea of using a potty
Leave a potty around. Show the child other children using a potty. Play with dolls that wee. Read books such as 'I want my potty' by Tony Ross.

Handling accidents

Nearly all children have 'accidents' at some time or other, but especially around the time that they are no longer wearing nappies. Older children sometimes have accidents because either they are afraid of asking where the toilet is, or they are so interested in what they are doing that they forget to go!

We can help children when they have an accident by:

- reassuring the child – they may need a cuddle or a friendly word
- moving them to a quieter place before washing and changing them
- being quite matter of fact – as if accidents happen and that it is not a big issue
- changing and mopping up as quickly as possible.

Older children are often very upset and embarrassed when this happens and they may prefer to sort themselves out alone – i.e. wash themselves and get changed in a separate room.

For our own protection against HIV and hepatitis we should always wear disposable gloves when dealing with accidents.

Case Study

You are working as a classroom assistant with six-year-old children. You realise that Claire has a wet patch on the back of her skirt. You mention this to the teacher who asks you if you can 'sort her out'.

Questions
1 *What would you say to Claire so that she is not embarrassed in front of her friends?*
2 *How could you make Claire feel better about what has happened?*

Signs of illness or abnormality

When helping children to use the potty or toilet, you should look for any signs of illness or abnormality – for example, you may notice that children are having difficulty in passing urine or a stool. Any concern needs to be passed on to the parents or, if this is not appropriate, to the supervisor or line manager.

Examples of common infections and difficulties include:

- thrush – itchiness, white discharge
- nappy rash – red rash
- constipation – difficulty in passing stools with pain
- cystitis – pain when passing urine
- kidney infection – blood in the urine.

Abuse

Unhappily, some signs – including marks or bruising – may indicate abuse so it is essential that any concerns are passed on to the key worker or the supervisor. (Chapter 3, pages 68–71 looks in more detail at abuse.)

Knowledge into Action

In your workplace, find out the following information.

1 *Where spare changes of clothes are kept.*
2 *What the procedures are when taking children to the toilet.*
3 *At what age children are allowed to go to the toilet by themselves.*

Clothing and footwear

Dressing children can be part of an early years worker's role, especially if children are being cared for at home. Nannies may be responsible for choosing items of clothing from a child's wardrobe in the morning or a childminder may keep sets of children's clothes in case of an accident.

Selecting clothes for children

- Clothes should be comfortable, easy to put on and washable.

- Cotton is often chosen as it is soft, absorbent and allows the skin to breathe.

- Choose clothes that allow children to be active – e.g. a garment that is too big may restrict a child's mobility.

- Choose clothes that are appropriate for the weather and the types of activity.

- Follow parents' wishes – e.g. Muslim girls may need to wear trousers.

- Check that clothes are clean – underwear should be changed every day.

Caring for clothes

- Always follow manufacturers' washing instructions.

- Sort out clothing according to colour and washing instructions.

- Check pockets before putting items in a washing machine.

- Check which type of washing powder is used, as some children's skin can react to certain detergents.

- Make sure that items are properly dried before being put away.

- Check that clothes such as jumpers and coats are labelled, if children are going into group settings.

Knowledge into Action

Note down what children in your workplace tend to wear.

1 *Who is responsible for providing aprons?*
2 *Do the children have separate clothes and footwear for physical activity?*
3 *Who decides whether children need to wear coats?*
4 *Where is the spare clothing kept in case of accidents?*

Footwear

Caring for feet is important for everyone as corns and blisters can make walking difficult and painful. Particular care needs to be taken with children as the bones in their feet are soft and still forming. Shoes need to be the right size and width for the child otherwise permanent damage to feet may be caused. Shoes need to be wide and long enough to allow growth, but not so big that they rub and cause blisters and corns.

Socks, tights and babygrows also need to be checked as, if they are too tight, they can stop the foot from developing. Care must also be taken to cut children's toenails as these can make their feet sore.

For many families on a low income, buying correctly-fitting shoes is difficult as they are expensive and young children's feet grow quickly. This means that many parents pass down shoes to younger children or buy second-hand shoes. Although understandable, this is not recommended as the shoe will have formed to the shape of the previous child's foot.

Think about it

Children's clothing and footwear can be expensive:

Working in small groups, find out the cost of providing the following items for a four-year-old child. You can use catalogues or look in shops.

Underwear and sleepwear
A pair of pyjamas
3 pairs of pants
3 pairs of socks
1 vest

Day wear
2 T-shirts
2 pairs of trousers
1 sweatshirt
1 apron

Outdoor wear
1 anorak or coat with hood
1 pair of gloves

Footwear
1 pair of leather shoes or sandals
1 pair of slippers
1 pair of wellingtons
1 pair of plimsolls

1 *What is the total amount to clothe this child for two or three days?*
2 *Why is it useful to have plenty of changes of clothes?*

Caring for children's hair, skin and teeth

Bathing and washing children may be part of an early years worker's responsibility – for example, if children are being cared for at home. This may include looking after children's hair, skin and teeth. If early years workers have this responsibility, it is important for them to discuss children's needs with their parents, especially if children have skin conditions – such as eczema – or if the religion of the family means that certain practices relating to bathing or hair care need to be followed – for example, Muslims may only wash under running water.

Looking after children's hair

In recent years, there has been an increase in outbreaks of head lice in pre-school settings and in schools. Headlice are parasites that live close to the scalp. They are sometimes known as nits as this is the name given to the eggs that they lay. Regular combing with a fine-toothed comb can prevent and kill headlice. The comb pulls the live lice out and damages the eggs.

Brushing and combing hair

If you are responsible for washing and combing hair, you need to follow parents' wishes – for example, some children may have braids or dreadlocks that should not be brushed or Afro-Caribbean children may need oil rubbed into their hair.

- Hair should be combed or brushed twice a day.
- Check for headlice or nits (the eggs).
- If hair is tangled start with a wide-toothed comb and then use a brush.

To make it more enjoyable:

- Give toddlers a doll of their own to brush.
- Encourage older children to brush their own hair.
- Let children look in the mirror while you are brushing.

Washing children's hair

Young children may need to have their hair washed several times in a week depending on their activities! Many young children get food and play materials such as dough in their hair as they tend to touch their heads with dirty hands. Older children may only need their hair washing once or twice a week unless they have been particularly active in their play and are sweaty. Most children have their hair washed as part of their shower or bath time and it is important to discuss with parents any fears or particular needs that children have. Many parents also like to use conditioners on children's hair as it makes it easier to comb.

Some younger children find hair-washing distressing as they do not like getting water on their faces.

Good practice – hair-washing

✔ Use mild shampoo that does not sting.

✔ Encourage children to get their hair wet themselves by playing with the water.

✔ Have a flannel or towel to hand so that children can wipe their eyes.

✔ Do not put too much shampoo on the head so that there is less to rinse off.

✔ Encourage children to rub their heads with shampoo. Show them the 'froth' in a mirror.

✔ Rinse as much of the shampoo out of the ends of the hair before tackling the scalp.

✔ Shield children's eyes when rinsing the scalp with a towel or flannel and encourage children to tip their head backwards.

✔ Keep talking or singing to children as your are rinsing.

✔ Have a towel ready to wrap them up in.

Think about it

You are caring for Darren who is three years old. He needs to have his hair washed because there is paint in it. His mother has warned you that he hates having his hair washed and tends to scream and kick. She thinks that he is afraid that the water is going to get in his eyes.

1 *How can you show Darren that he really needs his hair washed?*
2 *What can you do to involve Darren in the hair-washing process?*
3 *Why will it be important to be well prepared when you wash his hair?*

Caring for children's skin

Good skin care is important for everyone. Skin plays a vital role in our overall health and keeping it in good condition means keeping it clean and dry and, at certain times, moisturised. Protecting skin from the sun is also vital which means that we must be aware of the need to use protective skin creams on children as well as keeping them covered or out of the sun in the summer.

As children have different types of skin and many children may have skin conditions, it is essential for early years workers to find out from parents how they should look after children's skin – for example, a child with severe eczema may not be able to use soap on their hands or face and children with dry skin may need moisturisers or oils.

Haddon Davies

Hand-washing

Developing good hand-washing routines with children is important to prevent infections and stop germs spreading. It also gets them into a habit for when they are older.

- Keep nails short.
- Wash hands after going to the toilet, after playing outside and touching animals.
- Wash hands before eating or drinking.
- Use a nail brush if there is dirt under the nails.
- Dry hands thoroughly – each child should have their own towel.

Washing the face and body

Bath or shower time is usually a source of great pleasure for children and is often part of a bedtime routine. Children enjoy playing with the water and we can often wash younger children while they are playing.

Good practice – baths and showers

✔ Where early years workers have responsibility for washing and bathing children, they must always discuss the needs of children with parents. This is especially important where children have skin conditions such as eczema or where the religion of the family means that certain practices need to be followed – for example, Muslims wash under running water.

✔ However sensible children may seem, you should never leave them unsupervised in a bath or a shower. Children may turn on the hot water and scald themselves or they may slip and drown.

The bottom and genital areas of children need to be washed each day, although older children should be encouraged to wash themselves in these parts. Each child should have their own towel and flannel to prevent the spread of any infection. After the bath or shower, it is important that skin is thoroughly dried to prevent soreness. Younger children have folds of skin under their arms and neck that need to be patted dry.

Although many children have a bath or shower before going to bed they will still need to have their hands and face washed in the morning and younger children will need to have their faces and hands washed after meals.

Caring for children's teeth

- Brush teeth with a small-headed toothbrush after meals.
- Brush teeth in a circular way.
- Avoid sugary drinks and sweets between meals.
- Use toothpaste with fluoride to strengthen teeth.
- Regular visits to the dentist can help children get used to someone looking at and probing their teeth.
- A good diet with foods rich in calcium and vitamins can help children form healthy teeth (see Chapter 5, pages 101–2).
- Sugar is often the main cause of dental decay. Dentists recommend that if sugary foods are given they should be eaten at the end of a meal and that teeth should be cleaned afterwards.

Supporting hygiene routines

When we are caring for young children we should always be looking at ways to help them become independent. Personal hygiene routines can be learnt by children if we encourage them to be a part of them from an early age. This means that we may give a toddler the flannel so that they can wipe their face first or we may encourage a four-year-old to have a go at cleaning their teeth by putting a mirror in front of them. As children become older our role may just be that of reminding or praising them for washing their hands or supervising them at bath time.

There are also many topics or themes that we can bring up with children to help them understand the importance of hygiene. Information about health and hygiene topics can be gained through health promotion units, health and dental clinics as well as through professional organisations.

Topic	Activities	Visitors
Teeth	Looking in the mirror at teeth Counting teeth and marking them on a chart Looking at animals' teeth Practising using a toothbrush with a model	Dentist
Hands	Hand printing Drawing around hands Feely bags Looking at ways in which we use our hands – e.g. to make music, to eat with	Anyone who uses their hands in their work – e.g. musician, lace maker, watch repairer etc.
Hair	Looking at animals and their skin and fur Making a chart showing different colour hair Looking at different ways of styling hair	Hairdresser

Portfolio activity

Ask your supervisor if you can plan an activity that will help children to learn about their body.

1   *Write down a plan for this activity. This should include:*
    • the age of the children
    • what they are going to do
    • what equipment is needed
    • your role in the activity.
2   *Carry out the activity.*
3   *Write about how you felt the activity went.*
4   *What did the children learn from this activity?*
5   *What did you learn from doing this activity?*

Equipment

There are many items of equipment relating to the physical care of children. Some items – for example, novelty toothbrushes – are designed to encourage children's independence and to make an activity, such as cleaning teeth, more fun. Other items – for example, bath mats – are needed for safety.

Think about it

Look at the chart below and consider the reason for these items. Choose five items and find out their cost. This activity can be done in pairs or in groups.

Item	Reason	Cost
Bath mat	To prevent children from slipping.	
Bubble Bath		
Children's toothbrush		
Strawberry-flavoured toothpaste		
Inner seat for toilet		
A 'grow tall' step	A stool that allows children to reach washbasins, cupboards etc.	
Musical potty		
Shower ring	To stop shampoo from going into children's eyes.	
Fine-toothed comb		

Unit test

Quick quiz

1   Which activity will **best** promote gross manipulative skills in a child of three years?
    a   painting
    c   threading
    b   jigsaws
    d   clay

2   Physical activities for children are **most** important to:
    a   build up stamina
    b   make friends
    c   teach children to share
    d   promote confidence in movement.

3   Many children aged two can:
    a   draw recognisable pictures
    b   use scissors
    c   walk down stairs with help
    d   use a spoon to feed themselves.

4   An early years worker is planning to take a group of children outdoors to play on the equipment. The early years worker should **first**:
    a   line up the children
    b   check the equipment for safety
    c   make sure that children are wearing appropriate clothes
    d   tell the children that they need to be sensible.

5   An early years worker can **best** help children who are resting by:
    a   telling them to be quiet
    b   making them lie down
    c   allowing them to play in the homecorner
    d   reading them a story.

Short answer questions

1   Why is it important to check with parents before washing items of children's clothing?

2   Give three examples of activities that can help fine manipulative skills.

3   What is a percentile chart for?

4   Why do children need to sleep?

5   Name two signs that may mean that children are ready to move out of nappies.

Providing Food and Drinks for Children

This chapter looks at the importance of diet in children's overall development and the role of the early years worker in understanding children's needs. Most settings offer children a drink or snack as part of their routine and there are some jobs where early years workers are responsible for the preparation and cooking of food. This means that you need to know what to give and how to prepare it safely.

The importance of food

Food and water are essential for life. The food that children eat is especially important as it helps them to grow and gives them energy so they can develop. Studies show that the food we eat in our childhood can make a difference to our health when we are older. Mealtimes are also opportunities for children to enjoy being together, learn about other cultures as well as develop healthy eating patterns.

In order to grow and develop, children's bodies need **nutrients**. The body needs several different nutrients to stay healthy. These are:

- carbohydrates
- fats
- proteins
- vitamins
- minerals.

To gain all the nutrients that the body needs, we have to eat a range of foods. This is what is meant by a balanced diet. At different times in our lives, our bodies need differing amounts of nutrients – for example, children for growth, adolescents during growth spurts and women when they are breastfeeding. One of the main differences between the diets of children and adults is the energy content.

For their size, children need more energy than adults. This means that children up to the age of five should be given full-fat milk and dairy products as they need more calories.

The chart below shows the nutrients in common foods and why the body needs these nutrients.

Nutrient	Benefits to the body	Examples of foods
Carbohydrate	Gives energy	bread, pasta, flour, potatoes, yams, banana, plantains and vegetables, sweet potatoes
Protein	Helps the body to grow and repair cells. In children protein is linked to growth.	meat, eggs, fish, milk and dairy products, soya wheat, corn oats, pulses, beans and peas (The proteins below the dotted line need eating with other foods to work well – e.g. beans on toast.)
Fat	Gives energy and helps the body to absorb vitamins A and D	butter, margarine, vegetable oil, as well as hidden fats in meat, fish and dairy products
Vitamin A	Good for eyes and eyesight	carrots, milk, apricots, fatty fish, margarine
Vitamin B (There are a number of vitamins in the vitamin B group.)	Good for nervous system, helps release energy from other foods	bread, meat, yeast, pasta, flour, rice, noodles
Vitamin C	Good for skin and gums	oranges, lemons, grapefruit, blackcurrant, potatoes, kiwis
Vitamin E	It is not fully understood how this vitamin is used	vegetable oils, green leafy vegetables, milk, nuts, wheatgerm
Vitamin K	Helps blood to clot	present in most vegetables
Vitamin D	Good for teeth and bones	milk, margarine, cheese, yoghurts and other dairy products
Iron	Helps the blood to carry oxygen	red meat, broccoli, spinach, plain chocolate, egg yolk
Calcium and phosphorous	Good for bones and teeth	milk, cheese, butter, yoghurts and other dairy products
Fluoride	Good for teeth and bones	water (added), sea fish

What happens if a diet does not contain enough nutrients?

Eating a diet that meets the body's requirements is important for everyone. The right balance of nutrients can help us to fight infection and prevent diseases. Food also gives us the energy we need to enjoy life!

Children who are not eating enough or who are not eating a balanced diet can:

- lack energy

- fail to gain in height or weight

- have less resistance to infection – e.g. colds, sore throats

- be less alert mentally (studies have shown that diet affects cognitive development).

Calcium and vitamin D in children's diets

Calcium is only taken in by the body when there is also vitamin D. Where children do not have enough calcium and vitamin D in their diets there is a risk of stunted growth because calcium is needed to make strong bones and teeth. Children who do not have enough vitamin D may develop a disease called rickets. Milk, cheese and other dairy products are good sources of calcium and vitamin D.

> White bread contains chalk! By law manufacturers have to add chalk to white bread because the chalk contains calcium.

Nutritional values of foods

The energy that food gives us is measured in kilo calories or in kilojoules. Most wrapped foods have labels that show how many kilo calories or kilojoules are in them.

The table below shows how much energy children are likely to need per day at different ages. It is interesting to note that boys need more energy than girls.

Boys	k. calories	Girls	k. calories
Under one year	780	Under one year	720
One year	1200	One year	1100
Two years	1400	Two years	1300
Three–four years	1560	Three–four years	1500
Five–six years	1740	Five–six years	1680
Seven–eight years	1980	Seven–eight years	1900

(Source – *Manual of Nutrition MAFF 1993*)

Some food labels also give a breakdown of the main nutrients.

Think about it

TYPICAL NUTRITIONAL INFORMATION				
	Per 100g		Per 50g Pack	
Energy	2257	kj	1129	kj
	540	kcal	270	kcal
Protein	6	g	3	g
Carbohydrate	48	g	24	g
Fat	36	g	18	g
INGREDIENTS				
potatoes, vegetable oil, salt.				

Label from crisps

Look at these two labels and decide which of these products would be the best for children.

ADDED INGREDIENTS		
(greatest first): peach, sugar, water, glucose syrup, modified starch, milk protein, stbiliser (pectin), flavouring, citric acid, colour (lutein). Minimum 7% fruit.		
CAUTION		
ALLERGY ADVICE: MAY CONTAIN MINUTE TRACES OF NUTS		
NUTRITION		
TYPICAL VALUES	PER 100g	
Energy Value (calories)	341 kj (81 kcal)	
Protein	3.7 g	MEDIUM
Carbohydrate (of which Sugars)	14.6 g (10.5 g)	HIGH MEDIUM
Fibre	0.4 g	MEDIUM
Sodium	0.1 g	MEDIUM
PER POT (150 g)		
Energy Value (calories)	512 kj (122 kcal)	

Label from yoghurt

Some groups of foods are particularly good for children.

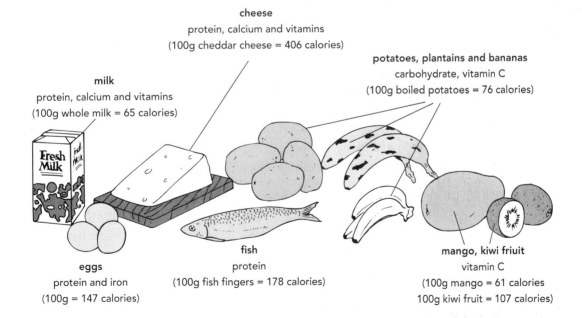

cheese
protein, calcium and vitamins
(100g cheddar cheese = 406 calories)

potatoes, plantains and bananas
carbohydrate, vitamin C
(100g boiled potatoes = 76 calories)

milk
protein, calcium and vitamins
(100g whole milk = 65 calories)

eggs
protein and iron
(100g = 147 calories)

fish
protein
(100g fish fingers = 178 calories)

mango, kiwi friuit
vitamin C
(100g mango = 61 calories
100g kiwi fruit = 107 calories)

To plan a balanced diet, it is important to look at what children eat over a few days. A balanced diet needs to be varied so that different foods are used. The chart below shows a sample menu for four days. Notice that a range of different foods have been used.

	Day 1	Day 2	Day 3	Day 4
Breakfast	Milk Cereal with banana Toast	Milk Porridge Apple	Milk Yoghurt Toast	Orange juice Cereal Toast
Mid-morning	Diluted apple juice Fruit scone	Lassi (yoghurt drink) Banana	Diluted orange juice Rice crackers	Milk Cheese straws
Lunch	Pitta bread filled with tuna and sweetcorn Fresh mango Water	Macaroni cheese Broccoli Fresh fruit salad Water	Cheese and spinach Rice salad Blackcurrant mousse Water	Trinidad stew (made with plantains) Sweet potatoes Yoghurt and banana Water
Mid-afternoon	Diluted fruit juice Cheese and biscuit	Hot chocolate Dried fruit mix: 1 (raisins, apricots)	Milk shake Home-made biscuit	Diluted fruit juice Raw carrot sticks
Tea	Three-bean sausage stew Bread rolls Pancakes Milk	Cold chicken pieces Rice salad Strawberry mousse Milk	Jacket potato with a choice of fillings Stewed apple and yoghurt Milk	Home-made pizza Salad Home-made ice cream Milk

Portfolio activity

You have been asked to look after a five-year-old for a day.

1 *Write a plan of the meals, snacks and drinks that you could give to this child (include breakfast).*
2 *Explain how your menu plan would give the child all the nutrients needed for a balanced diet.*

Providing drinks for children

Drinks are just as important as food in keeping the body healthy. Children who do not drink enough are likely to become dehydrated. This can be serious as the body needs water to do many things including to control temperature.

Drinks need to be offered several times during the day particularly if it is hot. The best drinks for children are considered to be water and milk. Water is good because it is pure and quenches children's thirsts while milk contains many nutrients including calcium and protein. Sugary and sweet drinks not only cause dental decay, but they can spoil children's appetites.

Knowledge into Action

1 *What drinks are offered to the children in your workplace?*
2 *Do all the children have the same drinks?*
3 *At what times are drinks offered?*

Foods to avoid giving to children

- **Nuts** are not recommended for children under five years because, although nutritious, there is a danger of children choking on them and also some children have a violent allergic reaction to them – particularly peanuts. If children are known to be allergic to nuts, adults have to be extremely careful when buying shop-made products such as biscuits where nuts may be a hidden ingredient.

- **Sugary foods and drinks.** Although sugar does provide energy, it can also cause dental decay. Sweets and sugary drinks fill children up without giving them any other nutrients. It also means that children develop a taste for sweet things and may dislike other more nutritious foods.

- **Undiluted fruit juices.** Fruit juices can be good for children, but they need to be watered down because otherwise the acid in them can cause tooth decay.

- **High-fibre foods** such as bran. Although adults need fibre in their diets, children do not need as much. Fibre fills up the stomach which means that there is less space for foods that can give children the energy they need.

- **Salt.** Children do not need extra salt in their diet and it can affect their kidneys. Eating salty foods such as crisps can mean that they develop a taste for salt. As there is a link between salt and high blood pressure in adults, it is better that children do not crave salty foods.

- **Uncooked eggs.** The advice is that children should not eat uncooked or partly cooked eggs because of a disease called salmonella which is a type of food poisoning. Examples of foods which should not be offered include home-made mayonnaise and boiled eggs with runny yolks.

How much food should children be given?

The best guide as to how much food to give is the child themselves.

Some children may eat a lot at one meal and less at another. Following a child's appetite is often the best way of deciding how much food to give, providing the food that is offered is nutritious and varied. Appetite is often a guide to children's needs. Children tend to eat more just before a growth spurt and less if they are feeling poorly.

Knowledge into Action

The best way of learning how much children eat is to observe them eating!

1   *Ask your supervisor if you can observe children when they are eating.*
2   *What do they eat first?*
3   *How much food are they given?*
4   *Do they leave any foods?*

Should children be offered snacks?

Three meals a day suits adults very well, but children can get hungry between meals. This is because children's stomachs are smaller and providing a snack for them can give them the extra energy that they need.

- **Good snacks** help keep children going without spoiling their appetites and are nutritious – e.g. slices of apples, oranges, bananas, dried fruit, a slice of bread or savoury biscuit with a drink of diluted juice or a glass of milk.

- **Poor snacks** fill children up with sugar or fat that stops them from being hungry at the next meal and does not provide many nutrients – e.g. sweets, crisps, biscuits and sugary drinks.

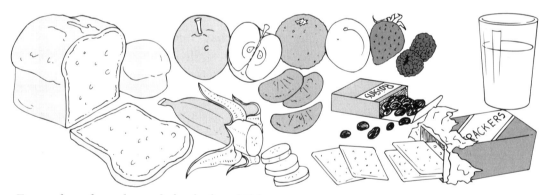

Examples of good snack foods for children

Portfolio activity

A good idea for an activity that is also a healthy snack is taste testing. Children can taste different types of apples and raw vegetables such as cucumber and carrots. Children can be involved in washing, cutting and presenting the taste tray. If appropriate, children can also draw fruit.

1   *Ask your supervisor if you can carry out an activity about taste.*
2   *Write about how you prepared this activity.*
3   *What did the children gain from this activity?*
4   *What did you learn from doing this activity?*

Preparation and storage of foods

It is most important that early years workers handling food know how to do so hygienically. Food poisoning actually kills around 40 people a year and young children are a vulnerable group. Most food poisoning is caused by bacteria multiplying on food and then being eaten. Bacteria need water, food and warmth in order to grow.

There are three principles in preventing food poisoning caused by bacteria:

1 Stop the bacteria from getting onto the food.

2 Stop the bacteria already on food from spreading.

3 Destroy the bacteria on food.

Stopping bacteria from getting onto foods is an important first step. The kitchen area must be clean and anyone handling foods must have good personal hygiene. Remember that bacteria grows when there is warmth, water and food. This means that when washing hands you must dry them thoroughly.

Always cover foods.

Wash hands thoroughly before handling food and during preparation, for example after handling raw meat.

Keep animals out of food preparation and eating areas.

Make sure raw and cooked foods are stored separately.

WAYS TO STOP BACTERIA FROM GETTING ONTO FOODS

Avoid handling foods with hands where possible. For example, use spatulas, spoons.

Regularly wipe and disinfect work surfaces and chopping boards.

Preventing the spread of bacteria in foods is done by storing foods safely. This does not completely stop bacteria but does slow it down. Bacteria grows quickly when it is at room temperature or in a warm area such as in the sun. The 'danger zone' is between 5°C and 63°C. Between these temperatures bacteria grows rapidly.

Many raw foods already contain bacteria when they come into the kitchen – for example, meat, eggs and dairy produce. This is why separating raw foods from cooked foods is essential.

Food group	Examples of food	Storage Keep in airtight containers
Dry foods	rice, flour, pulses, baby milk, couscous	Do not allow to become damp. Bacteria cannot grow whilst they are dry.
Perishables	meats – raw and cooked, dairy products – e.g. cheese, milk, butter, eggs, fish	Keep in the fridge. The fridge temperature must not be above 4°C.
		Cooked foods must be covered and kept in a separate place in the fridge.
Vegetables and fruit	root vegetables, carrots, sweet potatoes, yams, apples, plums plantains, tomatoes etc	These should be kept as cool as possible and off the floor.
		Root vegetables such as potatoes need to be stored in the dark. Do not eat green potatoes.
		Fruit and vegetables lose their vitamin C if they are not eaten whilst fresh.

Good practice – storing food

✔ Always read manufacturers' instructions when storing food.

✔ Do not eat foods that are past their sell by date.

✔ Once a tin is opened, store the contents in a covered container in the fridge.

✔ Keep fridges at 1–4°C.

✔ Keep freezers at −18–23°C.

Destroying bacteria on food means heating foods up to a temperature of 72°C. Foods need to remain at this temperature for several minutes to kill off bacteria.

If food is only slightly warmed through, bacteria will flourish, so when reheating any food make sure that it is piping hot.

When using microwaves to cook or heat food, you must follow manufacturers' instructions as well as stirring the food to ensure that the food has reached 72°C.

Good practice – preparing meals

✔ Tie your hair back.

✔ Wash your hands.

✔ Wear an apron.

✔ Read manufacturers' cooking instructions when using frozen or chilled food.

✔ Keep work surfaces clean and disinfected.

✔ Wash your hands and the chopping board after handling raw meat.

✔ Make sure that hot food is cooked thoroughly to a temperature of 72°C.

✔ Keep food covered.

Portfolio activity

Ask your supervisor if you can prepare a snack or help to prepare a meal in your workplace.

1 *Write down how you did this task.*
2 *What type of snack or food did you prepare?*
3 *What steps did you take to make sure that food was prepared hygienically?*

Poverty and children's diets

There is a strong link between poverty and health. A good diet helps people to stay healthy and studies show that families on low incomes may not always be eating healthily.

Families can find it hard to give children the right types of foods for the following reasons.

■ They may not have proper cooking facilities. If they are living in cramped or shared accommodation they may not have a cooker or all the equipment needed to make a proper meal.

■ They may not have enough money to buy all the ingredients needed to cook a healthy meal – e.g. one stock cube is needed, but they are sold in packets of 6; 100 grams of cheese is needed but it is sold in packets of 250 grams.

■ They tend to buy foods in small quantities and do not always have spare money to benefit from offers such as 'Buy two get one free.'

■ Cooking foods means using gas or electricity. When money is short it is cheaper to buy foods that re-heat quickly or are sold hot.

■ Families may shop at small shops where prices are higher, because they do not have transport to get to larger shops.

- Sometimes fruit and vegetables at small shops is not as fresh as in larger shops.

- Parents who are surviving on a low income are more likely to suffer from depression and may not have the mental energy to think about cooking.

- Some parents may not know how to cook or understand what makes a healthy meal.

Case Study

Jane is living in bed and breakfast accommodation with her two children aged three and four. There is a shared kitchen down the corridor which has a fridge and a small cooker. The kitchen is not safe for the children to be in and Jane doesn't like leaving them on their own in the room. She does not use the fridge because she has found that other people take the food. She tends to buy foods that she does not need to cook and that she knows the children will eat. She once tried cooking some pasta and sauce, but they would not eat it and so it was a waste of her money and time.

Parents like Jane in the case study are more likely to buy processed foods such as pies, tinned soup and crisps because they are cheap and filling. They are often tasty and there is little preparation involved. Families on low incomes cannot afford to waste food and therefore tend to buy foods that they know their children like. This means that children are often not eating a variety of foods which makes it harder for them to enjoy new tastes. Children, if asked, may say that they would like a packet of crisps rather than an apple.

Processed foods

Many families on low income tend to eat processed foods as they seem cheap. Diets that rely on processed foods tend not to provide the body with all the nutrients it needs.

The cooking and preparation of processed foods mean that vitamin C is lost and that high quantities of salt and sugar are added. Processed foods also lack protein, as it is cheaper for the manufacturer to put in other things such as starch and fat.

Helping children to eat a balanced diet

We have looked at the importance of eating well and why food is important to help children's growth. This next section looks at ways of encouraging children to eat.

Being a good role model

A good starting point is our own attitudes towards food. Children need to see good role models if they are to develop good attitudes towards eating healthily and enjoying food. For example, if we tend to eat our own food in a rush, we may be inclined to be impatient with young children who are often slow eaters.

Think about it

1   *What foods did you like as a child?*
2   *Do you still enjoy them?*
3   *What foods did you not like?*
4   *Do you like them now?*
5   *Were you told to eat all your food up before you could have pudding?*
6   *Do you eat when you are depressed?*
7   *Do you sit down to eat or do you tend to wander around?*
8   *Do you enjoy eating meals with friends?*

You may enjoy going through these questions with a friend.

Making meal times fun

We can help children to eat a balanced diet by making meal times fun. Children are more likely to eat when they feel happy and relaxed. The way food is served and presented to children is important. We can present food in a variety of ways to children.

- Pretend to have picnics or parties and bring along favourite dolls and toys.

- Cut food into interesting shapes – e.g. pizza into stars or triangles.

- Arrange food on plates to make pictures.

- Allow children to serve themselves.

- Give food special names – e.g. 'Peter Rabbit's carrots' or 'Humpty Dumpty's potatoes'.

- Make sure that food is easy for children too eat – e.g. not difficult to chew.

Size of portions and food preferences

Sometimes when adults are concerned about how much children are eating they tend to make the atmosphere negative. Sometimes it is better to put small quantities on a plate and offer a second helping rather than put so much on a plate that the child feels overwhelmed. We can ask children how much they would like and this can make them feel more relaxed as they feel they are in control.

As children grow up their tastes often change. Foods that were eaten without comment are refused and others that were left untouched are loved. This is quite natural and providing children are still eating a balanced diet it is not really a problem.

Case Study

Look at this conversation between a child and an adult. The child has not really eaten much lunch, but wants a pudding.

Adult: Finish this up before it gets cold, we're all waiting for you!
Child: I don't feel hungry.
Adult: You can't have any pudding unless you eat this all up.
Child: But I don't like it.
Adult: Yes, you do and I made it especially for you.
Child: I don't want it.
Adult: You might not want it, but there are children starving in this world and you are *not* having any pudding until you eat it up!

Questions

1 *How does the adult try to make the child feel guilty?*
2 *Will the child feel any more like eating now?*
3 *How would you handle this situation?*

Introducing new foods

One of our roles in caring for children may be to introduce them to new tastes and foods. Trying out new foods is a learning opportunity for children and may help them develop tastes for other foods. Sometimes children are reluctant to try out new foods and so the way we present them is important. Where children feel involved they are more likely to say that they like a new food. They can do taste tests or help by preparing, cooking or serving out the food.

Maths and science
Food provides wonderful maths and science opportunities. Children can count out the number of place settings and put plates and cutlery in each place. They can measure ingredients with spoons and cups. Children also enjoy seeing how food changes as a result of the cooking process – e.g. watching food brown or cheese bubble.

Independence and self-esteem
Children can feel grown-up and responsible when doing simple tasks such as serving out food and pouring out drinks, as well as helping clear away at the end of meals.

USING FOOD AS A LEARNING OPPORTUNITY

Social language and skills
Eating with others is fun. Children can learn that eating is part of being sociable and we can use mealtimes as a way of sharing with other people. Children can pass items around to each other and simple manners can be encouraged by sitting with the chilren and acting as a good role model. Older children can also enjoy helping younger children and can often do things such as peel satsumas and bananas for them.

Writing and drawing
It can be quite fun for children to make up their own menus or make place-names for each other. Children can also make tablecloths by drawing pictures on sheets of paper before the meal.

Forcing children to taste something does not work and may put them off the new food for longer. A more effective way is to say how much you like it or to put children with others who do eat the food.

Think about it

Michael is six years old and does not like eating vegetables. His parents have asked you to encourage him to eat more vegetables.

You have decided to do this by encouraging him to try some new vegetables and also by involving him in the preparation of the meal.

1 *Think of some vegetables that Michael may not have tried before.*
2 *Work out a meal that could include these vegetables.*
3 *Consider how Michael could be involved with the preparation of this meal.*

Respecting dietary customs

For thousands of years food has played a major part in people's lives and in their religions. Food has been used to celebrate festivals and life events – for example, marriage, birth and even death. Recognising the significance of food and how it is eaten is important so that we can meet all children's needs by respecting their

Food	Muslim	Jew	Sikh	Hindu (mainly vegetarian)	Rastafarian (mainly vegetarian although take milk products)	7th Day Adventist
Lamb	Halal	Kosher	Yes	Some	Some	Some
Pork	No	No	Rarely	Rarely	No	No
Beef	Halal	Kosher	No	No	Some	Some
Chicken	Halal	Kosher	Some	Some	Some	Some
Cheese	Some	Not with meat	Some	Some	Yes	Most
Milk/yoghurt	Not with rennet	Not with meat	Yes	Not with rennet	Yes	Most
Eggs	Yes	No blood spots	Yes	Some	Yes	Most
Fish	Halal	With fins, scales and backbones	Some	With fins and scales	Yes	Some
Shellfish	Halal	No	Some	Some	No	No
Cocoa/tea/ coffee	Yes	Yes	Yes	Yes	Yes	No
Fast periods	Ramadan	Yom Kippur				

culture and religion. Knowing which foods are not permitted and checking with parents about children's dietary needs is essential if parents and children are to feel that their values are respected.

On page 113 is a chart that shows the main dietary customs of the major religions where certain foods are restricted or forbidden.

The word 'some' means that some members of these groups may eat these products.

Halal or Kosher meat

Jews and Muslims will only eat meat if it has been killed in a certain way. This is what is meant by kosher and halal. Meat that has been killed in this way is bought at specialist butchers.

There are other reasons why children may have different diets from other children. It can be by choice – for example, vegetarian – or because of a medical condition.

Vegetarians and vegans

It is important to find out whether the parents wish their child to have a vegetarian diet or a vegan diet and find out how best this can be provided.

Vegetarians do not eat meat or fish, but will eat products that come from animals – for example, milk and eggs.

Vegans do not eat any food that comes from animals or fish.

Diabetes

This is a medical condition that means that the pancreas finds it difficult to regulate the sugar levels in the body. Most diabetics avoid sugar in their diets, but need to take regular snacks. If you are caring for a child with this condition, it is essential to find out more information from parents and you might have to record how much food a child has eaten.

Coeliacs disease

Children with this condition are not able to eat foods with gluten in them. Gluten is commonly found in cereals such as wheat, oat and corn. As many products are made with wheat flour – for example, ordinary bread, biscuits – it is extremely important to check that foods are suitable.

Celebrating festivals with food

There are numerous festivals that we can celebrate with children. Marking festivals with food provides many learning opportunities for all children. Children can gain by tasting new dishes, finding out about new foods and ways of cooking. We can ask parents if they have any recipes or equipment that we can use. Some parents may be keen to come in and help. Where possible food should be as authentic as possible rather than stereotypical. This means making sure that food is prepared correctly and tastes as it should.

The following chart shows some ideas of festivals that can be celebrated.

Chinese New Year		Late January or early February
Jewish New Year	Rosh (Hoshanah)	Usually September
Muslim New Year	(Al Hijrah)	14 weeks after Ramadan
Rastafarian New Year		7 January
Hindu New Year	(Divali)	October or November
Shrove Tuesday/Mardi Gras		40 days before Easter
Chinese Kite festival	(Chung Yang)	Late September or early October

Portfolio activity

Ask your supervisor if you can supervise a meal or snack time.

1 *Write down how you did this.*
2 *What was your role in the snack or meal time?*
3 *How did you make this an opportunity for children to socialise?*
4 *How did you help children to practise their social skills?*

Unit test

Quick quiz

1 Vitamin D is found in:
   a pork
   b milk
   c oranges
   d eggs.

2 A fridge should be kept at:
   a 2°C
   b 6°C
   c 8°C
   d 10°C.

3   A child with Coeliac's disease cannot eat:
   a   sugar
   b   peanuts
   c   bread
   d   eggs.

4   It is recommended that children under five should have:
   a   full-fat milk
   b   semi-skimmed milk
   c   skimmed milk
   d   condensed milk.

Short answer questions

1   Name two ways in which an early years worker might encourage a child to taste a new food.

2   What is the name of the disease that is caused by lack of vitamin D?

3   Fill in this sentence – Bacteria needs warmth, _____ and _____ to grow.

4   Name three sources of carbohydrates.

5   Which vitamin helps blood to clot?

Childhood Illness

In earlier times, childhood illnesses such as polio and diphtheria were fatal and large numbers of children died in childhood. Although times have changed, there are still diseases around that can kill children – for example, meningitis. This means that we must always be on the lookout for signs of illness in children and be ready to respond quickly if necessary. There may be times when, as an early years worker, you notice that a child seems unwell or you are asked to look after a child who is poorly. This means that you will need to know how to comfort and care for sick children. This chapter looks at ways of recognising that children are ill, how to care for them and also how to support parents when their children are not well.

General signs that children are not feeling well

There are often signs that children are not feeling well which show before the illness is apparent. Parents may say to us that their child is 'off colour' and this means that children are often incubating an illness. Incubation is the difference in the time between actually getting the germs and the first symptoms appearing. Incubation periods vary between illnesses, for example the incuabtion period of chicken pox is 10–14 days.

As early years workers we need to be able to identify the signs that children are starting to feel unwell. The following chart shows common physical and behavioural signs of coming illness.

Physical signs	Behavioural signs
Rings around eyes	Sleepy
Pale/greyish skin	Loss of appetite
Flushed cheeks	Quiet, reluctant to join in
Headache	Clingy, crying, whinging, irritable
Vomiting	Thumb sucking, babyish behaviour
Bedwetting	Upset sleep patterns

Knowing children well can often help parents and early years workers to realise that children are not their usual selves. For example, a child who is normally a good eater may not be feeling hungry or a child who is usually independent may ask for help with dressing. These may be signs that the child is feeling poorly.

The chart on page 118 shows some of the more common childhood illnesses.

Illness	Incubation	Signs and symptoms	Treatment	Complications
Common cold	1–3 days	Running or blocked up nose, sneezing, headache, tiredness, temperature.	Keep up fluid intake. Rest and sleep.	Ear infection, bronchitis
Chicken pox (Varicella)	10–14 days	Groups of red spots with raised white centres that become itchy on trunks and limbs. Slight fever.	Calamine lotion to relieve itchiness. Nails could be cut short to prevent scratching.	Scars caused by spots becoming infected.
Ear infection		Pains – e.g. earache, headache – persistent or intermittent vomiting.	Seek medical attention. Antibiotics, paracetamol.	Hearing loss – temporary. (Sometimes permanent where children have repeated infections.)
Food poisoning	½–36 hours	Diarrhoea, vomiting.	Fluids only for 24 hours. Seek medical assistance after 24 hours.	Weight loss, dehydration and, in severe cases, death.
Gastroenteritis (inflammation of the stomach lining)	Cause bacteria: 7–14 days Cause virus: ½–36 hours	Nausea, diarrhoea, vomiting.	Keep up fluid intake. Seek medical advice if symptoms are severe.	Weight loss, dehydration and, in severe cases, death.
German measles (Rubella)	14–21 days	Mild symptoms including a pink rash on head, spreads to trunk and limbs, sore throat and slight fever.	Rest if needed.	No complications but this disease can cause serious problems for unborn babies if the pregnant woman is infected. Children are at their most infectious a few days before symptoms show until one day after the symptoms disappear.
Measles	8–14 days Koplik spots appear in the mouth on inner cheek. These are bluish white spots that appear before the main rash.	At first: fever, runny eyes, sore throat and cough. Red rash (often blotchy) appears, often starting from the head and spreading downwards.	Rest, plenty of fluids and paracetamol if needed to treat fever.	Ear and chest infections and, in rare cases, encephalitis. (Inflammation of the fluid around the brain.)

Illness	Incubation	Signs and symptoms	Treatment	Complications
Meningitis, viral and bacterial	2–14 days variable	Fever, severe headache, nausea, stiff neck and blotchy skin rash that can look like bruising, drowsiness and dislike of light. Babies may arch back and their cry is high pitched. Symptoms develop rapidly.	Urgent and immediate medical attention. Antibiotics and observation.	Deafness, brain damage and death.
Mumps	14–21 days	Fever, headache, difficulty in swallowing with swollen face and glands in the neck.	Keep up fluid intake, rest, paracetamol for pain relief if necessary.	Meningitis orchitis. (Inflammation of the testes in young men.)
Tonsillitis		Very sore throat, fever, earache, headache and pain on swallowing.	Antibiotics and rest.	Ear infection – temporary, deafness (rare).
Whooping cough (Pertussis)	7–21 days	Spurts of violent coughing with child taking in a deep breath – 'whoop' sound made, vomiting.	Antibiotics in early stages, rest, reassurance and food after coughing attacks.	Nosebleeds, pneumonia, brain damage.

Children often develop symptoms quickly. A child who, in the morning, seems perfectly well may, in the afternoon, develop a high temperature. This is often because younger children's bodies have less resistance to infection than adults. It is essential that early years workers call for medical assistance if children are unwell. Where there is cause for concern a GP (family doctor) should be contacted or if you feel that the child is deteriorating rapidly, the ambulance should be called. (See Chapter 3, page 63 for information on calling the ambulance service.) In some illnesses – for example, meningitis – rapid diagnosis can mean that children's lives are saved. The symptoms of some of the more serious diseases are often similar to the mild ones. It is always better to check that children are not seriously ill, rather than worry about wasting a doctor's time.

Parents need contacting where there is the slightest concern and most children need their parents to be with them when they do not feel well.

Causes for concern

▧ Breathing – rapid or shallow and difficult

▧ Convulsions or fits

- Delirium

- Diarrhoea – for longer than 24 hours in babies under 12 months

- Dislike of being handled, fretful – in babies

- Fever – temperature of 38.3°C or higher

- Fever – temperature of 37.3°C lasting for over four hours

- Fontanelle (soft part of the head) of babies swollen or sunken

- Headache – severe especially if combined with any of the other symptoms in this section

- Lips and nails blue

- Neck stiff

- Pain persistent or acute – e.g. earache

- Rash

- Urine dark or abnormal

- Vomiting – for longer than 24 hours in babies under 12 months

- Weakness or rapid deterioration

- Yellowing of the skin or eyes (except in babies under six weeks).

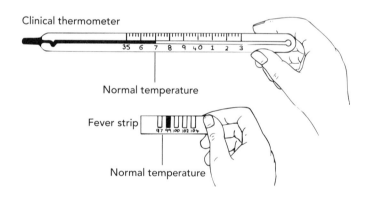

Taking children's temperature

Normal temperatures for children are between 36.5°C and 37.2°C. Temperature taken under the arm pit are slightly lower than those taken in the mouth. Children tend to have higher temperatures in the evening, after exercise and in hot weather.

Using a fever strip

The strip is put onto children's foreheads for a few seconds. The strip changes colour and shows the temperature of the child. The strips are easy to use, but are not as accurate as using a clinical or digital thermometer.

Using a clinical thermometer

There are different ways of taking the temperature of children using a clinical thermometer. Young children cannot put the thermometer in their mouths as there is a danger that they may break the glass. It is possible to take children's temperature by placing a thermometer under their armpit. This is probably the best way unless you have had further training.

- Check that the mercury is at the low point of the thermometer. If it is not, then shake the thermometer.

- Show the child the thermometer and tell them what you are going to do.

- Lift up the child's arm and put the thermometer under the armpit.

- Lower the child's arm and wait for at least two minutes.

- Read and then record the temperature and the time it was taken.

- Put the thermometer safely away.

The mercury in thermometers makes them dangerous if they are broken and care should be taken that they are kept out of children's reach.

Using a digital thermometer

Digital thermometers are easier to read and safer than clinical thermometers as they are not made of glass, although they are more expensive. The heat-sensitive end is put in the mouth for one to two minutes and a reading is shown in numbers.

Immediate action for high temperatures

High temperatures can be dangerous for children. They can have fits or convulsions that can cause lasting damage. There are some simple steps that we can take to bring down the temperature.

- Remove excess clothing – e.g. take a baby down to their nappy and vest.

- Dip a sponge or flannel in lukewarm water (*not cold*) and sponge the face and body.

- Open a window slightly to cool the air.

- Use a fan to cool the child down.

- Give the correct dose of paracetamol syrup (Calpol) if parents have given consent.

- Give the child plenty of reassurance and comfort.

- Offer sips of water to the child.

- Keep checking the temperature every ten minutes. Stop sponging when the temperature is down to 38.5°C to avoid chilling the child. Then cover the child with a light sheet. Watch out for signs that the temperature is rising again – e.g. flushed cheeks, drowsiness.

Identifying symptoms in children with varying skin tones

There are some signs of illnesses such as rashes that may look different depending on children's skin tones. Pale-skinned children may develop red rashes or spots whereas on a black or Asian child these may appear as raised patches. Pale-skinned children may look drained of colour whereas black or Asian children may look grey and have dark circles under their eyes when they are not feeling well. Check their lips and fingernails as well as if these are blue it may be a sign of lack of oxygen.

Whatever the skin tone of the children we look after, it is always easier to decide if children are poorly when we know them well. It is often by recognising that children are not 'themselves' that we may realise that they are unwell.

Case Study

You are babysitting for a two-year-old girl. She starts to complain of a headache and you notice that she is looking pale and feels hot.

1 *In pairs write down what you need to do next.*
2 *Role play a telephone conversation with the child's parents.*

Supporting children with asthma

Asthma is a condition that means that normal breathing becomes difficult. Children may wheeze and cough, fighting to catch their breath.

One in ten children in Great Britain has asthma. This means that many children have medication to either prevent an asthma attack or to help during an attack. They may have inhalers, volumatics or nebulisers that allow them to take the drugs. Where children have a history of asthma attacks, we must get information from the parent or a healthcare professional about how to help them use their medication. Young children are encouraged to learn how to use inhalers by themselves.

Signs that children are having an asthma attack

Signs
- Wheeziness
- Breathlessness
- Dry cough that is persistent
- Rapid breathing
- Difficulty in talking

Action
1. Keep calm and reassure children.
2. Allow children to sit or be in a comfortable position for them.
3. Allow children to self-administer their inhaler.
4. They may take another dose from the inhaler, if the attack has not completely eased up.
5. If there is no improvement after 5–10 mins – dial 999 for an ambulance.

If children turn blue or have blue lips during an attack, dial 999 for an ambulance immediately.

Asthma attacks can be very frightening for the child. They can get worse if the child begins to panic. This means that they will need reassurance from an adult. We can talk to them quietly and gently. It is often a good idea to either take them to a quiet place at the start of an attack or to keep other children away so that they do not feel crowded. We can sit them down, loosen clothing and encourage relaxed breathing not deep breathing. We can help children by knowing where their medication is kept and getting it at the start of an attack.

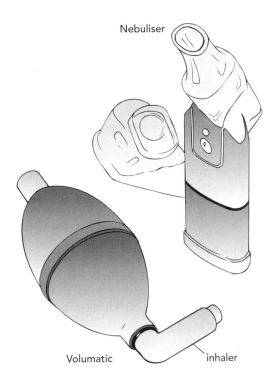

Nebuliser

Volumatic   inhaler

Making sure that you are giving the right inhaler

Some children have more than one inhaler. It is important that the correct one is given during an attack as the drugs in them work in different ways.

Preventive medication
The drugs help prevent attacks but will not help a child during an attack. The inhaler cases are often **brown** or **orange**.

Medication during an attack
The drugs work by reducing the inflammation of the airway walls allowing air to pass in more easily. The inhaler cases are usually **blue**.

Reassuring and comforting children who are not well

Children who are not feeling well are likely to feel frightened and unhappy. They may ask for their parents and need comforters such as teddies and blankets. Early years workers can help children by giving them plenty of reassurance. To do this we must stay with them even if they are drowsy. Children are helped in different ways and this can depend on their age and what is wrong with them. We could distract them by showing them a book or talk to them about what is happening and why. Some children cope better when they know what is happening 'Your tummy is telling you that it didn't like the lunch. It is letting us know that it doesn't want it and when it has given it all back, you will feel better.'

Some children will need physical reassurance and you may decide to hold their hands, rub their backs or sit them close to you.

As children pick up on the atmosphere around them, it is important that we are cheerful, positive and do not show signs of alarm.

Think about it

Look at these case studies in pairs.

Case Study 1
Finn is four years old and is feeling sick. He has been given a bucket and is waiting in the office for his father to come. You are waiting with him.

1 *What can you say to reassure him?*
2 *Why is it important for you to stay with him?*

Case Study 2
Danielle is two years old. You are caring for her in her own home. She has a slight temperature, a rash and is crying. You have contacted her mother, but it will take her an hour to get back.

2 *List some of the common illnesses that she may be suffering from.*
3 *At what point would you consider contacting a doctor?*
4 *How can you help Danielle while she is waiting for her mother?*

Caring for sick children

When we care for sick children, we may need to change our approach. The most important thing is to help the child get better again. This means that adults must not worry if children change from their normal pattern of behaviour. Children who are normally quite independent may ask to be fed or they may be more tearful.

There are some activities that we must carry out to help children get better and to prevent the spread of infection.

Hygiene

Keeping children clean helps prevent infection from spreading, but also makes them feel more comfortable and settled. A personal hygiene routine for a child includes:

- washing hands and face

- combing or brushing hair

- changing underclothes or nightwear each day

- having a bath or shower

- cleaning teeth – especially after meals

- changing bedclothes/making up the bed

- trimming finger nails (this is especially important if children have itchy rashes).

Where children are too poorly to have a bath or shower, they can be given an 'all over wash' using a flannel, towel and a bowl of water. We must always make sure that we dry children carefully and that they do not get cold.

Ventilation is important where children are being cared for. Early years workers need to make sure that children are kept warm, but some fresh air is needed to prevent bacteria from building up. This can be done by leaving a window slightly ajar or by airing the room while children are not in it.

Measures to prevent the spread of infections

Part of caring for sick children includes thinking about ways of preventing the spread of infection. Children who are recovering from an illness are more vulnerable to picking up another infection as their immune system is lowered.

Good practice – reducing the spread of infections

✔ Wash hands after touching any body fluids – e.g. vomit, saliva.

✔ Dispose of body fluids immediately – e.g. empty and disinfect potties straight away, throw tissues away.

✔ Sterilise and clean items used in food preparation in cases of gastroenteritis or food poisoning.

✔ Make sure work surfaces in kitchens are sterilised.

✔ Keep areas clean, tidy and aired – e.g. children's bedroom, lounge.

✔ Remove food that is unwanted and throw it away.

✔ Change water or drinks frequently.

✔ Use paper tissues rather than handkerchiefs.

Giving drinks and food

We must be careful to check that children are keeping up their fluid intake. This is important as children can become dehydrated. They may lose fluid through vomiting or sweating. Children can become very poorly if they dehydrate and we must look for signs that this is happening – for example:

- cracked lips, dry mouth

- passing less urine

- urine a dark colour

- headache

- sunken fontanelle in babies (the soft part of the head).

Some children may not feel like having lots to drink and may only take small sips at a time. Sometimes we can give children flavoured drinks if we have checked that this is all right with parents or doctors – for example, fruit drinks high in vitamin C, fruit juices. We can encourage them to drink by using straws, by giving them a 'special' beaker or by playing a game.

Children who are sick may not feel like eating or they may not be allowed to eat – for example, if a child has been vomiting. We must always check what they can have with parents or doctors. Children who have been vomiting may need to start by eating dry foods such as toast and crackers. Milk-based foods may cause them to vomit again.

Sometimes children may need some encouragement to eat – for example, it may be painful for them to swallow. They may need smaller portions or pieces. Some children may want to be fed rather than feed themselves. You can make up games or present food in fun ways to help them – for example, make a face out of food or pretend that you are a waiter.

Quite often we must follow the children's appetites, this means that there may not be set meal times and they may want small snacks instead. We can give foods that do not require much effort and slip down easily – for example, yoghurts, omelettes, mashed potatoes and minced meat, thick soups. Foods should be as high in protein and energy as possible – for example, we can add cheese and butter to potatoes and look for yoghurts that are made with full-fat cream.

Food to tempt sick children

Portfolio activity

Abeda is four years old and has chicken pox. She has some spots in her mouth and has not wanted to eat much.

1 *Plan a meal that may tempt her to eat.*
2 *Write about how you would present it and why it would be easy for her to eat.*
3 *Write an assessment of the nutritional value of your suggested meal.*

Administering medicines and treatments

There may be times when early years workers are asked to administer treatments or medicines.

Most early years settings have forms or books where the name of the child, the medication or treatment, the dosage and time is recorded. Parents are asked to sign the form or book so that we have written consent. This is important because if early years workers administer medicines without consent, they could be accused of assaulting the child.

It is important to know if medicines need to be taken before or after meals.

The chart below shows an example of a form that could be used to record consent in an early years setting.

Date	Name of child	Medicine or treatment	Purpose	Dosage/method and storage	Signature of parent	Time treatment given and by whom
4.3.98	Eliza Wilson	Ampicillin	For ear infection	One 5ml spoonful at 1 pm. Keep in fridge		Given at 1.05 pm by Sarah

Where children are on regular medication – for example, treatment for asthma or epilepsy – a 'one off' signature from parents would be sufficient. It would be advisable to find out as much as possible about this condition and the medication including the side effects of any drugs – for example, some drugs for epilepsy can cause drowsiness.

Knowledge into Action

Ask your supervisor about the policy on giving medicines.

1 *Find out who is responsible for storing the medicines and who gives the medicines.*
2 *Are there any children in the early years setting who need inhalers?*
3 *Where are these kept?*
4 *Write down the answers to these questions.*

Giving medicines to children

▦ Before giving any medicine it is vital to check the label and instructions:

▦ Is it for the right child?

▦ How much needs to be taken?

▦ Does the bottle need shaking?

▦ Should food be taken before or after the dose?

Most medicines for children come as a liquid or syrup and are given either by syringe or spoon. Spoons should be marked with dosages – for example, 5ml. An ordinary teaspoon is not the same as a medicine spoon.

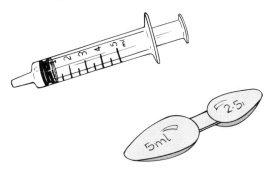

Some children enjoy their medicine and take it easily. Some medicines may not taste good and we need to find ways of getting children to take them. We can have a pleasant drink ready or something to distract them. Some early years settings may have syringes that make it easier to give children medicine.

If we are giving medicines to children we may also need to look out for side effects – for example, some antibiotics give children diarrhoea.

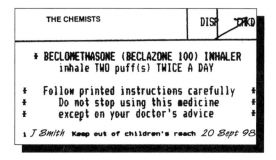

THE CHEMISTS   DISP   'D'KD

‡ BECLOMETHASONE (BECLAZONE 100) INHALER
  inhale TWO puff(s) TWICE A DAY

‡ Follow printed instructions carefully ‡
‡   Do not stop using this medicine   ‡
‡   except on your doctor's advice   ‡

1 *J Smith* **Keep out of children's reach** *20 Sept 98*

Storing and labelling medicines

Medicines need to be kept safe. Young children are curious and may try to imitate a situation they have seen. They may wish to try using an inhaler or see if tablets taste nice. Medicines should be locked away and kept out of reach.

However, not all medicines can be stored in a locked place. Some medicines – for example, antibiotics – need to be stored in a fridge, although they can be put towards the back of the fridge so that children cannot see them. All medicines need labels to show what they are and who is taking them.

Good practice – giving medicines

✔ Medicine that is not correctly given can be dangerous.

✔ Always check the dosage.

✔ Medicines that have no proper labels should not be given to children.

✔ When medicine is given a record should be kept.

Records of children's health

Most parents are happy to give early years settings details about their child's health. This can help us in caring for children. Some children may need regular medication because they have a long-term health need such as eczema or diabetes. It is important that settings are aware of these health needs so that arrangements can be made to store and give medicines.

There may be children who are diabetic and need to have regular snacks, but are not allowed to have sugary foods and sweets. There may be children who have epilepsy and we need to know how to help them if they have an attack. Records need to be kept up-to-date and anyone who needs to know about a child's condition should be told about it.

Case Study

You are babysitting for Mohammed who is three years old. His mother has asked you to give him a spoonful of medicine for an ear infection when he goes to bed.
When you get out the bottle, he runs away saying that he doesn't want to take it.

In pairs work out what you might say or do to encourage the child to take the medicine.

It is helpful if we know the name and telephone number of the child's doctor in case of an emergency. In a home environment, this information may be put near a telephone.

Any information we are given about children's health is sensitive and confidential and we must not pass on information without good reason. A parent may not wish other people to know that their child has epilepsy because they want their child to lead a 'normal' life.

Section D

Significant Health Factors

Long Term Factors (inc Allergies): *Asthma*

Continual Medication: *Ventolin inhaler (if necessary)*

Special Diet: *Dairy free*

Special Difficulties with Speech, Hearing, Vision: *None*

Name & Address of Family Doctor: *Dr Smith*

.... Telephone No: *01332 48579*

Records during an illness

When we care for children who are not well we must keep accurate records. These may help in deciding if they need further treatment. Our records need to have times and dates on them. The information that needs noting down will depend on the illness of the child, although we should always note down when we have given treatment or medicine.

Think about it

You are caring for a child who has been vomiting.

Write a list of the information that you would need to note down.

Identifying play activities for sick children

Children who are not well may have to spend some time in bed or resting. Some children may not need to stay in bed and will prefer to sit and be near us.

They may become bored and frustrated and we can help by providing some activities and playing with them. We need to remember that sick children often tire quickly and may lose their concentration easily. This means that any activity or game that we play should be short and easy for them to do. We can use a kitchen tray to put games and puzzles on if there is no table near a bed. Children enjoy doing activities and playing games that they have not done before. Sometimes we can borrow items from toy libraries which means that children have something new to play with.

The chart below gives a list of ideas that can be used with sick children.

Treasure box	A box of small toys or objects that the child has not seen before – books, finger puppets, cuddly toys. The objects can be changed frequently so that the child does not get bored.
Puppets	Finger puppets and hand puppets are a good way to play with children. Older children can use them and make up shows with them.
Jigsaw puzzles	These can be put on a tray so that they can move with the child. They need to be easy enough so that the child does not become frustrated.
Story board	Story boards often have felt figures and objects that children can attach and move around a board.
Binoculars and magnifying glasses	Children can watch what is going on outside and look at birds with the binoculars. The magnifying glass can be used to look at objects such as shells, feathers and plants.
Story tapes	There are a variety of tapes that can be used. The tapes mean that children can listen over and over again to their favourite bits.
Mobiles	Children can make simple mobiles – e.g. cut out shapes and tie them on twigs.

Card games	Children can play simple games – e.g. Snap, Happy Families. Cards can be put on a tray if children are in bed.
Table top games	There are many games that can be used – e.g. Lotto, Snakes and Ladders.
Drawing, colouring and sticking	Children can cut, stick and draw. Older children can be given kits to do. Providing new materials or interesting ones can make it more fun for children – e.g. glitter, glue or collage materials.

Case Study

Mark is three years old. He is starting to feel better after chicken pox, but needs to be distracted if he begins to scratch his spots.

Think of three activities that would be suitable to help Mark.

Recognising the needs of parents/carers

Parents of sick children are likely to be under many pressures. It is a distressing time for parents and we need to be as supportive as possible.

Common reactions from parents include:

Guilt

- They may not be able to take time off work.
- They may not have recognised that their child was unwell.
- They may feel that they could have prevented the illness.

Exhaustion

- Due to lack of sleep and from continual caring.
- Due to worrying.

Anxiety

- From lack of information.
- The child may not be showing progress.
- The parent may have other responsibilities – e.g. caring for other children or being unable to take time off work

To help parents we need to listen to their fears and reassure them. We may need to give them opportunities to care for themselves by getting them drinks and food. If we are looking after their children, parents must be able to feel that they can trust us to keep in contact with them.

Case Study

You are working as a nanny. Sarah is two years old and has whooping cough. Her mother has taken two days off work, but must now return as her employer will not give her any more time off.

1 *Plan some activities that you can do with Sarah*
2 *How can you make Sarah's mother feel better about leaving?*
3 *What information would you need to give to Sarah's mother and when?*
4 *In what circumstances would you contact Sarah's mother at work?*
5 *What would you do if you could not reach her?*

Roles of healthcare professionals

There are a number of healthcare professionals who may be involved in the care and treatment of sick children. They may give advice and instructions as to how children need to be looked after or they may need information from us about children.

Doctor (GP)	Diagnoses illnesses, prescribes medication or refers children for further treatment or diagnosis. They can give medical advice about caring for children.
Paediatrician	A consultant who specialises in the development and treatment of children. Often based at a hospital.
School nurse	Monitors children's development and the health of school-age children. Gives advice to parents and schools about illnesses. Has specialised training in children's development and health.
Health visitor	Monitors children's development and gives advice to parents. Sees children in their own homes as well as at clinics. Passes on all records to school nurse. Has specialised training in children's development
Practice nurse	Based in doctors surgery, gives advice to all members of the family as well as vaccinations and routine tests.

Unit test

Quick quiz

1 Which of these is the normal body temperature for a child?
   a 32°C
   b 34.5°C
   c 36.9°C
   d 38.3°C

2 A child who has asthma is becoming breathless. The early years or educational worker must **first**:
   a tell the child to sit down.
   b call an ambulance.
   c put the child in the recovery position.
   d rub the child gently on the back.

3 Which of the following signs is not a symptom of dehydration?

   a Cracked lips

   b Passing less urine

   c Hunger

   d Headache

4 Rubella is the medical term used for which disease?

   a Chicken pox

   b Scarlet fever

   c Food poisoning

   d German Measles

5 A child is vomiting and complains of a headache and a stiff neck. These are all symptoms of:

   a whooping cough.

   b meningitis.

   c chicken pox.

   d mumps.

Short answer questions

1 Name two illnesses where rashes appear.

2 What is the other name for whooping cough?

3 What is the incubation period for chicken pox?

4 What is the treatment for tonsillitis?

5 Arching of the back in babies is a sign of which disease?

Working with Young Children

Looking after children involves more than just caring for their physical needs and keeping them safe and happy. Part of a professional early years worker's role is to help them to learn about their world and to encourage their development. To do this we need to understand how children learn, our role in supporting children's learning and also which activities encourage learning.

An important message of this chapter is that learning should be fun and children learn best when they are enjoying what they are doing. The chapter is split into four sections:

1   *How do children learn?*

2   *The role of the adult in supporting children's learning and development.*

3   *Communicating and developing children's language skills.*

4   *Ideas for practical activities.*

1 How do children learn?

The human brain is quite complex and no one is really sure how exactly we learn. However, over the years psychologists, who study human behaviour, have devised some theories. In this section, we are going to look at three theories and consider how they might influence early years workers working with children.

Social learning theory

This theory, first put forward by **Albert Bandura** (born in 1925), covers many aspects of child development and so is referred to again in Chapters 8, 9 and 11.

The social learning theory suggests that children learn by looking at the behaviour of adults and others around them and then imitate what they have seen. To show this Bandura carried out an experiment in which he showed three groups of children a short film about an adult hitting an inflatable doll. Each group saw one of these endings to the film:

Ending One   The adult was praised and given sweets.

Ending Two   Nothing was said to the adult.

Ending Three   The adult was smacked and told off.

Bandura then looked to see how children behaved when they were left alone with the same doll. He found that children who saw endings one and two were more aggressive with the doll than the children who saw ending number three. He came to the conclusion that the children who had seen endings one and two were more aggressive towards the doll, because they had learnt from watching the adult that it was acceptable to hit the doll.

Linking theory with practice

Most early years workers accept that there is a link between children's learning and what they see.

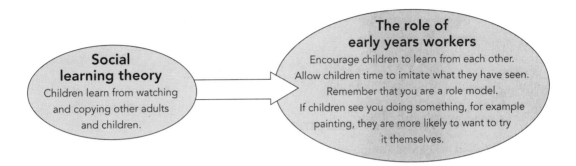

Social learning theory
Children learn from watching and copying other adults and children.

The role of early years workers
Encourage children to learn from each other.
Allow children time to imitate what they have seen.
Remember that you are a role model.
If children see you doing something, for example painting, they are more likely to want to try it themselves.

Behaviourist theories

There is a group of psychologists that believes that our learning is shaped by our direct experiences. One of the most famous theories was put forward by **Burrhus F Skinner** (1904–1994). In simple terms it states that we repeat experiences that are enjoyable and avoid experiences that we have not enjoyed. In this way we learn skills and types of behaviour. For example, if a child is given praise or has enjoyed doing a puzzle, they are likely to do this again.

Skinner called things that would make us repeat an activity positive reinforcements. There are many different types of positive reinforcement – food, praise and money are common positive reinforcements for all of us!

This theory is the idea behind trial and error learning. We may try something out and if it is successful, we learn from this and repeat the experience. For example, a baby girl shakes a rattle and hears a noise. She is pleased with the noise and so shakes the rattle again. She has learnt that rattles can make noises.

Linking theory with practice

The behaviourist theory is widely accepted by early years workers not only as a theory of how children learn but also as a way of managing children's behaviour (See Chapter 11, pages 234–251).

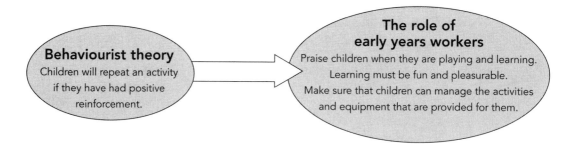

Cognitive development theory

This theory suggests that learning is a process and children need to pass through different stages. The most famous psychologist who worked with this theory is **Jean Piaget** (1896–1980), a Swiss biologist. He was working on intelligence tests when he became interested in finding out why children's logic was different from that of adults.

Piaget's main idea is that children develop logic based on their experiences and try to draw conclusions from these experiences. Sometimes these conclusions – or **schemas** as Piaget called them – are wrong, but understandable. For example, many young children think that all women must be 'mummies'. Their own experience is often that women are mothers and so they develop this schema. Eventually, they learn that some women are not mothers and so they have to adapt their schema.

From studying children carefully, Piaget concluded that there were stages of learning broadly linked to children's ages and children were not able to move from one stage of learning onto another until they were ready.

Age	Title	Stage of learning
0–2 years	Sensory motor	Babies are starting to find out about things around them and discovering what these things can be made to do.
2–7	Pre-operational	Thought processes are developing. Children are starting to use symbols in their play, although children often need to see things and feel them to learn about them. For example, five-year-olds find it hard to add up in their head, but can manage with counters.
7–11	Concrete operations	Children can think more logically. They can follow rules of games. They can use and understand symbols – e.g. letters and numbers.

Linking theory with practice

Although Piaget's work has been criticised because often children do things earlier than he suggested, the idea that children need to learn at their own pace has been accepted.

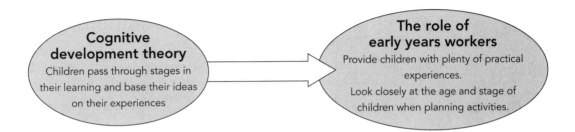

Cognitive development theory
Children pass through stages in their learning and base their ideas on their experiences

The role of early years workers
Provide children with plenty of practical experiences.
Look closely at the age and stage of children when planning activities.

(For more information on Piaget see Chapter 8, page 162.)

Piaget suggested that children's direct experiences help them to form their ideas.

Haddon Davies

Although research is still being carried out into how children learn, the main point to understand as an early years worker is that children need to be active in their learning. There must be plenty of opportunity for them to touch, feel and explore different materials. Children also need to enjoy what they are doing so activities for children must be suitable for their stage and adults must praise children.

Stages of play and learning

When planning activities and play experiences for children we may need to look at their stage of learning and understanding in order to provide experiences that are appropriate to their development. The chart belows shows the ways in which children play and learn at different ages. Play and learning have been brought together as children often learn through direct play experiences.

Age	Play and learning development
0–6 months	Watching adults closely Exploring by using the mouth and by touch Playing alone with toys such as rattles and baby gyms
6–12 months	Exploring by using the mouth and by touch Watching and copying adults Repeating movements such as dropping a rattle Enjoying simple games such as peek-a-boo Exploring toys alone
12–18 months	Learning through trial and error – e.g. banging two cubes and discovering the sound it makes Repeating actions that they have enjoyed Beginning to play with adults and notice other children Playing and 'talking' alone
18 months–2 years	Learning through trial and error Imitating other children and adults Exploring things with mouth Possibly carrying out repetitive actions – e.g. putting things in and out of boxes or scribbling on several pages Watching other children but not joining in Enjoying playing with adults as well as by themselves
2–3 years	Beginning to show some reasoning skills – although still learning by trial and error Imitating adults and other children Starting to use symbols in their play – e.g. a stick becoming a wand Beginning to play alongside other children Most of their play is 'pretend' play – e.g. telling off toys
3–4 years	Showing more reasoning skills and asking questions such as 'why' Starting to concentrate for longer on a play activity that interests them Recognising shapes and letters Solving jigsaw puzzles through a mixture of reasoning and trial and error Playing co-operatively together and taking turns Playing imaginatively – e.g. playing in the home corner, dressing up
4–6 years	Showing more understanding and using reason based on their experiences Starting to use and understand symbols – e.g. writing and reading Starting to understand simple rules in games Playing co-operatively, taking turns and enjoying table-top games
6–8 years	Enjoying using rules and understanding the need for rules Showing reasoning skills but still using some trial and error learning Playing in small groups and making up their own games which tend to have rules Enjoying playing competitive games but not always coping with losing Tending to play with children of their own sex

Knowledge into Action

Ask your supervisor if you can observe two children of different ages at play.

1   *Make notes on what they are doing and how.*
2   *How does this compare to the stages in the chart above?*

2 The role of the adult in supporting children's learning and development

This section looks at different ways in which early years workers can support learning and development and also when early years workers need to intervene.

When you are planning activities for children you need to think about your role. Are you going to take an active part in their learning or are you going to assist them in learning for themselves?

Adult-directed activity

Adult-directed activity

Some activities are called **adult directed**. This means that the children are gaining experience and skills by following instructions from an adult. They might be looking for insects on a nature walk or listening to a story. We need to think about adult-directed activities carefully. They can be very positive learning experiences, but we must also be careful that we do not use them as a way of controlling children.

Activities initiated by children

These are different from adult-directed activities because the children make the decisions and choices. Activities initiated by children are considered to be good for children because they help them to be creative, solve problems and be independent. Children might decide to pretend they are farmers or they might want to make a card to take home. We can help children by allowing them enough time to finish their games or activities and also by praising them. Children who have been playing happily have not wasted their time, they have been learning how to relate to others, which is a skill for life.

Structured activity

The idea of structured activities is that children are able to learn whilst exploring and playing. Structured activities help children to use materials and explore concepts that they might not otherwise do. They may practise different skills – for example, counting pretend money. (See Chapter 8, page 163, for more information on structured activities.)

Spontaneous activity

Spontaneous activity takes place when children adapt materials or equipment to play with. For example, they might use a sheet to make a tent. Children enjoy playing in this way although adults need to check that they are playing safely. Examples of spontaneous play would be activities such as bouncing on beds and sofas and using the climbing frame as a ship!

Learning opportunities in everyday routines

Children can learn through helping with everyday routines. They can experience soap on their hands and watch in which direction water goes down the plug hole. If we talk to children while we are carrying out tasks and look for ways of involving them, something as routine as putting on a coat can become a learning opportunity.

Learning through everyday routines not only helps children develop some important life skills – for example, being able to wash up – but it also gives them a sense of belonging and involvement.

Think about it

1   *In pairs, choose two of the following tasks and discuss how you could involve children in carrying them out.*
2   *Are there any safety considerations?*
3   *What age would they be suitable for?*

Hanging out washing	*Feeding a pet animal*
Tidying away jigsaw puzzles	*Preparing a sandwich*
Washing up beakers	*Planting bulbs*
Posting a letter	*Buying fruit in a shop*

When should adults intervene in children's activities?

We **always** need to intervene in children's activities:

▪ when they are in danger of hurting themselves

▪ if they could harm others

▪ if equipment is likely to be broken or damaged

▪ when racist, sexist or other offensive remarks are being said.

We **may** decide to intervene:

▪ when children are showing signs of frustration

▪ when children are running out of ideas

▪ when there is a learning opportunity that is too good to miss.

When we intervene in children's learning we need to understand the difference between taking control and supporting children. Look at the following example.

Mark is making a model. He is trying to glue a round shape onto a flat surface. It keeps falling off. He picks up the model and throws it down in frustration. The adult can intervene in two ways:

1 Taking control
'Bring your model here I'll do it while you play with something else.'

2 Support
'Would you like me to help you with that? I'm sure that together we can sort it out. Can you think of anything else that might make it stick?'

Why is support better than taking control?

Support means giving children help in such a way that they are still learning and are still in control of their activity. This is important as it gives children confidence in their abilities. We may decide that the children in the home corner are starting to run out of ideas. We could either tell them to stop playing and change activity or we could support their play by offering them some new equipment or asking if we can take a part too.

Knowledge into Action

Two children have been fixing together a train track. Now it is complete they do not seem to be playing with it and one of them has started to throw the trains around.

1 *Why do you think this is happening?*
2 *Write down how you might encourage them to play with it.*

Making the most of learning opportunities

Learning opportunities may also happen unexpectedly and should be used – for example, a rainbow might appear or children might be playing with water when they notice that some objects float while others sink. Early years workers should use these moments to help children think through what they are seeing.

Helping children to be independent, self-reliant and self-confident

We want children to grow up to be self-reliant, confident and able to make choices in their lives.

Children can be helped to become self-reliant by being encouraged to carry out everyday tasks – for example, wiping up their own spills, getting their own cups and plates out and tidying away. Taking control and doing everything for children may mean that such tasks are done quickly but it also means that children are not allowed to take responsibility. This is why you must encourage children to do as many things for themselves as they can. By being praised for their efforts they will also gain confidence.

Children also need praise when they have had a go at something even if they may not have been successful. Look at this example:

Think about it

Rajeet spills food down his favourite jumper. He tries to remove it with a cloth, but there is still a stain. What would be the best thing for the adult to do and say?

1   *Do nothing and praise Rajeet for cleaning his jumper.*
2   *Tell Rajeet to take his jumper off so that the stain can be removed.*
3   *Praise Rajeet for his efforts and say that he is too young to clean it properly.*
4   *Praise Rajeet for his efforts and say that some stains only come off with soap and that he can help wash it.*

Encouraging self-direction in children

Learning to concentrate and finish tasks is an important life skill. Most children develop these skills through being supported by an adult. We may praise them when we see that they are starting to become frustrated or give them some support and help so that they can finish the task.

Good practice – supporting children's learning

✔   Make sure that activities are suitable for the age/stage of the children.

✔ Look out for children who are feeling frustrated as this can lead to feelings of failure.

✔ Praise children as they are playing and learning.

✔ Help children by offering suggestions rather than telling them what to do.

✔ Encourage children to find their own solutions by asking questions that will help them to think through a problem..

Portfolio activity

Ask your supervisor if you can supervise and support children during an activity.

1 *Write down the age of the children and what they were doing.*
2 *What do you think the children gained from this activity?*
3 *How did you help them to learn for themselves?*
4 *What did you learn from supervising and supporting these children?*

Why do stereotyping and labelling stop children from learning?

Children need to be confident enough to try out different experiences and ways of playing so that they can learn. When children feel that they cannot or should not try something, they miss out on a learning opportunity. Stereotyping and labelling children creates situations where children may not feel that they can try out an activity. A child who overhears an adult saying that he is a 'bit slow' may not believe that he can do something and so does not even try or a girl who is praised because she is always clean and tidy may avoid playing in the sandpit.

This means that as early years workers, we must make sure that all children are actively encouraged to take part in activities and given plenty of praise.

Adapting the materials and approach we use to meet children's needs

Some children may need extra support so that they can learn. We may need to think creatively about the learning opportunities we offer to make sure that children with special or particular needs can benefit from them.

■ **Layout and presentation can be changed**. For example, in one playgroup, where a girl had mobility needs, all the activities and equipment came to her. The painting, story time and even the rabbit were brought to her so that she could have the same opportunities as the other children.

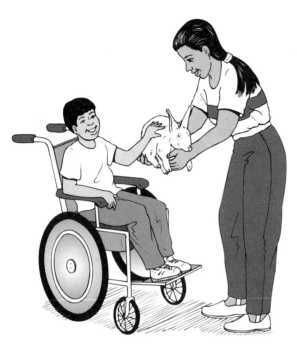

- **Specialist equipment and materials** can be used to help children with special needs. These may be borrowed from toy libraries or from charities.

- **Early years settings can adapt materials**. For example, one nursery made some dressing-up clothes which meant that children in wheelchairs could put them on more easily.

- **Early years settings may try different approaches** for children with learning difficulties. There is often no single right way for an adult to support children's learning. We need to recognise that what works well for some children will not be as effective with others.

Portfolio activity

Some children may be missing out on learning opportunities without us realising it. A quiet or shy child may not be confident enough to play with other children or use certain pieces of equipment.

1   *Look at two children in your workplace.*
2   *Over a session, record what they have been doing.*
3   *Have they both had the same learning experience, amount of adult attention and opportunity to use materials?*
4   *Think of practical ways to support children who may be missing out on learning opportunities because they are shy or quiet.*
5   *Ask your supervisor if you can try out one of these ways if there is a child in the workplace who would benefit.*
6   *Write about how you encouraged this child*

3 Communicating and developing children's language skills

Children need to talk and express themselves in order to learn. Language and thought processes are connected.

One of the more important aspects of caring for children is to promote their language skills so that they can express themselves clearly. We need to work with children in different ways according to their age and stage of development. The chart opposite shows the stages of language development and the role of adults in supporting this development.

Age	Stage	Role of adult
0–6 months	Babies are trying to communicate. They make eye contact and babble. They imitate and repeat sounds.	Good eye contact, running commentary and repetition of phrases – e.g. 'I think youy're feeling hungry now, aren't you?' As babies begin to babble they need praise and recognition that they are trying to communicate.
6–18 months	First words are made. One word may stand for several things. Children begin to point to attract adult's interest. They respond to pictures of animals and familiar objects. By 18 months most children are using 50 words.	Getting down to the level of the child and making eye contact is important. Children need to feel that they are being understood and listened to. Rhymes, songs and books can be introduced. Children need plenty of adult input and running commentary – e.g. 'It's time for a bath now. You like your bath, don't you?'
18 months– 3 years	During this time children's vocabulary increases quickly. By the age of three children are putting sentences together and are beginning to use questions. Children enjoy and are able to follow stories and remember rhymes. By three years some children are using 900 words.	Adults need to allow children enough time to think and answer. They must be patient as children often enjoy repeating questions and asking for stories and rhymes over and over again. We can help children with their pronunciation and grammar by using the same words but correctly – 'I felled down' – 'You fell down did you? Shall I look at your knee?'
3–8 years	By the age of five most children have a vocabulary of 3000 words and are using complex sentences and questions. By the time children go to school, they can often understand simple jokes and enjoy stories. By eight years children can use language in many different ways – e.g. to socialise, to express a need, to recount and predict events.	Adults need to extend children's vocabulary and help them to use language as a way of thinking. We can use open questions. This means asking questions where children have to give more than a one-word answer. For example, 'Why do you think the ice melted?' Children need to have time to think and may stammer if they rush to explain something. We need to show them that we are listening by, for example, nodding our heads and making eye contact. They may use words that they have heard without understanding their meaning – e.g. swear words – and we may need to explain that some words are not nice. Stories and rhymes are still needed and enjoyed even when children can read for themselves.

Common communication difficulties

Some children may find communication difficult for one of the following reasons:

- a physical condition – e.g. a cleft palate or enlarged tongue
- a learning difficulty – e.g. autism
- a hearing impairment either temporary – e.g. glue ear – or permanent
- a stutter or stammer
- shyness
- lack of stimulation and language input
- more than one language is being learnt.

Non-verbal comunication – i.e. pointing and bowing

Sometimes children may be understood by their families without being able to communicate with other people. In other cases the youngest child in the family may have its needs met so quickly by older children that they have not had to talk in order to get what they want.

Stuttering and stammering is common in children and is usually temporary. They may need time and sometimes feel more relaxed when talking to an adult by themselves.

If children have a speech difficulty they may be referred to speech therapists or other health professionals.

Good practice – communicating with children

- ✔ Make eye contact.
- ✔ Smile and look patient.
- ✔ Allow children time to think about what they want to say.
- ✔ Do not finish sentences for them.
- ✔ Do not interrupt to hurry them along.
- ✔ Listen to what children are saying!
- ✔ Correct any grammar by echoing back their sentence correctly – e.g. 'He **took** your ball did he?'
- ✔ Ask open questions – e.g. 'What are you doing?' rather than closed questions that can be answered with only one word – e.g. 'Are you enjoying that?'

Think about it

Look at this conversation between an adult and a child who is drawing.

Adult: Are you enjoying that?
Child: (nods head)
Adult: What's it meant to be?
Child: It's my mum and my house and my sister and.... (adult looks away)
Adult: Oh that's very nice. When you've finished remember to hang up your apron.

1   *What mistakes has the adult made in this conversation?*
2   *In pairs, write your own conversation between an adult and a child who is drawing.*
3   *Why would your conversation help to develop a child's language?*

Talking and listening activities for children

There are many activities that children enjoy which encourage them to talk and listen. Activities where young children must listen to others often work best in small groups as they can find it hard to wait for their turn.

The chart below shows some examples of types of activity that could be used.

Activity	Benefits
Peek-a-boo (8–12 months)	This is a traditional game that has variations in many cultures. Babies learn to communicate and make eye contact with adults. We can sometimes see babies pull something onto their head in order to show the adult that they want to play the game again.
Meals and snack times (4 months–8 years+)	Talking and socialising at meal times should start from babyhood. Meals and snack times can be times in the day when children can talk and listen to each other in a relaxed way. They might talk about their favourite food or what they are going to do next as well practising their social skills and table manners.
Telephones and walkie-talkies (15 months–7 years)	Telephones often encourage children to speak and talk. At 15 months they may babble and say 'bye'. Older children enjoy having real conversations with each other either in the home corner or using walkie-talkies.
Puppets (15 months–8 years+)	Puppets can help children to talk and listen. Children who are not comfortable talking in front of others can use the puppet to talk for them. Babies enjoy watching puppets. Puppets come in all sorts of shapes and sizes and can be made easily. Finger and sock puppets are particularly easy for children to make themselves. Children from five years enjoy putting on puppet shows.
I-Spy (3–8 years)	Children from about three can begin to enjoy this traditional game. We can vary it to meet children's needs. We may ask children to guess what we are looking at or we may tell them the sound it begins with.
Board games dominoes, picture lotto, card games – e.g. Happy Families (3–8 years)	There are many games that can help children to talk, ask questions and listen to others. Younger children will need adults to sit with them as they play, whereas older children who understand rules can play by themselves.

Activity	Benefits
Feely bag Objects are put into a bag or box and children have to guess what they are feeling. (4–8 years)	Children can guess and discover what they are feeling. Older children can describe what they are feeling to other children as part of a game. The adult may elaborate to extend the children's vocabulary. 'Is it soft? Does it feel furry? Can you squeeze it?'
News time/circle time This is a common activity in schools and some nurseries. Children sit in a circle or as a group and take it in turns to talk. (4–8 years)	Children can talk about what they have been doing or bring something in to show. In small groups it can help children to listen to others and to gain confidence in talking to more than one person. We may need to be sensitive to children who do not have anything to show or may not have done anything that they have enjoyed. In some early years settings children can choose a book or a toy in the setting and say why they like using it instead.

Helping children to participate

It is easy for quiet children to be forgotten during talking and listening activities, especially if there are older children with them. In some early years settings we can ask older children to put up their hands if they wish to speak, but with younger children this is not appropriate.

Children who seem to find it difficult to talk in front of others may need us to help by asking questions that will lead them through what they wish to say. If children need encouragement to express themselves, then we can make a special effort to build a relationship with them. We can look for moments in the day when they can get some individual attention – for example, sharing a book together, helping tidying away.

Think about it

Choose two activities from this list and write down why they would be good for developing language in four-year-olds.

Jigsaw puzzle	Cooking	Playing in the sand	Dough
Small world play – e.g. playmobile	Painting	Planting bulbs	

Portfolio activity

Ask your supervisor if there is a child in your workplace who needs support with language.

Talk to your supervisor about the needs of this child and plan an activity that will encourage the child to talk and listen.

1   *Write about this activity.*
2   *How did the child benefit from doing this with you?*
3   *What did you learn from this activity?*

4 Ideas for practical activities

Songs, rhymes and musical activities are a wonderful way to develop children's language. They can learn new words, rhythms and rhymes. Children enjoy doing actions that go along with songs and being part of a group.

There are also benefits when children start learning to read. Studies show that children who know nursery rhymes learn to read more quickly. We can start using nursery rhymes and singing to children from a very early age.

Children do not listen to how well we sing, only to the words, tune and pattern. It is always better to take a deep breath and sing rather than worry about what you sound like!

Think about it

How well do you know your nursery rhymes?

See how many of these questions you can answer. You may enjoy doing this with someone else.

1 *Who stole a pig?*
2 *How do cockles and shells grow?*
3 *What did the king of Hearts do to the knave?*
4 *Who was eating bread and honey?*
5 *Who put Pussy in the well?*

Rhymes and songs can be found to fit in with a particular topic or theme – for example, Incey Wincey spider to go with a topic about rain or animals. We may also be able to find some songs in other languages. It is good for children to hear as many types of music as possible. This means playing classical music as well as jazz, pop and as much music from other countries and cultures as we can find.

We can also make music using our hands. Most children enjoy clapping. They can clap in time to music as well as taking it in turns to clap out the sounds in their names. Older children enjoy playing games where they must follow the clapping rhythm of a leader.

Musical instruments

Most early years settings have some musical instruments. Sometimes these are home-made ones – for example, shakers made by putting rice into bottles or a beater can be used to hit a saucepan lid. Young children do not need tuned instruments to have fun. They can learn a lot about making sounds from experimenting with drums, shakers, rattles and bells. Wherever possible we should try to show children as many instruments as possible. Sometimes parents can bring in instruments to play and show the children – for example, bagpipes and horns.

Ideas for percussion

Name the instrument

A child goes behind a screen and chooses a percussion instrument. They play it in short bursts. One child is then chosen to identify the instrument. The other children can give them clues to help them – for example, 'It is big,' 'It is made of metal.'

Simon Says

Similar to the traditional game, this can be played in two different ways.

1 Instead of saying 'Simon says' a pattern is clapped. When no pattern is clapped the children should not follow the action.

2 Following on from the first idea, all the actions are replaced by sounds made by the body – eg. clapping, stamping, humming.

Hot and cold with instruments

An instrument is hidden and one child is asked to find it. The other children play their instruments loudly when he is close to it and softly when he is 'cold'.

Stand up, sit down

The adult plays a pattern on a drum over and over again. A child who is hidden plays a shaker. When the shaker is being played at the same time the children stand up and when the shaker stops the children sit down.

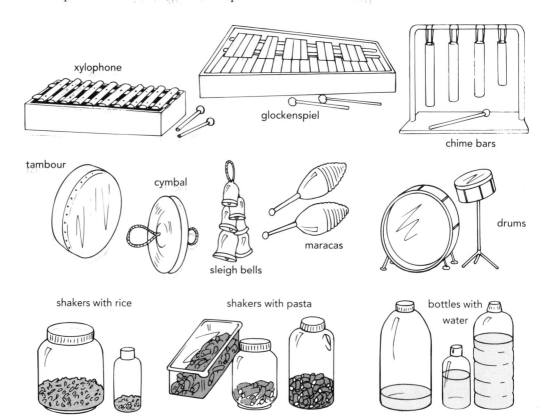

xylophone

glockenspiel

chime bars

tambour

cymbal

sleigh bells

maracas

drums

shakers with rice

shakers with pasta

bottles with water

Pass the beater

The children sit in a circle and a beater is passed round to the song 'Pass the beater, round and round, when it stops make a sound.' The child with the beater must go to the middle and play the instrument.

(Any instrument could be used – e.g. triangle, tambourine.)

Knowledge into Action

Ask your supervisor if you can plan an activity involving music or rhymes.

1   *Write down the age and group size of the children.*
2   *Write about your activity and the benefits of this activity for the children.*
3   *How did you prepare for this activity?*
4   *Did the children enjoy the activity?*
5   *What did you learn from carrying out the activity?*

Books and stories for children

Books are not only sources of information but also of great pleasure to most children. Listening to stories, sharing books with adults as well as curling up in a chair with a book help children to escape and develop their imagination. Providing books for children from a very young age can help their language skills by increasing their vocabulary as well as giving them a good start with reading.

Books for all ages

Babies of eight months are fascinated by images and by 15 months most children are trying to turn pages in books!

Age group	Stage/role of adult
1–2 years	Children like simple picture books. They recognise objects in their own lives. By two years they may have a favourite book.
3–4 years	They listen to simple stories. They want the same stories repeated. At around three years, they pretend to 'read' books. At around four years some children recognise their names and words in their environment. Counting books and nursery books are often particularly popular with this age group.
5–7 years	Children are beginning to learn to read. They still need to be read to and enjoy having stories read to them. They begin to enjoy a wide variety of books including joke books and factual books.

Setting up a book area

Book areas are places where children can sit or lie down and read or share a story. In home environments, a shelf of books in the sitting room may act as a book area, whereas in large early years settings a corner of the room may be used. When choosing a place for a book area, it is important to make sure that there is enough room for all the children to sit down so that story time is comfortable.

To make this area a special and comfortable place it could be:

- Carpeted – to allow children to feel able to stretch out.

- Well lit – to prevent children's eyes from being strained.

- Quiet – to help children to concentrate and use their imaginations.

- Attractive – to stimulate children's curiosity (cushions, displays of books).

Choosing books for children

Below is a list of some of the kinds of books available.

- picture books

- pop-up or flap books

- feely books

- poetry and rhymes

- factual books – e.g. animals, ships, going on holiday

- joke books

- cartoons

- dual-language books

- big books that can be shared with groups of children

- story books.

When we choose books it is important to think about how the book is going to be used. If it is going to be read to a group of children, we may decide to choose a book with clear large pictures and print so that all the children can see it. Some books have few words and may be good for children who are ready to start reading. Young children often enjoy books where words or phrases are repeated. This means that they can predict what is going to happen next and enjoy saying the words at the same time as the adult.

Stereotyping in books

Images and words in books can be powerful. We need to make sure that they do not stereotype any group of people. For example, not all grandmothers have grey hair, sit in rocking chairs and knit. When choosing books, we need to look carefully for any hidden messages. Is the villain fat and ugly? Do men always do the driving? Do girls always need rescuing?

We should also check that there are positive images of people. For example, we may find that in some books there are no pictures of older people having fun, or of people with black skin.

Knowledge into Action

Using five children's books, look at them and consider these questions:

1   *How are disabled people portrayed?*
2   *Are all the images of white people?*
3   *How are women portrayed in the book? Are they in traditional caring roles, such as making dinner, caring for children?*

Books in different languages and showing a range of cultures

A wide range of books can help children understand that there are different languages and ways of seeing the world. Children often enjoy looking at photos of children from cultures different from their own. Some books are dual-language, which means that two children with different home languages can share and appreciate the same book. For children who speak more than one language or whose culture is not shared in the early years setting, they are essential. They show children that their home life is valued and recognised.

Books for children with particular needs

Sharing a book that is about other children in similar circumstances can help children. They may enjoy the story and then feel ready to talk about how they are feeling. Children's charities are often able to give advice about books that can help children with particular needs – for example, books to help children who have lost a parent or close relative.

Providing a range of books

In order to build a selection of books there are a number of places where we can go.

Public libraries have children's sections and some even have story sessions. This makes them an excellent source of books for early years workers who are caring for children in home environments – there may not always be a large selection of books in the home.

Another source of books is the Health Promotion Unit run by the health authority. This is particularly useful for books about health, the human body, safety and accident prevention.

Good practice – reading a story to children

✔ Story time is an enjoyable part of most children's day. It is a time when they can relax and rest as well as learn. Here are some hints that may help you to feel more confident when you read or tell a story to children.

✔ Spend some time preparing for the story.

✔ Read through the book that you want to use. Think about whether it is going to be about the right length for the age of the children. Sometimes it may be better to read two short stories rather than one long one.

✔ Prepare more than one story in case there is a change of plan and you find that you have more time than you thought.

✔ Make sure that the children are comfortable and settled before you start. Sometimes you can help children to be ready by showing them the book, saying 'I think this is a book that you're really going to enjoy,' and praising those children who are ready to start.

✔ Be positive and enthusiastic as you read.

✔ Vary the tone of voice and the speed at which you read. Sometimes you may speak very quietly to help children to listen carefully.

✔ Change words or sentences if children are not going to understand them. Sometimes you may need to miss out a couple of pages if the children are losing their concentration or you may decide to say 'I think that we'll finish this another day and sing a few rhymes instead.'

✔ Prepare some visual aids such as puppets or props to make stories come to life. Consider using visual aids with nursery rhymes – e.g. pictures of currant buns, ducks and sausages.

✔ Try to involve children in the story. Ask them questions – e.g. 'Can you see the mouse?' Be careful to keep a balance between asking questions and getting on with the story. You may need to say to a child 'After this story, you can tell me about your rabbit but I think we'll just finish this first.'

Reading a story

Portfolio activity

Ask your supervisor if you can read a story to a group of children.

1   *Write down the number of children in the group and their ages.*
2   *What type of book did you choose?*
3   *Explain why you chose this book.*
4   *Explain how you made the story interesting for the children.*
5   *How did the children react to your story?*
6   *What did you learn from doing this activity?*

Cooking with children

Most children enjoy eating and this means that cooking is often a favourite activity. As it requires some adult assistance and supervision, children often cook in small groups or individually. Working in small groups helps children to learn to share and gives them plenty of opportunity to talk, listen and watch. Children are also learning about food: where it comes from and how certain processes – for example, whisking – can change it. Children are also able to learn about healthy eating and hygiene in the kitchen. It is also a wonderful opportunity for children to taste food from different cultures.

Choosing ideas and recipes

When we are thinking about a cooking activity we need to think about:

- age and size of the group
- experiences children may have already gained
- equipment that is available
- cost of ingredients
- time available
- learning outcomes
- dietary considerations – e.g. some children may be allergic to nuts.

It is often a good idea to try a new recipe by ourselves first so that we can find out how easy it is and if the children would enjoy the food. We can also decide how safe it will be for children at the same time. Good recipes for children allow them to be involved in the preparation and cooking for most of the time.

Some easy ideas for children

Dish	Ingredients	Method	Learning potential
Sandwich	Bread, margarine/ butter, cheese/cold meat/banana or other fillings	Butter bread with flat knife. Add fillings.	Children can make a savoury meal by themselves. We can look for different types of bread and can also toast the bread.
Egg salad	Lettuce, tomatoes, eggs, sweetcorn, oil, vinegar and a pinch of salt	Put eggs in pan and boil for 10 minutes. Plunge eggs into cold water. Wash the lettuce and tomatoes and drain. Make salad dressing (equal quantities of oil to vinegar – e.g. 2tsps oil – 2tsps vinegar.) Arrange lettuce in a bowl or plate and cut tomatoes in half. Spoon on sweetcorn and then peel eggs and cut them. Sprinkle with dressing.	Children can see the change in the egg when it is hard-boiled. Different types of lettuce can be used and children can mix their own dressing easily. They can see that the oil does not want to mix with the vinegar.
Quatre, Quatre cake	Egg, self raising flour, margarine, sugar	The idea of this recipe is each ingredient weighs the same as the egg. If the egg weighs 100g you put in 100g of flour, 100g of sugar and 100g of margarine. Mix margarine and sugar together until pale. Add in egg and flour. Bake in a greased cake tin or as fairy cakes in a moderate oven for 15 minutes or until firm to the touch.	This is an old French recipe which works very well with the old-fashioned type of scales. The egg acts as the weight and children can see when the other ingredient – e.g. sugar – matches the weight of the egg. This gives children an understanding of the difference between mass and volume. There may appear to be more flour than sugar, but their mass is the same.
Baked bananas	Bananas, butter, brown sugar and lemon juice	Peel the bananas and put them on a greased dish. Put knobs of butter on them. Cut a lemon in half and squeeze out some juice. Sprinkle with brown sugar. Put in a hot oven for ten minutes or microwave for around three minutes or until the bananas are soft and brown.	This is a simple dish for young children to do. They can peel the bananas, squeeze the lemon and sprinkle the sugar. They can learn that there are different types of sugar and banana. They can also see how baking a dish can change the way the ingredients look.

Note: Children should not eat any foods or mixtures that contain raw eggs – for example, licking out the bowl after making cakes.

Learning outcomes for children

Children can learn a lot about maths and science from cooking. They can see the difference in colour, texture and shape when food is cooked. Part of the cooking process can also involve experimenting – for example, when cooking cakes, one cake can be left out to see what happens or one group of children can use plain flour and another group can use self-raising flour. Children can carry out simple taste tests. We can ask one group to use brown sugar and another white sugar.

Children should be encouraged to weigh, measure and count as they cook. Look out for recipes that use cups as measures, as this allows very young children to do some measuring.

Playing games with children

Games are organised activities that allow children to play together in a structured way. They can help children to learn the social skill of turn taking. Babies quickly learn to enjoy peek-a-boo, whilst older children enjoy playing games together that have rules. We need to choose games according to the needs of the children we are working with. For example, children under three years old find it hard to sit for any length of time and do not understand the idea of rules They may need games that are short in length and where they can be physically active.

Children can learn different skills from a variety of games whilst having fun.

Types of game	Examples of games	Links to desirable outcomes
Table-top games	Lotto, snap, matching games, counting games	**Personal and social development** – sharing and turn taking **Mathematics** – counting, matching, sorting **Language and literacy** – communicating with others and learning new vocabulary.
Physical games	Hopscotch, follow-my-leader, hide and seek	**Personal and social development** – working with others, turn taking **Physical development** – gross motor skills, co-ordination.
Party games	Pass the parcel, musical statues	**Personal and social development** – being part of a group, turn taking **Creative development** – moving to music.

Young children need the support of adults to be able to take turns and understand what they need to do. Some children may need an adult to be their partner if they do not like losing or if they find it hard to concentrate. As children get older, we can encourage them to play by themselves, although we may need to keep an eye on them in case emotions are running high.

Think about it

Here is a list of games that are often played with children.

Follow-my-leader	Kim's game	Football	Draughts	Bingo
Hunt the thimble	What's the time Mr Wolf?	Oranges and lemons	Musical statues	
Obstacle races	Hide and seek	Snap	Picture lotto	Hopscotch

Choose five games from the list and write down:

- the maximum and minimum number of children required to play it
- the age group that can play
- the equipment or space that is needed to play the game
- whether it is competitive or non-competitive.

Playing a game with individual children can be a good way of building a relationship with them. We can make games ourselves to suit the particular needs of the children we are working with. For example, sensory snap – each card has a texture and the idea is to match the textures.

Are competitive games good for children?

This is a difficult area. There are advantages and disadvantages to games being competitive and sometimes the competitiveness of a game depends on the adult who is supervising it and the reward for winning. Parents have different views about competitiveness that may need to be taken into consideration when planning games.

The table below shows some of the arguments used for and against competitive games.

What do you think?

Advantages	Disadvantages
Can boost self-esteem for children who find reading and writing difficult – e.g. they may not read well, but are able to run fast and win races.	Can lessen self-esteem. Children may not try out activities because they do not wish to fail or lose.
Team games can help children to work together.	Children may blame one child who they feel has let them down.
Competitive activities encourage children to succeed – e.g. they may play a sport for their country.	Competitiveness breeds jealousy and can cause fights and arguments.
Our society is competitive and children need to cope with not always winning.	Competitiveness makes people think only about what they can get rather than about others.

Portfolio activity

Look at the types of games that are used in your workplace.

Ask your supervisor if you can play a game with some children.

1 *Write down what the benefits of this game are for the children.*
2 *How did you carry out this activity?*
3 *What did you learn from doing this activity?*

Unit test

Quick quiz

1 A group of children notice that it is snowing. They stop what they are doing to look. The early years worker should **first**:
   a Tell the children that they should get on with what they are doing.
   b Look for a book about snow.
   c Stand with the children and talk to them about what they are seeing.
   d Get out the scissors to make paper snowflakes.

2 A child goes over to the art table because she wants to draw a picture for her mother. This is an example of:
   a adult-led activity
   b spontaneous activity
   c structured activity
   d parallel play.

3 Songs and rhymes can best help children to:
   a play together
   b be creative
   c join in a group
   d develop language.

4 A simple game of lotto can promote:
   a counting skills
   b matching skills
   c communication
   d turn taking.

5 Which of the following concepts are **best** promoted through a cooking activity:
   a floating and sinking
   b soft and hard
   c weighing and measuring
   d sorting and matching.

Short answer questions

1 Why should books have positive images of disabled people in them?

2 Name two untuned musical instruments.

3 Why might some parents not wish their children to take place in a sports day?

4 Give an example of positive reinforcement.

5 Give three reasons why some children have difficulties in communicating?

Play and the Young Child

Play is an extremely important part of children's lives, although there are different ideas as to how it should be provided for children. This chapter looks at different approaches to play and different issues – for example, your role in providing play opportunities for different ages of children. It also looks at creative, pretend, physical and manipulative play in detail.

Early approaches to play

Today play is accepted and encouraged. Every town has a toyshop. Children's organisations campaign for play to be seen as a basic right for all children in the world.

Society's attitude towards play has changed enormously in a century. This change has happened gradually although current pre-school education has been strongly influenced by two people whose thoughts and approaches were quite different – **Frederich Froebel** and **Maria Montessori**.

Frederich Froebel (1782–1852) is famous because he was one of the first people to believe that children need to learn from doing and playing rather than being taught. This approach is often called **child-centred** learning. In 1837 he set up a kindergarten, which in German means literally 'a children's garden'. The kindergarten was for children aged between three and seven years. Pretend play was encouraged both indoors and outdoors as Froebel felt that children learnt about the world through directly exploring materials such as wood and feathers. He also encouraged learning through number and finger rhymes. At the time his ideas were considered to be very unusual and it was not until after his death in 1852 that the idea of kindergartens spread in Germany and were also taken up throughout Europe.

Maria Montessori (1870–1952) worked with poor children in Rome in the 1900s. Her approach was different from Froebel's in many ways. She did not believe that pretend play was useful and felt that children needed **structured learning** and developed equipment that would allow children to experience concepts such as shape, size and order. Montessori felt strongly that young children were more receptive to learning than at any other age and it was important not to waste this time in their lives – learning could not be left to chance. Children were encouraged to work quietly when using the equipment and were individually guided by an adult. The idea of structuring play has become an accepted part of early years practice. Today, Montessori's ideas and the equipment she designed are still popular and there are many Montessori method nurseries.

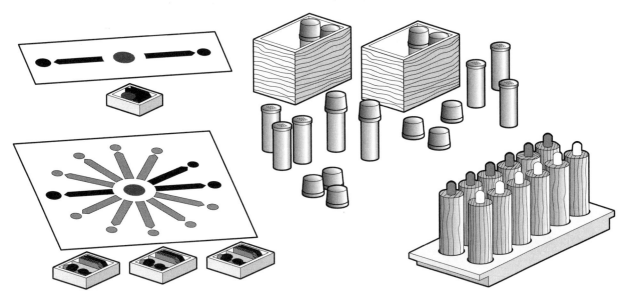

Montessori equipment

The aim of this equipment is for children to learn about size. Children are asked to order these objects according to their size.

Why do children play?

This question is still asked by child psychologists – people who study children and their development. It is an important question because if we know why children need to play, we can make sure that we give them the best equipment and environment to play in.

There are two theories that many early years workers agree with:

1 Play is needed to practise skills that are needed later on in life.

2 Play is needed for children to understand concepts – e.g. number, space and time.

Play as practice

The idea behind this theory is that children need to play so that they can practise skills they have seen. This is part of the **social learning theory**. This theory is based on the idea that children learn through copying what they have seen others do. Early years workers who believe in this theory would place a lot of importance in providing pretend play situations for children. This theory would explain why children in other countries play in different ways depending on what is considered important in their culture.

(The social learning theory explains many different aspects of child development and so it also referred to in Chapters 7, 9 and 11.)

Play is needed to gain concepts

In Chapter 7 (pages 136–7), we looked at **Piaget's** theory that children passed through stages when learning. Piaget was also interested in the way children played and he put forward a theory that children passed through three stages of play. Piaget suggested each stage built on the knowledge and experience of the one before and it was through play that children gained an understanding of their world. Piaget's ideas are widely accepted and this has meant that pre-school settings and schools use play as a way of helping children to learn. Early years workers who believe in this theory concentrate more on allowing children to discover and use play materials for themselves.

Piaget's stages of play

Age	Type of play	Common features of this stage
0–2	Practice or mastery play	Children are concentrating on controlling their bodies. Play allows them to explore their bodies – e.g. babies put their feet in their mouth. Children are exploring their environment and are keen to see how they can affect it. A child might drop a toy over the edge of the cot or bang a toy against another. Play tends to be repetitive.
2–7	Symbolic play	Children are using language as a means of communicating and this is reflected in their play. Children are learning to use symbols in their play. This means that a child might use a stick to stand for a magic wand or an empty plate might have a pretend meal on it.
7–11	Play with rules	Children are developing an understanding of rules. They play with board games and devise their own games. They are becoming logical in their thoughts.

Knowledge into Action

See if you can look at these theories in action:

Play as practice

Ask your supervisor if you can observe a child's play in the homecorner or playground.

1 *Is any of the play echoing adult life – for example, children saying that they are going shopping or children pretending to cook?*

Play is needed to gain concepts

Ask your supervisor if you can observe children who are in the 'symbolic play' age group.

2 *Are they using symbols in their play – for example, children using a stick to stand for a gun?*

Issues in play

It is hard to imagine that something as pleasant as play can cause argument, but there are some issues around play that early years workers do not always agree on! It might be interesting to find out what staff in your workplace feel.

- **Guns and war games.** Some early years workers feel strongly that children should not be given guns to play with and they will stop children from playing any type of war games. They feel that if society is to become a less violent place, acts of aggression need to be stopped in childhood.

- **Superhero play.** This is where children copy of actions of popular heroes such as pop singers and film and television stars. Some early years workers feel that superhero play may encourage gender stereotypes as boys often pick up on the supercop image and girls often pick up on the 'sex symbol' image.

- **Television.** There are early years workers who feel very strongly that children should not watch television. They argue that children should be active and that television does not encourage children's overall development.

Think about it

In pairs, decide what you think about these two issues:

1 guns
2 television.

(As a child did you ever play with guns or watch television?)

Free or structured play

Some pre-school settings believe that play should be directed by adults. This is often called **structured play**. Others feel that true play comes from the child not the adult – this is sometimes called free play. Many early years settings plan both free and structured play into their days. You will need to be able to support both types of play.

Free or spontaneous activity. This allows children to play at their own pace and use the materials and equipment around them in their own way. The element of choice in free play helps build children's self-esteem. Children may use the climbing frame as a ship or collect leaves in the garden to make a secret nest for birds. You can support this type of play by making a large range of materials available to children and making sure that children have enough time to develop their play.

Structured play. This is where adults shape the play activities. Structuring play means that adults can help children to develop particular areas of skill or knowledge. For example, an adult might plan play around the theme of 'people who help us'. The adult may decide to make the homecorner into a hospital, and by playing alongside the children, introduce new vocabulary to them.

Children learn through play

As adults we may see that children are having fun while they are playing, but if we look more closely we can see that they are often very intense in their play and concentrate on what they are doing. They are also developing skills and learning through their play. Look at these areas of development and see how play may encourage them.

Physical benefits. Children learn many physical skills – for example, fine manipulative skills are learnt through playing with small equipment, whereas balance, co-ordination and gross motor movements are developed through vigorous physical play.

Cognitive benefits. Children learn about the world around them through exploring and touching materials. For example, they may gain an understanding of colour through painting and an understanding of volume and capacity by pouring water into different sized containers.

Language benefits. Play allows children to learn communication skills in a natural way. A good example of this is when children are playing pretend games they often use words and phrases that they do not understand but wish to try out.

Emotional benefits. Play has been shown to help children with emotional development by developing children's confidence and making them feel good about themselves. Pretend play also allows children to explore roles safely and act out their feelings.

Social benefits. There are many types of play activity where children can learn to be with others. They may work co-operatively using construction toys or they may simply play alongside other children using pretend play to explore relationships. Social skills such as turn taking, sharing and listening to others can be learnt through play.

Cultural benefits. Children can learn about the world around them through play. This means that their play often reflects the cultural backdrop. Studies have shown that children in different countries play in different ways – reflecting the values of their society. In this country, there are many cultures living side by side

and play can be used as a medium for children not only to identify with their family's culture, but also to learn about other cultures.

Behavioural benefits. If play is challenging and enjoyable, children are likely to concentrate and develop self-reliance. Think of how much more you learn when you are enjoying yourself! Boredom and frustration are often factors in poor behaviour. This means that we must make sure that play activities are interesting and varied.

Knowledge into Action

Ask your supervisor if you can look at children playing.

1   *Is the play structured or free?*
2   *Briefly describe what the children are doing and write down what you feel children are gaining from the play.*
3   *How are the adults supporting the play?*

Stages of social play

Learning to play with other children is a gradual process. As children grow and develop they become able to play together, although there are times when children who can play co-operatively will choose to play alone – for example, if they are doing a jigsaw or practising a physical skill such as using stilts.

The way children play together can be put into four stages:

1   Solitary

2   Parallel

3   Associative

4   Co-operative

1 Solitary play. Up until the age of about two years children usually play alone. They explore equipment and their environment, but seek reassurance from adults and enjoy games directed by adults such as peek–a-boo.

2 Parallel play. From about two years, children seem to be more aware of each other, although they may not communicate or try to play together. Parallel play is children playing alongside each other. Children may play side-by-side in a sandpit, each one playing intently in their own way.

3 Associative play. From the age of about three, children look to see what other children are doing and may copy them. Children may stand at the edge of older children's games

4 Co-operative play. By about the age of three and a half, most children are able to play co-operatively. This means that they actively play together. They talk and decide about their play. You may hear children say things like 'Let's be lions.'

By the age of seven, most children are able to play games with rules together and if you ask them what they are doing, they are very sure of what the game is about.

Knowledge into Action

Ask your supervisor if you can observe two children playing in your workplace.

1 *Write about how they are playing.*
2 *What equipment are they using?*
3 *How are they playing together – for example, are you seeing co-operative play?*
4 *What skills do you think they are gaining through their play?*
5 *How are these skills being developed?*

Choosing play materials and equipment

Early years workers need to be able to provide materials and equipment that children will enjoy using and that also help their development. In order to choose equipment and activities, it is important to look at children's age and stage of development. The chart below shows what play equipment children may enjoy using at different ages.

Age	Play needs of the child	Indoor equipment	Outdoor equipment
1–2	The child is mobile and gaining gross motor and fine manipulative skills. The child needs plenty of opportunities to strengthen their muscles and develop co-ordination.	Push and pull toys Toys that make music Dolls Trolleys Building bricks Posting toys	Paddling pool Baby swing Small slide
2–3	Children are starting to notice and play with other children. Their language is increasing and much of their play is pretend play. Children are gaining confidence in physical movements and enjoy playing outside. Children of this age can be easily frustrated and have a short concentration span – less than 10 minutes – so they need opportunities to be independent in their play and a range of activities. There should be plenty of equipment as children find it difficult to share with each other.	Dressing up clothes Home corner equipment – e.g. tea sets, prams, cooking utensils, pretend telephones Building blocks Toy cars and garages Dolls and cuddly toys Dough Paint Jigsaw puzzles Musical instruments	Paddling pool Sand and water tray Slide Climbing frame Swings Sit and ride toys Tricycles

Age	Play needs of the child	Indoor equipment	Outdoor equipment
3–4	Children are starting to co-operate with each other and enjoy playing together. Most of their play is pretend play. Pieces of dough become cakes; tricycles become cars! Children enjoy physical activity, gaining confidence in being able to use large equipment – e.g. climbing frames. They are also developing fine manipulative skills and beginning to represent their world in picture form.	'Small world' play – e.g. playmobile, duplo figures Dressing-up clothes Home corner and equipment Dough and other malleable materials Water and sand Construction toys such as train tracks, building bricks Jigsaw puzzles	Climbing frame Slide Paddling pool Tricycles Bicycles with stabilisers Balls and bean bags
4–6	Children are more interested in creating things – e.g. making a cake, drawing cards and planting seeds. Children enjoy being with other children although they may play in pairs. Children are beginning to express themselves through painting and drawing as well as through play. Children are enjoying using their physical skills in games and are confident when running and climbing.	Materials for junk modelling Cooking activities Dough and other malleable materials Jigsaws Home corner Construction toys Small world play – e.g. Duplo people Simple board games	Mini gardening tools Skipping ropes Hoops Climbing frame Slide Tricycles Different size balls
6–8	Children are confident and can play well with other children. Children are starting to have particular play friends and are able to share ideas about their play. Games that involve rules are played and rules are added and changed as necessary! Most children enjoy physical activity and play organised games. Sometimes this age can be very competitive. Children are also keen on making things – either of their own design or by following instructions.	Creative materials – e.g. junk modelling, crayons, pieces of card and paper Board games Jigsaw puzzles Complex construction toys Books Collections – e.g. stamps, stickers	Balls Hoops Bicycles Roller-skates Skipping ropes Climbing frames Slides Swings

Portfolio activity

Ask your supervisor if you can put out some play equipment for a group of children.

1 *Write down the age of children you were working with.*
2 *Explain why you chose this equipment*
3 *How did the children use the equipment?*
4 *What have you learnt from doing this activity?*

Choosing and buying equipment and materials

Play equipment and materials can be expensive and careful thought needs to be given to choosing them. Early years settings will want to ensure that they get good use out of their toys.

Checklist for toys and equipment:

- Does it have a safety mark?

- Can it be used in different ways?

- How many children are able to use it at a time?

- How easy is it to store?

- Can it be cleaned or washed easily?

- Are new parts easily available, if needed?

- What age of children will most benefit from it?

Play opportunities in everyday life

There are wonderful play opportunities for children in everyday life that do not require commercial equipment. In a home environment children can play with pieces of pastry, pour water into plastic cups and help to wash up. In larger early years settings children may be able to clear away, help with cooking activities, empty bottles and make musical instruments and jugs for pouring water. Children can also learn while tidying away. This helps them to feel more confident.

Supporting children with special needs

It is now accepted that children who have special needs should still have the same play opportunities as other children. This means that early years settings may need to adjust their layout and choose equipment and materials according to the play needs of children rather than their age.

Providing an effective play environment

Children need us to help them play. Organising play activities is part of most early years workers' daily work. Activities and equipment need to be varied and well presented, but also suitable for the age of children.

Step-by-step guide to organising play

Space and layout

- Is there enough room for children to move between activities safely?

- Are the fire exits clear?

- Are activities that need water near a sink?

Equipment

- Is the equipment suitable for the age of children?

- Is the equipment clean?

- Has the equipment been checked for safety?

- Have broken or incomplete toys been removed?

- Is there enough equipment for the number of children playing?

- Can children reach the equipment so that they can be independent in their play?

Preparation (allow plenty of time)

- Will children need aprons?

- Do tables need protecting?

- Are there cloths to hand for wiping up spills?

- Is there a dustpan and brush ready to sweep up sand?

- Is there enough paper out for painting and drawing?

- Is there space to dry paintings?

- Does the room or outdoor setting look pleasant?

- Do the activities look inviting and appealing – e.g. fresh paint, dressing up clothes laid out, books displayed in the quiet corner?

Supporting children's play

- Look out for children who may need practical help, such as needing help putting on dressing-up clothes.

- Ask children if they need help. This makes them still feel in control and does not undermine their confidence.

- Look out for children who are becoming bored or stuck. Offer help or further materials.

Keeping play safe

- Listen and watch for signs that children's play is becoming over-excited – e.g. shouts, or silence (see Chapter 3, page 52).

- Intervene quickly if you see children doing anything potentially dangerous – e.g. waving sticks around.

- Explain why they cannot play in this way firmly, but give them ideas on how to carry on playing.

Helping children to resolve arguments

Where possible help children to resolve disputes themselves by allowing them the opportunity to think through the problem and arrive at their own solutions – for example, by saying 'You both want the trike, what would be fairest?'

Clearing away (allow plenty of time!)

Where possible involve children in tidying away. Cleaning should be done by adults.

- Make sure that puzzles and board games are put away complete.

- Sterilise or wipe down toys that have been handled.

- Wipe down aprons and empty water tray.

- Rake through sand and throw away debris.

- Fold or hang up dressing-up clothes.

- Put clay in an airtight container.

- Throw dough away if it has been out for several sessions.

- Check that paintings are named.

- Wipe tables with disinfectant.

- Vacuum carpet.

- Sweep and wash floor, once equipment has been put away.

Case Study

Mark and Rajeet are playing chase with Jo. They are clearly having a good time. Mark picks up a stick and starts waving it at Jo to stop him from getting nearer. He is shouting 'go away you lion'.

Questions

1 *Why would you need to intervene at this point?*
2 *What could you say to make Mark understand that he needs to put the stick down?*
3 *Why might you consider taking the stick away?*
4 *How could you encourage them to carry on playing together?*

Portfolio activity

Ask your supervisor if you can help set out an activity or play equipment and help with the supervision and clearing away.

1 *Write about how you made the activity or equipment look attractive to children.*
2 *What steps did you take to make sure that everything was safe and hygienic?*
3 *Write about how you supported the children during their play.*
4 *What was your role in clearing away?*
5 *What did you learn from doing this task?*

How play can fit into a curriculum programme

Since the introduction of a National Curriculum in the late 1980s, children's learning and play experiences have been structured and organised. In schools, children's learning and play experiences are linked to the National Curriculum which clearly sets out learning targets, while many pre-school settings link their activities to an early years curriculum called Desirable Outcomes, first introduced in 1996. The aim of the desirable outcomes is to prepare four-year-olds for school, although most nurseries use the desirable outcome framework for planning many of their activities throughout the nursery.

The Desirable Outcomes were due for review in 1999, but at the time of writing, they had six headings:

1 Personal and social development. This covers areas such as turn taking, sharing, independence and self help skills.

2 Knowledge and understanding of the world. This looks at helping children to understand their environment, other people and the difference between man-made and natural objects.

3 Mathematics. This is about encouraging children to compare, sort, match and count as well as recognise shapes and patterns.

4 Language and literacy. This area looks at encouraging children's communication skills, including speech and listening. It also looks at helping children to enjoy books and recognise that printed words have meanings.

5 Creative development. This covers a range of activities that help children's imagination and self expression – e.g., music, painting and dance.

6 Physical development. This covers children gaining confidence in large and small movements.

Below is a week's curriculum plan which shows how a nursery may plan using the 'desirable outcomes'.

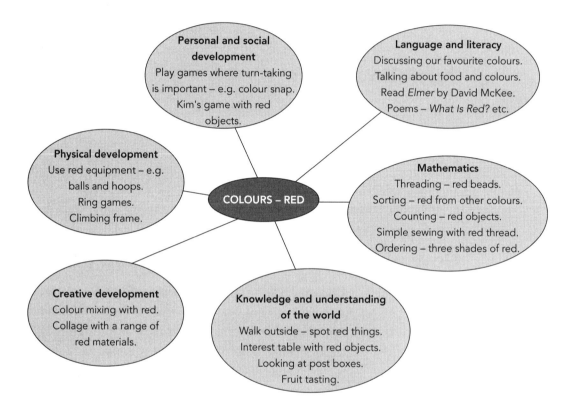

Different types of play

Most early years workers plan for children to play in different ways because this allows children to use and develop several skill – for example, playing on a climbing frame develops gross motor skills and a sense of balance whereas playing in the homecorner is more likely to encourage language.

Play is therefore often put into four groups:

1 creative play

2 pretend play

3 physical play

4 manipulative play.

As an early years worker, you need to understand the benefits of each type of play and know how to provide for it. This section looks in detail at how these types of play can benefit children of different ages. Planning different play activities also helps nurseries to cover the 'desirable outcomes'.

Creative play allows children to express themselves using materials rather than words. Creative play helps children to discover properties of materials as well as giving them the opportunity to use language and develop fine physical skills.

Adults can help children by providing a range of materials and by encouraging children to experiment with them. We must make sure that the emphasis is on enjoying the process and discovering the materials rather than on producing an end product.

Material	Benefits	Provision
Sand and water	**Physical development.** Hand-eye co-ordination and fine manipulative skills are developed through using the equipment – e.g. pouring with jugs. **Cognitive development.** Properties of the materials are explored through touching them – e.g. water is runny, sand does not pour when wet. **Language opportunities.** Children tend to chat as they are playing. **Emotional benefit.** Builds confidence – sand and water are activities with no right or wrong way. Helps release tension and aggression. **Social skills.** Children take turns with equipment and can play in different social groupings or by themselves.	**Indoors.** Purpose-built trays are often used. Water can be played with in a sink and sand can be put into a baby bath if needed. **Outdoors.** Sand pit, paddling pool. **Safety.** Make sure that these activities are closely supervised. There is a risk of drowning or sand being thrown in children's eyes. Outdoor sandpits need covering after use to prevent access by animals. Keep floors clear as both sand and water can make them slippery. **Equipment for sand play.** Bottles, jugs, scoops, animals, toy cars, sieves, spades. **Equipment for water play.** Funnels, bottles, jugs, items that float and sink, boats, beakers, sponges.
Dough, clay, Plasticine etc	**Physical development.** Fine manipulative skills and hand-eye co-ordination, through rolling, cutting and pounding. **Cognitive development.** Learn about elasticity of these materials and experience making different shapes and forms. **Language opportunities.** Children enjoy talking about what they are doing. They may use some objects in pretend play. **Emotional benefits.** Releases aggression, makes children feel in control, no wrong or right way to play. **Social skills.** Children take turns with equipment although probably choose to play individually.	Table and protective covering. **Safety.** Dough needs to be changed frequently. Enough salt must be added to prevent children from eating it. **Materials.** Dough: it is important to make different types up – e.g. stretchy dough, cooked dough, smelly dough, Plasticine, clay, other modelling materials. **Tools.** Rolling pins, cutters, scissors, boards, plates, modelling tools.

Material	Benefits	Provision
Junk modelling and collage	**Physical development.** Fine manipulative and gross manipulative skills and hand-eye co-ordination through cutting, sticking and holding. **Cognitive development.** Helps children develop spatial awareness – size, shape and proportion. **Language opportunities.** Develops vocabulary if unusual materials are made available for children. **Emotional benefits.** Gives children sense of satisfaction and ownership when they have finished. Enjoyment through handling and problem solving. **Social skills.** Turn taking and sharing of materials and equipment. Develops independence and self-reliance through completing their own project.	**Indoors.** Table with protective covering. **Safety.** Make sure that small items cannot be swallowed by younger children. Do not leave scissors around. **Materials.** A wide range is needed so children can make choices and develop their own ideas – e.g. different size boxes, glue, sellotape, paper, cardboard, foil, plastic lid tops, lace, pasta, sawdust, newspaper, magazine, fabrics, bottle tops, sweet wrappers, sequins etc. **Equipment.** Scissors, aprons.
Paint and drawing	**Physical development.** Fine manipulative skills and hand-eye co-ordination through making marks and scribbles. **Cognitive benefits.** Putting marks on paper helps children to learn about communicating by using signs. This is the first step towards reading. **Language opportunities.** Children tend to talk as they draw and paint. It is part of their thought process. **Emotional benefits.** Children can express themselves visually – e.g. they can paint angry pictures. They also enjoy seeing their work displayed. This gives them confidence and a sense of achievement. **Social skills.** Children learn to take turns and share.	Painting easel, table, wall covered with polythene **Materials.** Different types of paints – powder, acrylic, poster and ready-mixed – chalks, pastels, felt tips, charcoal, different coloured paper, card. **Equipment.** Different types of brushes for painting, rollers, items for printing, sponges.

Strong links to desirable outcomes. Creative development, physical development, knowledge and understanding of the world, personal and social development.

Stages of development

By observing children's stage of development we can see what types of equipment and materials they may benefit from – for example, a child who is beginning to model shapes with dough may be ready to start with clay which could then be painted.

Looking at children's pictures of people is also interesting as it can show not only their stage of fine manipulative development, but also their understanding of themselves.

4–5 years

5 years

6 years

Stage	Drawing of people	Dough
One	Scribbling with to and fro movements	Banging and pounding
Two	Circular movements are made	Rolling and starting to form shapes
Three	Large head with arms and legs Children know what they are drawing	Rolling and cutting out shapes easily Using tools
Four	Head, trunk, legs and arms as well	Beginning to make other simple features – e.g. eyelashes 3D models

Think about it

You have been asked to work with a group of children to make paper hats for a party.

1 *How can you make sure that each child makes a hat in their own way?*
2 *What equipment and materials would you need?*

Pretend play

Pretend play is where children talk to toys or objects and make up games using characters. It is also known as imaginative play. Children act out what they see and feel using words. As children get older and they are able to co-operate, we see that they take on roles: 'You're the mummy and I'm the baby and the baby's being naughty!'

When children are playing in this way, it can be called role play. This type of play helps children to develop language and communication skills as well as helping them to act out situations. Children also learn to socialise through this type of play. This type of play also has emotional benefits for children as they can act out their fears and fantasies.

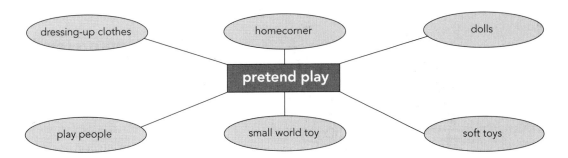

Strong links to desirable outcomes – language and literacy, creative development, personal and social development.

From about the age of 18 months children start to pretend in their play. A doll might be picked up and cuddled or put into bed as if it were a real baby. Pretend play can take many different forms depending on the stage of children and their play needs.

Different forms of pretend play include:

Role play   Children take on a role in their play – e.g. a fireman, a baby.

Socio-dramatic   Groups of children play co-operatively together taking on
                  different roles.

Domestic play   Children act out activities that they see happening at home –
                  e.g. ironing, telling off a doll or mumbling about making the
                  tea!

Imaginative play Children act out things that they have experienced such as
                  going shopping or swimming and adapt them to suit their play
                  needs.

Fantasy play   Children pretend that they are doing something that they may
                  have seen or heard about – e.g. having a baby or going on an
                  aeroplane.

Superhero play   Children try to take on the characteristics of a current TV idol
                  – e.g. pretending to be a footballer or a police detective.

Children also enjoy using equipment such as small world toys, dolls and cuddly
toys to pretend play with. They might get out farm animals and make noises for
each of the animals or, with a set of play people, they might give each one a name
and a character.

Knowledge into Action

1   *Ask your supervisor if you can observe and listen to children playing in a 'pretend way'.*
2   *Briefly describe their activity and write down how you think their play is helping their language
    development.*

Setting up pretend play areas

It is possible to set up pretend play
areas in most early years settings. In
a home environment, children may
play under a table or behind a sofa,
whereas in larger early years settings
children may play in purpose-built
home corners. Pretend play can also
take place outdoors and children
enjoy using tents as well as finding
areas in gardens where they can hide
away.

Children often prefer to be able to keep their play private as it is their own world, although we must always make sure that we can see or hear what they are doing.

Equipment for pretend areas

Equipment does not have to be shop bought. Cardboard boxes can be turned into cars, televisions and cupboards. A good range of materials allows children to extend their play although too much equipment out at one time might overwhelm them. Where possible, equipment should be varied from week to week, so that children's play does not become too repetitive. As children gain a sense of their cultural identity through pretend play, it is important that all children's home backgrounds are reflected in the choice of items.

Dressing up clothes

■ Clothes that reflect other cultures – e.g. saris, tunics.

■ Uniforms and clothing that help children to be in role – e.g. bus driver.

■ Hats, shoes, glasses and other accessories – e.g. bags and suitcases (belts are not recommended).

■ A plastic-coated mirror for children to look at themselves in, adds to their play.

Props for domestic play

■ Plates, dishes, cutlery, chopsticks, spoons, cooking utensils – including those from other cultures – e.g. woks

■ Telephone

■ Bedding, towels

■ Child-sized furniture – e.g. cookers, beds, tables and chairs

■ Prams, pushchairs, cots and dolls

■ Shop tills, shopping baskets, paper bags, toy money and notes

■ Pretend First Aid kit

■ Dolls of both genders and different skin colours

■ Cuddly toys.

Pretend play and the curriculum

Pretend play fits well into an overall curriculum plan. We can change the pretend area to match the theme. A nursery working to a theme of 'people who help us', might turn the pretend area into a hospital. The aim of this is to encourage children to explore the theme of hospitals and use the equipment in a different way.

Adults can either play alongside children – for example, pretending to be a doctor – or they can increase understanding by inviting visitors in or by reading a story that fits in with the theme.

Providing varied themes in this way can increase children's vocabulary while at the same time extending their play. Children may also enjoy making props to fit the theme – for example, making dough cakes for a bakery.

Ideas for themes could include hospitals, vets' practices, bakers, post offices, cafes.

Intervening in children's pretend play

There are three situations when we need to intervene in children's pretend play:

To ensure safety. You must intervene when play is likely to become dangerous – for example, if children are becoming over-excited or aggressive.

To support and extend play. You may decide to intervene when children's play seems to be repetitive and running out of steam. You may offer to play alongside them or add more equipment.

To challenge racist or other offensive remarks. You must always challenge racist or other remarks, even if children are saying them as part of their role. These situations need handling sensitively (see Chapter 1, page 13).

Think about it

A local playgroup has been given £200. You have been asked to draw up a list of possible equipment that they could buy. The playgroup is particularly interested in buying equipment that would encourage pretend play.

Write out a list for them and include some reasons for your choices. Where possible include prices.

(This activity can be done in pairs or small groups.)

Physical play

In Chapter 4 (pages 74–86) we looked at why physical exercise was important in developing children's bodies and maintaining their health and also at the safety aspects of providing physical activity.

In this section we look at how children play when exercising and at equipment that can help children's physical play.

Children enjoy running around playing chase, throwing, catching and climbing. Physical play helps children to develop muscles, stamina and co-ordination of their movements. It can help children to develop an awareness of space and gives them confidence. You may hear children say 'Look at me, I can jump!'

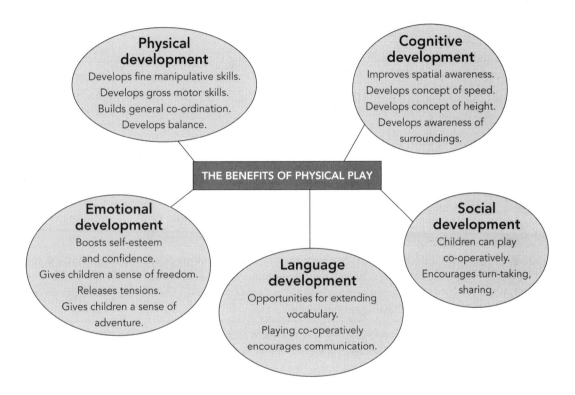

Strong links to the desirable outcomes – physical development, personal and social development.

Physical play with large equipment

Children are able to develop many skills through using large equipment.

Most early years settings are able to provide some large equipment for children to work with. In home environments where there may not be enough space or resources, children can be taken to a local playground where there may be a range of equipment. Equipment can often be adapted for children with special needs – for example, harnesses can be added to swings and grippers can be attached to bars of climbing frames. Specialist equipment is also available – for example, tricycles that are strengthened for larger children who cannot use a bicycle.

The following chart shows types of large equipment for physical play and the play potential for children.

Equipment for Physical play

Type of equipment	Play and developmental potential	Age range
Trampolines	Children enjoy bouncing and this allows them to develop their sense of balance while giving them a sense of achievement. Jumping and bouncing strengthens leg muscles and builds stamina.	3–8 years Some trampolines have handles, which means that children from three years can use them safely.
Seesaws and rockers	Children enjoy working in pairs and can enjoy the sensation of moving from side to side. Balance and co-ordination skills are improved.	Rockers can be suitable for children of eighteen months. Seesaws are generally for children aged between three and eight years.
Play tunnels	Play tunnels can be used in many ways. Children can use them as places to hide as part of a game. They can also be used as part of an obstacle course and link can often into other pieces of equipment such as tents. Play tunnels can develop co-ordination between the arms and legs and general agility.	2–6 years Younger children may become frightened in a tunnel and older children may get stuck.
Slides	Slides help children learn to climb and build up confidence in balancing. Children enjoy the sense of achievement from completing the movement. They enjoy the sense of risk-taking and challenge as they climb.	18 months–8 years+ Different heights of slide are available ranging from two steps upwards.
Swings	Swings give children much pleasure as they enjoy the rhythmic movements. As they learn to co-ordinate their movements they build up strength in the legs and upper body as well as their ability to balance.	From 9 months–8 years+ Baby swings are available which prevent children from falling out.
Climbing frames	Co-ordination and balance are developed through climbing. Leg and arm muscles are strengthened and children enjoy the challenge and the feeling of adventure. Climbing frames can be used as part of a game – e.g. it becomes a house or ship. Co-operative play is often seen when older children are using climbing frames.	From 3–8 years+ There are a variety of styles of climbing frame available.
Ropes and rope ladders	Children enjoy learning to climb up ladders. This helps their sense of balance and co-ordination. They enjoy the challenge of this activity. Ropes can be used to swing on which strengthens arm muscles. Ropes can be used as part of children's games.	From about 4 years
Sit and ride toys Tricycles Bicycles Go-karts	These are versatile and popular with children. They can make moving around part of their games and can play co-operatively together. Many skills are developed, including the ability to judges speed, steer and pedal. Leg muscles are strengthened and general co-ordination is developed.	1–8 years+ The range of equipment means that very young children can enjoy feeling mobile.

In many playground areas, large pieces of equipment such as slides and climbing frames are joined together to form a single unit. This allows more children to play together and allows children to make physical play into more of a game.

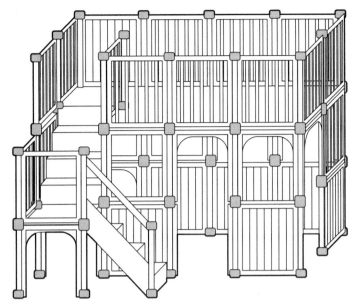

Integrated play equipment

Helping children to practise skills

There are some physical skills – for example, throwing and catching, pedalling and balancing – that need practice. To help children gain these skills, adults can structure play activities which are fun yet concentrate on areas that need developing without making children feel frustrated. Bringing out equipment or thinking of activities that children have not used before helps them to come to an activity feeling confident – for example, ideas for helping children to throw and catch might include using different size balls, beanbags, frisbees and airballs.

Children can be asked to throw beanbags into hoops or see how far they can throw an airball.

Knowledge into Action

1 *Make a list of any large equipment in your workplace.*
2 *Observe how children use this equipment.*
3 *Are there any pieces of equipment that seem to be particularly popular?*
4 *How do children use these pieces of equipment?*

Think about it

1 *Can you think of three activities that would encourage a group of five-year-olds to practice their throwing and catching skills?*

Stereotyping in physical play

By the age of three, most children are aware of their gender and by the age of five, most children are tending to play with members of their own sex. As physical play is so important in children's overall development it is essential that, although children may choose to play according to gender, their play is not limited by this. Early years workers can help by being good role models and making sure that their comments encourage all children to participate in activities. If children seem to avoid choosing equipment the early years worker could structure an activity that includes skill – for example, an early years worker working with six-year-olds noticed that the boys were not picking up the skipping ropes and that the girls were not using the footballs. She organised an obstacle race that included skipping and dribbling a football.

Portfolio activity

Ask your supervisor if you can supervise and support physical play.

1   *Write down how you encouraged all the children to use the equipment.*
2   *Write down how you made sure that the children played safely.*
3   *What physical skills did the children develop through their play?*
4   *What did you learn from doing this activity?*

Manipulative play

Manipulative play can also be called construction play. Most manipulative play encourages children to build or to fit equipment together. Examples of manipulative play include jigsaw puzzles, interlocking shapes and train sets that fit together. Children gain much satisfaction from this type of play as they are able to see the end product. Self-esteem is also boosted as many types of equipment do not have a right or wrong way of using them – for example, Duplo bricks can be made into a tower or can be used to make a wall. Through manipulative play children are also able to develop their fine manipulative skills as well as their gross motor movements. Children might turn and twist small pieces to fit together which encourages their fine skills or, with larger equipment such as foam blocks, they might use their whole bodies for lifting and carrying.

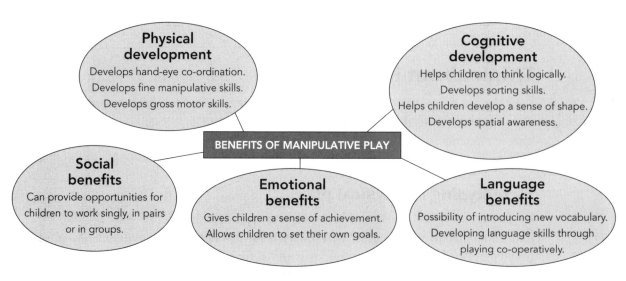

Strong links to the desirable outcomes – personal and social development, physical development.

There are many types of equipment to encourage manipulative play. Not all equipment needs to be commercially manufactured. Jigsaw puzzles can be made out of cardboard and older children can make their own by doing a drawing, sticking it down and then cutting up the pieces. In the same way children can have a lot of fun from moving around cardboard boxes.

Manipulative play

Name and description	Benefits	Age range
Shape sorters	These early toys help young children to recognise shapes as well as encouraging them to use their hands and problem-solving skills. Young children may need adult help if they are not to become frustrated. These activities help children's confidence and they gain a sense of achievement.	From 12 months
Duplo Brightly-coloured plastic blocks that fit together. Animals and people are also available.	Encourages pretend play and allows children to use their fine manipulative skills. Muscles in the hand are also strengthened and hand-eye co-ordination is developed There is no 'right or wrong' way to use this equipment which means that children gain confidence.	18 months–5 years
Lego Small bricks that fasten together. There is a large range of parts available which means that children can make many things – e.g. cars, houses, gardens.	The small parts mean that children's fine manipulative skills and hand-eye co-ordination are developed. There is huge scope for children to make intricate models with this equipment.	**From 5 years** The small parts in some of these kits could be dangerous for younger children.
Jigsaw puzzles A variety of puzzles are available including tray puzzles where children can slot in shapes, floor puzzles for group play and small-piece puzzles.	Jigsaw puzzles help children's spatial awareness and develop fine manipulative skills. Problem-solving skills are also developed along with matching skills. Floor puzzles allow pairs of children to work and play co-operatively together. A range of tactile puzzles is available for children with sensory impairments.	From 15 months–adulthood
Interlocking train sets Pieces of track that join together like a puzzle. Trains and wagons are then put onto the track.	This equipment promotes fine and gross manipulative skills. Children often use this equipment on the floor either as a solitary activity or in pairs and small groups. Children gain a sense of satisfaction from forming the track. This equipment also encourages pretend play.	From 3–8 years
Large foam blocks These blocks are coloured and children can use them to hide behind and clamber over. They are large but not heavy.	These blocks can help children's gross manipulative skills. Children can use them for physical play and through play can increase their spatial awareness. Lifting large blocks can make children feel strong and in control, promoting their self-esteem. This equipment can provide opportunities for social play and solitary play.	From 18 months

Name and description	Benefits	Age range
Large wooden blocks Blocks of different sizes and shapes that can be built up to make walls or shapes.	This equipment promotes gross manipulative skills. Children can use this equipment as part of their pretend play. They might make a boat or bus with it. Spatial awareness is developed and children are able to play by themselves, in pairs or in small groups.	**From 2 years**
Constructo straws, octons, meccano and K'nex Types of small shape-based construction toys that fit together.	This type of equipment allows children to make shapes using their fine manipulative skills. They develop spatial awareness and understanding of pattern and shape. Older children enjoy following instructions to make models which promotes their problem-solving skills.	**From 5 years**

Linking stages of development to manipulative play

The chart below shows how most children gain their skills and at what age, although it is important to remember that children gain skills at different rates.

Age	Manipulative skills	Suggested types of equipment
12 months	Picks up toys Moves toys from hand to hand Takes cubes out of cups and boxes	Stacking beakers, push and pull toys
18 months	Builds tower of three bricks Turns several pages in books Manipulates simple toys – e.g. pulling strings, pushing buttons	Posting toys, tray puzzles, toys that make music, wooden bricks
2 years	Can build tower of six bricks Manages a jigsaw of four pieces Beginning to use preferred hand	Peg board, tray puzzles, Duplo
3 years	Threads large beads Snips and cuts with scissors Matches shapes	Floor puzzles, Duplo, train sets, cars, jigsaw puzzles with 8–12 pieces
4 years	Can cut in a straight line Manipulates toys with confidence Dresses and undresses Can manage simple sewing cards	Duplo, large wooden blocks, foam bricks, train sets, jigsaw puzzles, octons
5 years	Laces shoes Cuts on line Makes simple model from bricks Beginning to control pencil and write	Lego, constructo straws, wooden bricks
6-8 years	Increased confidence in small fine movements Can untie knots and bows Can use both hands to assist in tasks Cuts out shape accurately	Equipment for this age group depends mainly on their interests. Small bricks allow them to make intricate models.

Portfolio activity

Ask your supervisor if you can plan and set up one of the following types of play:

- Creative play
- Pretend play
- Physical play
- Manipulative play.

1 *Write down how you planned for this type of play.*
2 *How did you make sure that the equipment was appropriate for the age of the children?*
3 *How did you make sure that the play activity was safe?*
4 *What benefits did the children gain from playing in this way?*
5 *What did you learn from this activity?*

Unit test

Quick quiz

1 Which of these play activities is most likely to encourage fine motor skills?
   a playing in a home corner
   b playing on a climbing frame
   c playing with large foam blocks
   d playing with sand.

2 When choosing equipment for a group of children, an early years worker should first consider:
   a age and stage of children
   b colour of equipment
   c size of equipment
   d play potential of equipment.

3 Solitary play means that children:
   a do not have any friends
   b are playing by themselves
   c are feeling lonely
   d are playing a board game.

4 Two children are starting to argue in the home corner over a piece of equipment. The early years worker should:
   a wait and see what happens
   b tell the children to do something else together
   c take one child out of the homecorner
   d ask if they need some more equipment.

5   Which of these pieces of equipment could be used to promote manipulative play?
   a dressing-up clothes
   b interlocking train set
   c seesaw
   d dough.

Short answer questions

1   What is meant by the term free play?

2   Name three toys that a three-year-old would enjoy playing with.

3   Why is it important that play equipment is put out attractively?

4   Why is it important that boys and girls play with a range of materials and equipment?

5   Name two types of equipment that would encourage physical play?

Emotional and Social Development

People have a strong need to be together. We work, socialise and live near or with other people. Being with other people is a skill that children need to develop. They need to learn to share, communicate with others and understand how their behaviour affects other people. This means

WANTED-
STABLE,
CARING
ADULT

that the emotional and social development of children is an essential part of their overall development. In this chapter we explore the theories of emotional and social development, the stages children pass through in their development and ways of supporting and encouraging children to develop.

This chapter also looks specifically at children's fears of separation, loss and anger and how as carers we can support and help them to manage their strong feelings and emotions.

Theories of emotional and social development

There are many theories about emotional and social development of children. Some of the key questions are:

- How do we get our personalities?

- Are we born with them?

- Are our personalities formed as a result of our experiences?

- Are there stages in developing our personalities?

It is important for early years workers to have some understanding of the theories as they have changed the way in which children are cared for.

This section looks at three influential theories:

1 Social learning theory.

2 Psychoanalytical theories of Freud and Erikson.

3 Attachment theory.

1 Social learning theory

In Chapter 7 (page 134) we looked at the social learning theory as a theory to explain how children learn. The social learning theory suggests that children learn by looking at the behaviour of adults and others around them. They then imitate the behaviour they have seen. This theory suggests that children's social development could be affected by other people. This means that when children see influential people – for example, parents and teachers – showing desirable social skills – for example, being kind and generous – they are more likely to show this behaviour themselves.

Linking theory with practice

The social learning theory has implications for early years workers. If children learn behaviour from others around them – including other children – we need to be good role models for them.

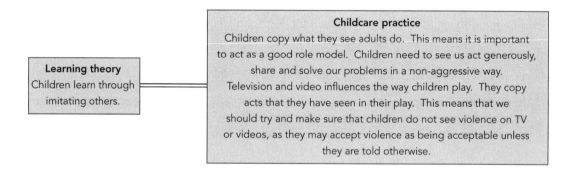

Childcare practice
Children copy what they see adults do. This means it is important to act as a good role model. Children need to see us act generously, share and solve our problems in a non-aggressive way. Television and video influences the way children play. They copy acts that they have seen in their play. This means that we should try and make sure that children do not see violence on TV or videos, as they may accept violence as being acceptable unless they are told otherwise.

Learning theory
Children learn through imitating others.

Knowledge into Action

In your workplace, observe some children who are pretend playing for a few minutes.

1   *Write down any phrases or actions that you think children have learnt through watching adults.*
2   *Look out for any play that suggests children have been influenced by television – e.g. pretending to be a character from a programme.*

2 The psychoanalytical theories of Freud and Erikson

These theories look at how children's personalities may be shaped by their experiences at different stages of their development. There are many different versions of these theories but Freud's and Erikson's are well known.

Sigmund Freud (1856–1939) is famous for being interested in what people say and do unconsciously – for example, sucking a pen, saying something they did not mean to.

He came to the conclusion that children had instinctive needs. He also felt that our personality was likely to depend on how our physical needs were met at different stages in our childhood. He thought that at different stages in childhood, particular areas of the body gave children pleasure and that at each stage children need to be allowed to experience these. Freud warned that children's personalities are affected by not successfully passing through these stages.

The following chart shows Freud's psychosexual stages.

Stage	Age	Area of physical pleasure	Link to overall development
Oral	0–1	Mouth, lips	Children using mouth to feed Weaning takes place
Anal	2–3	Anus	Children gain control of bladder and bowel movement Toilet training takes place
Phallic	4–5	Genitals	Children gain awareness of gender and have to accept that they are either girls or boys Boys and girls have to understand they cannot marry their mother or father Children often begin to play with members of the same sex
Latency	6–12	None	Freud felt that this was a period of calm

Linking theory with practice

Freud's theory, although famous, has been heavily criticised. However, it may have influenced early years practice in the following ways:

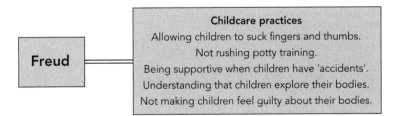

Freud

Childcare practices
Allowing children to suck fingers and thumbs.
Not rushing potty training.
Being supportive when children have 'accidents'.
Understanding that children explore their bodies.
Not making children feel guilty about their bodies.

Eric Erikson (1902–1994) was influenced by Freud's work, but felt that the stages children passed through were linked to their social development. He also considered that people's personalities carried on developing for the rest of their lives. Erikson proposed eight stages through which we need to pass. His theory was that in each stage there is a decision or dilemma that we have to face. He felt that the support given by other people in each stage affects our personalities. The table below shows Erikson's early-childhood stages, the 'dilemmas' we have to face and the affect of these on our personality.

The first part of Erikson's stages of development

Age	Stage and dilemma	Affect on personality
0–1	Basic trust Mistrust	**Optimism** Children need to decide if the world is a safe one where their needs can be met or whether it is dangerous and unpredictable. Erikson felt that the mothers or primary carers are very important for children during this stage. If children are shown consistent care and love their outlook on life is likely to be more positive.
2–3	Autonomy Shame	**Willpower** Children are starting to be mobile and aware that they can do things for themselves. They need to decide whether or not to try to be independent, knowing that if they try and fail they will feel ashamed. Erikson thought that the role of carers is encouraging and praising children but not allowing them to do things they might fail.
4–5	Initiative Guilt	**Purpose** Children are interested in their world. They may want to ask questions and try to play. If they are not encouraged to do so they may start to feel guilty and stop taking the initiative.
6–12	Industry Inferiority	**Competence** Children are starting to find out how things work to make things. By listening to teachers and comparing themselves with their friends and peers they come to think of themselves as either competent or inferior. Carers need to praise children and make sure they feel they can do things.

Linking theory with practice

Erikson's theory suggests that primary carers and adults can help children during the stages of development.

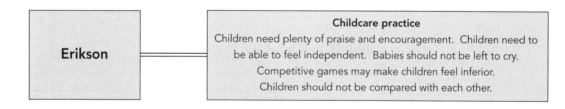

| Erikson | **Childcare practice**
Children need plenty of praise and encouragement. Children need to be able to feel independent. Babies should not be left to cry.
Competitive games may make children feel inferior.
Children should not be compared with each other. |

3 Attachment theory

Attachment theory looks at the needs of children to have a strong stable relationship with their **primary carers** – that is, mothers, fathers or whoever is the main person looking after them. It is increasingly accepted that the attachment children have with their primary carers and their ability to relate to others are linked. The theory is that only when children have a secure relationship with their primary carer can they go on and develop wider relationships. It is now accepted that babies and young children can form several close relationships or attachments and that it is only when their primary carer is not available and no substitute attachment is formed that emotional harm can be done. This means that babies and young children can be cared for successfully by people other than their primary carer. However, it is important that these other carers build a stable relationship with the child.

John Bowlby (1907–1990) is the best-known theorist on children's need to be with their primary carers. There were three aspects to his theory of attachment:

1　Children who have been separated from their parents are more likely to suffer from psychological problems later in life.

2　Attachment is an instinct in babies. They must form an attachment by the time they are 12 months old.

3　Babies and young children's fear of strangers is instinctive. In nature, animals will only follow their mother, which prevents them being attacked by other animals.

Linking theory with practice

The theory of the need of children to have an attachment to their primary carer or a substitute has changed many early years practices.

Attachment theory	Childcare practice
Children need a strong attachment.	Parents are encouraged to stay overnight when their children are in hospitals. Children are allowed to visit their parents in hospitals. Parents are encouraged to stay and settle their children in childcare settings before leaving them. The keyworker system is widely used. This means that when children are in daycare settings, they have one person in particular to care for them. This gives them another attachment. It is now recognised that the emotional care of the child is as important as they physical care.

Mckenzie heritage picture archive/Embeke Waseme

The stages of emotional and social development

There are different stages to the emotional and social development of children and, although ages can be given, the age at which children reach different stages may vary greatly. The speed at which children are able to start playing and co-operating with other children and leaving their primary carer often depends on individual circumstances – for example, younger children in the family may learn to play quickly as there are other children around them. As with other areas of children's development, it is more important to build up a picture of their emotional and social development than to concentrate on what is 'normal' at a particular age.

The stages of emotional and social development

Birth to one year	During the first year, babies learn to play and communicate their needs. They laugh, smile and make eye contact with their primary carers and family. These are important social skills.
1 month	Watch primary carer's face
3 months	Smile and coo Enjoy being handled and cuddled
6 months	Laugh and enjoy being played with
8 months	Fear strangers
9 months	Play peek-a-boo Discriminate between strangers and familiar adults
12 months	Are affectionate towards family and primary carers Play simple games – e.g. pat-a-cake
1–2 years	During the next year children learn that they are separate from their primary carers. They recognise, and begin to use, their names. They begin to explore independently. At about the age of two they begin to show anger and frustration if their needs are not met immediately. They do not recognise that other people have needs as well. During this year children start to play alongside other children.
15 months	Start to explore environment when adult is close by Start to use words to communicate Have a stronger feeling of being an individual
18 months	Have increasing vocabulary Point out objects to familiar adults Explore environment and show some independence but still need familiar adults Show strong emotions – e.g. anger, fear and joy
2 years	Play near other children (parallel play) Begin to talk when playing (pretend play) Imitate adults' actions Show strong emotions, including jealousy
2–3 years	This is an important year in children's lives and there is great progress in their social and emotional development during this time. It is often a difficult year for both children and carers as the children come to terms with their independence and strong desires. Tantrums and strong feelings at the start of the year lessen as children gradually develop more language and physical skills. Early years workers need to support and reassure children who are starting to leave their primary carers during this year. There is a wide variation in the way children progress over the year so it is hard to put specific times to these steps.

During this year most children will:	• move out of nappies • have a strong sense of identity, including gender and age • be happy to leave their primary carer for short periods • start taking an interest in other children and playing with them • show concern for other children – e.g. telling someone if baby is crying • start to wait for their needs to be met.
3–4 years	This is a more settled year for children. They grow in confidence, as they are able to make friends and play with other children. Their language and physical skills have developed. They show social skills – e.g. turn taking, sharing and concern for others. Emotionally children still need reassurance from their immediate carers, but are more independent and may play by themselves for longer periods. Strong emotions are still felt and quarrels and temper tantrums still occur at times.
During this year most children will:	• be affectionate towards family, friends and carers • want to help and please primary carers and other familiar adults • imitate (in play) actions seen – e.g. putting teddy to bed, feeding dolls • share playthings • play with other children – mostly pretend play • show concerns for other people – e.g. rubbing back of crying baby.
4–6 years	Haddon Davies *'I got to the top!'* In some ways the expression 'I can do' sums up this period of a child's life. Emotionally, most children feel confident and express themselves in terms of their achievements – e.g. 'I got a sticker today' or 'Look at me, I can climb this now'. They may start to use words and actions in imitation of other people. Playing with other children is increasingly important and some children start to make close friendships. At this time, children start to play with members of their own sex, which may link to their understanding of gender roles.
6–8 years	Children start to gain a sense of fairness and justice, which means they can share equipment and materials more easily. By the age of seven, children have started to become more self-aware and can be critical of their efforts. They may stop drawing if they are not happy with what they are producing. Children start to be influenced by adults and children who are not family members. Having a friend or group of friends becomes increasingly important to them and is sometimes a source of sadness. Children start to compare themselves to their peers and may need adult reassurance to cope with this.

The link between emotional and social development and overall development

As we have seen in other chapters, children's overall development is linked together and this is especially true of emotional and social development. Emotional and social development relies on children having opportunities to become confident. A difficulty in one area – for example, not being able to speak clearly – means that children's social development is affected because other children find it harder to play with them.

Portfolio activity

Ask your supervisor if you can observe a child in your workplace.

Look at the way in which this child interacts with other children and make notes for about three minutes.

1   *Is this child able to play co-operatively?*
2   *Did the child use any speech to play with the other child or children?*
3   *Did the child make any eye contact or use body language while playing?*
4   *Write down what you have learnt from looking at this child's social development.*
5   *Compare your notes to the stages of social development given earlier in this chapter.*

The importance of self-image in children

Our self-image is what we think of ourselves. This is sometimes called self-concept. As children get older they gradually build up a picture of what they think they are like. The first step in this process is during the first year of life (at about 9–12 months) when children start to understand that they are separate to their primary carers. By two years children are starting to refer to themselves by name and by three years, most children know their age and whether they are a boy or a girl. At around six years, children are starting to say things like 'I'm clever' or 'I'm naughty' as well as statements like 'I'm tall' and 'I can run fast.'

Children learn about themselves through listening to adults and other children and by watching the reactions of others. In this way they gain a view of themselves. It is essential that children develop a positive view of themselves as this will affect their self-esteem and in turn their confidence.

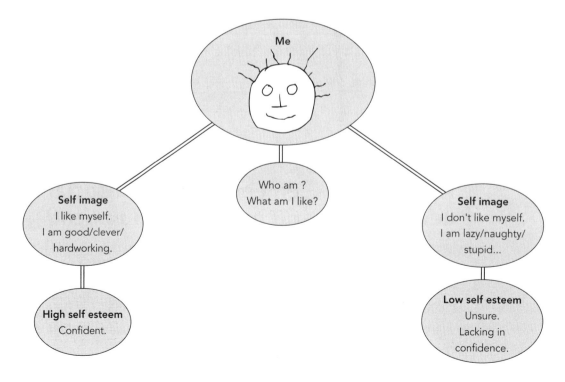

Self-esteem is based on self-image. Self-esteem is about how highly we value ourselves. Children who have high self-esteem are more likely to fulfil their potential because they are confident about themselves and their abilities. They are more likely to try out new activities, can cope better with failure and are ready to make friends.

The role of adults in building children's self-esteem

As children's self-image and in turn self-esteem is mainly based on adults' reactions to them, it is important that early years workers make children feel wanted and loved at all times.

Good practice – helping children to be self-reliant and independent

✔ Do not talk negatively about children.

✔ Give children simple tasks appropriate to their age and stage – e.g. a child of 18 months could collect their shoes.

✔ Do not set tasks that may end in the child feeling they have failed.

✔ Give children plenty of praise and encouragement.

Think about it

Think of some simple self-help tasks that children of the following ages might be encouraged to do. Think of three tasks for each age range.

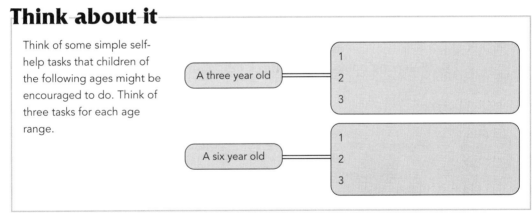

A three year old
1
2
3

A six year old
1
2
3

Helping children to see positive images to avoid stereotyping

The 1989 Children Act recognised the need for all children to develop positive self-images regardless of race, gender or disability.

From about three years, children become aware of their gender. Over the next few years they try to work out what being a girl or boy means. To do this they look at the adults around them and also look out for signals sent to them – for example, a boy might be told that he should be brave if he falls while a girl might be given more comfort when she falls over. This sends the boy the message that boys need to be stronger than girls. In the same way, children from about the age of four start to become aware of their culture and race. Again, they are trying to work out what this means for them.

This means that as early years workers we must make sure that children see a wide range of people performing a wide variety of roles, otherwise they may come to some limiting conclusions – e.g. girls can't be doctors, boys can't cook, black people are poor, Chinese people can only cook.

Think about it

As early years workers we must also be aware that language can also reinforce stereotypes. Traditionally girls have been brought up to be more aware of their looks than boys and to be quieter and less active.

Look at these words and consider if they are more likely to be used about boy or girls.

Helpful	Bookish	Rogue	Boisterous	Sweet
Pretty	Rough	Kind	Spiteful	Difficult

The role of the early years worker in helping children to establish a positive identity

There are many ways in which we can help children to feel positive about their gender and family background.

- Welcoming parents and other family members. Building a relationship with children's families shows them that we value their family background. (See Chapter 10, page 218.)

- Selecting books and pictures that show people in many roles.

- Making children feel they belong – e.g. by having objects in the homecorner that reflect their culture and traditions.

- Making sure we treat and value children in the same way.

- Actively encouraging children to have a go at activities that might be considered gender-orientated.

- Encouraging visitors who are good role models to come and talk or work with children.

- Avoiding separating children by gender.

Supporting emotional and social development

As early years workers we need to be able to provide both a safe and stimulating environment for children and one that will help their emotional and social growth. To do this we need to look at the emotional and social needs of children:

- love and affection

- security and stability

- opportunities to socialise.

These are discussed below.

Portfolio activity

In your workplace ask a child over the age of four to tell you about himself or herself.

1 *Listen carefully to what the child says and make notes if you can.*
2 *Look at this list and consider the child's attitude about these subjects.*
   - Qualities – e.g. I am good or I am kind
   - Achievements – e.g. I can dance
   - Physical features – e.g. height, colour of hair, colour of skin
   - Family – e.g. I have a brother
   - Gender and age – e.g. I am a boy
   - Possessions – e.g. I have a dog.
3 *Do you feel that the child you talked to has a positive self-image?*
4 *Write down what you have learnt about this child from carrying out this activity.*

Unconditional love and affection. This is a basic need for children. When they feel loved and valued they develop a positive self-concept. It is important they feel accepted and loved unconditionally – i.e., for who they are not for what they can do or look like. A positive environment for children is a warm, welcoming one where they feel wanted and appreciated. This gives them a sense of belonging.

Security and stability. A positive environment is a secure one where children feel they are being protected and cared for. Although we encourage them to be independent and give them opportunities to explore, they still need to feel there is someone to turn to and who will take over if needed. This makes them feel safe.

Children also need stability, especially if there is some upheaval in their home lives. We can provide stability for children by making sure rules and boundaries are firm and consistent, responding in predictable ways and, above all, by making sure we are always there for them.

Children also feel more secure when they can see a pattern and an order to their lives. As early years workers we can help them see this by explaining what they will be doing when we are with them. We may say 'After your nap, we'll have a story.' or 'It's Tuesday today. What do we always do on Tuesdays?'

Opportunities to be with other children. Children need the opportunity to be with other children if they are to develop their social skills. In situations where early years workers are looking after only one child they may need to find ways to introduce the child to other children. Parents may be happy, for example, for the child to go to a club, parent-and-toddler group or playgroup. Early years workers have an important role in helping children's social development by supporting them while they play and learn together.

Sometimes children who are unsettled try very hard to test adults. When this happens it is important for early years workers to stay calm and showing the child they are still valued. The children who are likely to behave in this way are often who feel insecure and this is their way of finding out who cares for them and whether they are in a stable environment. Look at the following example.

Case Study

Michael is four years old and has had five changes of nanny since he was two years old. At first he seemed to get on fine with Sarah, but recently his behaviour has been very poor. He often pinches her and looks constantly for ways to be disruptive. Today he has picked up the felt tip pens and started drawing on the walls, even though there was plenty of paper on the table.

1   *Why might Michael be showing this type of behaviour?*
2   *How should Sarah react?*
3   *Why is it important for Sarah to talk to Michael's primary carer?*

Factors affecting children's emotional and social development

There are many factors that can affect children's emotional and social development, both direct and indirect.

Direct factors

▪ **Genetic disorders** – e.g. Down' syndrome, autism and Asperger's – which mean children find it harder to form relationships with other people.

▪ **Poor attachment** to primary carers strongly affects children's emotional and social development. Studies have shown that from birth the strength of bond between children and their primary carers is particularly important. Reasons for difficulties in forming this bond include separation of baby and primary carer due to illness or prematurity, postnatal depression and inadequate parenting skills. Health visitors and other professionals routinely look out for such difficulties and aim to offer support to help primary carers who are finding it hard to care for and love their children.

Indirect factors

▪ **Lack of opportunity to socialise** can cause children to feel different from other children, which can lower their self-esteem. For example, a child living on a farm might not meet many other children or a child whose parents are travellers might not stay long enough to make friends.

- **Position in family** can affect children's emotional and social development. For example, an only child might not have many opportunities to play and socialise whereas a child from a large family might suffer from jealousy and fear of competition from their siblings.

- **Poverty** can lead to limited opportunities. For example, a child living in bed and breakfast accommodation might feel different from other children because of where they live or what they wear.

- **Cultural differences** can make some children feel different and uncomfortable. A child might be the only one wearing a certain type of clothing or a child's family might be isolated in the community, limiting opportunities for friendship and socialisation.

- **Impaired or delayed language development** can mean that children are unable to communicate with other children. They may stutter and be laughed at by other children or their speech delay may result in frustration and difficulties in controlling their anger.

Helping children who have difficulties in relating to other children

You can help children by acting as their guide and staying alongside them when they are with other children. You could start by involving only one or two other children in an activity. After several successful guided activities and plenty of praise, children might then be able to cope with a less structured situation.

Examples of guided activities might include:

- cooking

- playing board games

- doing a floor puzzle with another child

- playing on a dough table.

Case Study

Stephen has a speech impairment that means that he stutters when he is nervous. He is five years old and has started to go to school. He is not very confident at playing with other children and once in the playground an older child began to imitate his stutter.

The speech therapist has helped Stephen and now suggests that he needs to start playing with other children in order to gain confidence. Stephen now has a classroom assistant to help him in the mornings.

Questions
1 *Why is it important that Stephen trust his classroom assistant?*
2 *Why might his classroom assistant choose activities that involve Stephen working with one other child to begin with?*

Supporting children's emotional and social development

There are many ways that we can support children's emotional and social development.

Praise and recognition	Showing affection and unconditional love
Praise children for their efforts, not just their achievements. Praise children for being helpful, kind and generous. Praise children for playing well either together or by themselves.	Greet children and their parents in a warm way. Take time to listen and talk to each child as an individual. Make each child feel that they are special through labelling items such as their pictures and by making the homecorner reflect their home background.

Social skills include being able to share, take turns, listen to others as well as being able to behave in a way that is appropriate to the people you are with. As many of these skills are learnt through copying adult behaviour, it is essential that early years workers act as good role models for children. Children need to see adults co-operating, sharing and talking to each other in a respectful way.

It is worth noting that every culture has different social codes of politeness – for example, looking someone in the eye can be considered rude in some cultures, especially if it is a child who is looking. The codes for eating also vary and if you are working with children from a culture different from your own it is important to check what these are.

Helping children relate to others and feel part of a group

Children learn how to co-operate with others through direct experience. By encouraging children to work and play together we can help them to gain this experience and in doing so to learn to value and respect each other.

Providing a stable environment
Make sure that children understand what is happening to them.
Give reasons and help them understand the routine.
Encourage children to play with familiar toys and comfort objects.
Repetitive play not only builds skills, but it also gives children security.
Explain the rules and boundaries to children.
Older children may come up with their own sets of rules.

Boosting self-esteem
Encouraging children to be independent.
Displaying pictures and other items they
have made.

The early years worker can help children by providing activities appropriate to their likely stage of social development. For example, with toddlers we could provide activities that children find enjoyable – for example, dough or sand – and which, at the same time, bring children together. However, we would not expect them to share and pass equipment at this stage. With older children we could set up a game that they could play together and help them to take turns and work out the rules.

There are some activities that help children to co-operate as part of a group – for example, circle time and story time. Circle time allows children to show and share what they have been doing with other children. Children benefit from being part of a group and from learning to take turns and listen to others. When organising this type of group activity, it is important to consider the age of the children as well as their attention span. Children under the age of three will find it difficult to sit for over more than five minutes without some activity.

Portfolio activity

1 *Ask your supervisor if you could help serve a meal or snack in your workplace.*
2 *Write down how you helped to make this a social occasion.*
3 *What social skills did the children show during this time?*
4 *What did you learn by carrying out this activity?*

Helping children to gain self-help skills

Self-help skills allow children to be independent. They include skills like dressing, washing hands, brushing hair and pouring drinks. Children's self-esteem grows as they gain these skills because they are then able to take control of these small areas of their lives. As early years workers we need to encourage children to have a go at being independent while at the same time not expecting them to fail. Many self-help skills require physical co-ordination and some practice. This means that children's efforts should always be praised and, where possible, tasks are broken down into steps that are appropriate for children's stage of development.

The following flow chart shows the steps involved in getting dressed for children aged between one and two years.

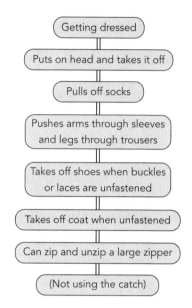

Getting dressed

Puts on head and takes it off

Pulls off socks

Pushes arms through sleeves and legs through trousers

Takes off shoes when buckles or laces are unfastened

Takes off coat when unfastened

Can zip and unzip a large zipper

(Not using the catch)

Knowledge into action

1   *Choose one of the following self-help skills and show how it could be broken down into steps.*

> Brushing teeth
> Hanging coat on peg
> Combing hair
> Folding clothes
> Washing face
> Getting out toys and equipment
> Washing hands
> Blowing nose

(You may like to do this in pairs.)

Separation from carers

For most children separating from their primary carers is a big step. It is important that we understand how children are likely to react to this separation.

Research carried out on the separation of children from their primary carers suggests that there is a pattern to their anxiety. This is often referred to as **separation distress**. There seems to be three stages to this process.

Stage	Signs
One – Protest	Anger, crying loud, frustration
Two – Despair	Listless, quiet, not participating in activities
Three – Detachment	Withdrawn, plays by self, does not interact with adults or other children

Children will only go through all three stages if the care they are receiving is inadequate and if they are not quickly reunited with their primary carer. Children who have reached the detachment stage seem to have 'separated' from their primary carer and are no longer interested in the carer or others around them.

Age and separation

- Babies under six months are unlikely to show any signs of distress, as they will not have formed a strong attachment with their primary carer.

- Children between the ages of one and three years are more likely to show signs of distress when leaving their primary carer.

- Older children who have had experience of the primary carer leaving and then returning are more likely to cope with short periods of separation.

Bubbles/Ian West

Helping children who are showing signs of distress

Ideally children should always be left with people with whom they have built up an attachment. This is not always possible and so many early years workers will see children who are in the first stage of the distress syndrome. In this situation it is vital not to ignore them, as they will then feel abandoned! Wherever possible children should be allowed their comforter as this can help them to feel more secure.

Good practice – helping children who are showing signs of distress

- ✔ It is better for just one person to try to settle the child.

- ✔ Unless they are being cared for in an emergency you should contact the primary carer if children have not settled in after 15 minutes or so.

✔ Hold and cuddle the child.

✔ Read stories or involve the child in a quiet activity with you.

✔ Older children may feel better if they draw a picture that they can give to the primary carer when they return.

✔ Do not leave children to 'get on with it'.

Helping children to adjust to new early years settings

There may be times when we know that children are going to be changing early years settings or carers. Children might be moving onto school, leaving the area or changing childminder or nanny. Supporting children through a change can help them to feel more secure and settle in more quickly. It is important to work with parents when preparing children so that we can reinforce anything they have said to the children as well as passing on any concerns that children may have mentioned to us.

Ways of helping children to prepare for a change

Children are likely to have many concerns about any change.

Common concerns of children

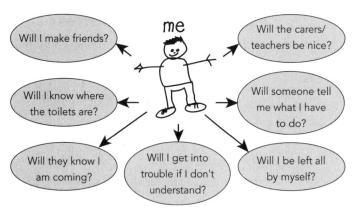

Ways to prepare children for change include:

▨ reading books on topics like starting school, going to hospital and starting playgroup

▨ arranging a visit to the new early years setting

▨ involving children in any preparations – e.g. packing a bag, buying items of clothing

▨ encouraging children to ask questions and take these seriously.

Think about it

Jason is four years old and he is due to go into hospital for a few days. There will be times in the day when his mother will not able to stay with him.

1 *How can you help Jason to prepare for this change?*
2 *Why is it important for Jason to take his comforter with him?*

Settling-in policies

In earlier times children were abruptly separated from their primary carers. Children were taken from their parents' arms crying and no period for adjustment was allowed. The work of John Bowlby and other people has shown early years workers that children need time to settle in. Most early years settings now have a 'settling-in' policy which is designed to help children adjust to the new environment.

Ideally, if early years settings or carers are working with very young children, the period of adjustment should be gradual. It is considered good practice for large early years settings to have a key worker system. This means that children are encouraged to form a relationship with one particular person who then acts as a substitute primary carer.

Flow chart showing how children might be helped to settle in

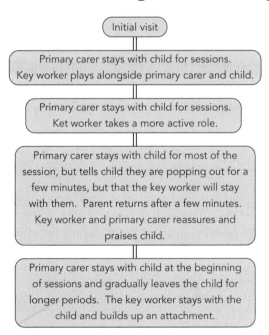

Initial visit

Primary carer stays with child for sessions. Key worker plays alongside primary carer and child.

Primary carer stays with child for sessions. Ket worker takes a more active role.

Primary carer stays with child for most of the session, but tells child they are popping out for a few minutes, but that the key worker will stay with them. Parent returns after a few minutes. Key worker and primary carer reassures and praises child.

Primary carer stays with child at the beginning of sessions and gradually leaves the child for longer periods. The key worker stays with the child and builds up an attachment.

The length of time between each stage depends on how well children are coping with the separation.

Sometimes the needs of the parents will mean that the normal settling policy cannot be used. For example, if a parent is taken suddenly ill and childcare has to be quickly arranged or a child is taken into local authority care and Social Services becomes responsible for placing the child. Sometimes parents may not be able to spend time settling children in because they are unable to take the time off work. In these types of circumstances we need to be flexible and work with the parent or whoever has parental responsibility to find ways of settling children in.

Multiple transitions

This means 'many changes' and applies to children who have experienced many early years settings or many different carers. There are a number of possible reasons for this, including the following.

- Children may have been taken into local authority care – either into children's homes or foster homes.

- Children may have experienced several carers due to childcare arrangements breaking down.

- Children may have moved with their families several times either as travellers or due to employment.

■ Children's family structure may have changed – e.g. a divorce and remarriage and several people sharing in children's care.

The effects of multiple transitions

Multiple moves from early years setting to early years setting or from carer to carer can make children feel very disorientated.

Children can feel a sense of loss and grief from not being with their friends or carers.

This means that some children regress. They may start wetting the bed, becoming clingy or sucking their thumb. Older children may detach themselves by not trying to form new relationships because they do not want to be hurt again.

It is essential that, when we are involved with children who have had many changes in their lives, we are patient and supportive. We need to win children's trust, which takes time. In early years settings, early years workers also need to think about activities that will help the 'new' child break into the existing friendship groups. We can ask another child to be a 'friend' to the new child or provide activities that encourage small groups to work together – for example, cooking activities or planting bulbs.

Think about it

Jamie has moved school five times in two years. He is six years old and has just started at his new school. He is clingy to his primary carer in the morning and does not want to join in with other children. You have been asked to work with him until he settles in.

What activities could you prepare that would:

1   *Help Jamie relate to the other children?*
2   *Help Jamie talk about himself and his fears?*
3   *Give Jamie more confidence?*

Reactions of parents

It is easy to forget that parents may also have some strong feelings when leaving their children.

■ **Guilt** because they are no longer caring for their child. Some parents may have had to return to work through need rather than through choice.

■ **Loss** because they are so used to caring for their child that it seems strange not to have them there all the time.

■ **Anxiety** that the child may prefer the early years worker to them. Especially when children are spending more time with the early years workers than with the parents.

To help parents with these feelings we must be able to reassure them that although we are caring for their child, they remain the most important people in the child's life.

Think about it

Kim is the youngest of four children and this is his first day at the early years setting. Kim's mother says to you on her way out 'that's the last of my babies gone now and he didn't even wave goodbye at the school gate.'

1 *How do you think that she felt when she said this?*
2 *Why was she disappointed that her child did not wave?*
3 *What can you say to make her feel more positive about her role as a mother?*

Kim waving to his father before going to school.

Portfolio activity

Find out your workplace's policy on settling in new children.

1 *How long does it take for most children to settle in?*
2 *Observe two children when they leave their primary carers.*
3 *Record how they cope with the separation.*
4 *What do they do after their primary carers have left?*
5 *Write down what you have learnt from observing the children*

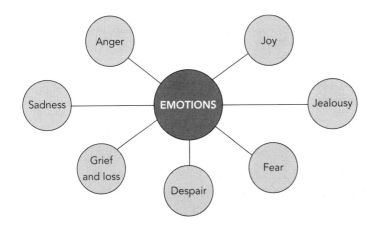

Helping children cope with their strong feelings

Young children can have very strong feelings that they are unable to contain. This means that when they are angry they may lash out and hit another child or when they are disappointed they may burst into uncontrollable sobs.

As children get older and have developed more language they are able to express these feelings in other ways. For example, an angry child might go to an adult to complain, rather than bite another child.

Anger is a common emotion in most children. In any situation where a child is angry and aggressive, it is important for the adult to stay calm and in control. If a child is violent, you must send for another adult to help.

- Talk quietly and firmly to the child.

- Move the child away from the situation if necessary to protect other children or equipment.

- Vocalise what the child is feeling – e.g. 'You are cross with Simon because he's not playing with you.'

- Distract a young child with another activity.

- Give an older child time and a place to 'cool' down.

- Praise the child for mastering their anger.

Activities that can help children to express feelings

Planning activities that allow children to be aggressive helps them to vent their feelings in a positive way. Activities are also needed to help them express other strong feelings.

Activity	Effect
Dough, clay and other malleable materials	Pounding, squeezing, pummelling and squashing down shapes can make children feel in control and strong.
Sand	Digging, moulding castles and towers and then pushing them down can make children feel satisfied.
Hammer and pegs	Children enjoy banging down on pegs with a hammer.
Drums and percussion instruments	Loud marching and banging can help children release tension.
Books and stories	Reading children's books or making up stories about children who are afraid or who are jealous can make children feel they are not alone.
Drawing and painting	Children can express the way they are feeling through drawing or painting. They might paint an angry picture or a sad face.
Role play	Home corners or other situations where children can act out their fears and frustrations can help them come to turns with what they are feeling.

Jealousy. Most people have had feelings of jealousy at some time in their lives. It is an emotion that most adults have difficulty in owning up to, as they often feel

"Well at least he's stopped hitting the others"

Home corner

Unwanted behaviour in children

guilty about their jealousy! Jealousy is often a sign of insecurity and children who are feeling jealous may be afraid that they are no longer loved or liked. Young children are most likely to feel jealousy towards a member of their family – for example, a baby brother or a step parent. We can help children who are feeling jealous by giving them more attention and extra reassurance. Becoming angry with children or ignoring them can make them feel more rejected.

Fears. It is quite common for children over the age of two to develop fears. They might be afraid of dogs, being left alone in a room or falling asleep by themselves. These fears are very real to children and adults need to provide plenty of reassurance and understanding. As children get older they may be able to talk about their fears, but with younger children we need to make them feel that we will be there for them and will protect them.

Case Study

Michael is three years old and is afraid that there are monsters in the toilets in the nursery. The early years worker decides to make a 'monster scaring' card with Michael. She tells him that this is a special card that will send any monsters away and that they will put it on the door of the toilet. Michael looks much happier when he has finished the card and says that this card will sort out any monsters.

Think of three reasons why making a card has made Michael feel better.

Sadness. There are many times when children feel sadness and disappointment and supporting children at these times shows them we really care for them. Children might burst into tears if their painting 'goes wrong' or if they do not win a game. We can help children in a number of ways, including:

■ expressing through words why they are sad – e.g. 'Are you feeling sad because you were looking forward to taking this home?'

■ helping them in a practical way – e.g. by offering to give them another piece of paper or by telling them they can play another game later

■ giving them plenty of attention – e.g. asking them if they would like to help us or reading a story to them.

Loss and grief. There may be times when early years workers need to support children through feelings of loss and grief. Children may have experienced the death of a family member or even a pet that they cared for. In the same way, children are affected by the separation of their parents and may experience feelings of loss and grief. The increase in divorce and separation of parents means that early years workers working in early years settings are likely to deal with children who are coming to terms with a change in their family structure.

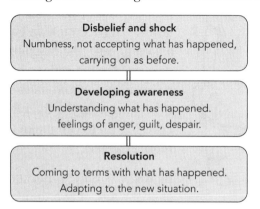

Disbelief and shock
Numbness, not accepting what has happened, carrying on as before.

Developing awareness
Understanding what has happened. feelings of anger, guilt, despair.

Resolution
Coming to terms with what has happened. Adapting to the new situation.

Work done on grief suggests that people go through stages in accepting their loss. Understanding the grieving process can help us identify where children may be in this process.

Helping children with feelings of loss and grief

It is important that children are allowed to go through a grieving process. The pace of this process depends very much on the child. Early years workers need to be ready to support children through this painful process sensitively. Where possible, close contact and discussions with parents should happen so that together the children's needs can be met. We need to remember, in such situations, that parents might also be coping with their own feelings.

Early years workers should provide a calm and reassuring environment so that children feel there is some consistency in their lives. We can encourage children to write about what they are feeling, paint pictures and use puppets and other imaginative play to express themselves.

Sometimes children may need specialist help in order for them to deal with their feelings and emotions. There are a number of specialists who can help children and their families. These include play therapists who use play as a way of helping children with their feelings.

Think about it

Freddy the hamster has died. He belongs to two children aged three and five.

Discuss in pairs:

1 *How would you tell them that he has died?*
2 *What activities could help them to cope with his death.*

Unit test

Quick quiz

1   Which activity will **best** help children to release aggression?
    a   jigsaw puzzle
    b   dressing up
    c   dough
    d   drawing.

2   Which activity will encourage social skills in a five-year-old who has difficulty in taking turns?
    a   Playing in the home corner with other children.
    b   Playing a board game in a group with an adult.
    c   Going for a nature walk.
    d   Doing a floor puzzle.

3   Children of 3 years normally:
    a   take turns and share
    b   play alone
    c   cling to parents
    d   have same sex friends.

4   How **best** could an early years worker prepare a child for going to a new school?
    a   Teach the child to read some words.
    b   Read a story about a child who is starting school.
    c   Invite another child to play who is also going to start school.
    d   Organise a visit to the school.

5   Which of these skills could be considered self-help skills?
    a   putting on a coat
    b   reading a book
    c   washing hands
    d   pouring a drink.

Short answer questions

1   What is meant by the phrase **multiple transition**?

2   What is the difference between self-image and self-esteem?

3   Name three ways in which an early years worker could boost a child's self esteem.

4   What is meant by the word 'attachment'?

5   Why is it important for babies and young children to have a key worker?

Parents and Carers

As an early years worker, you will need to be able to work with parents and carers. You will need to listen and talk to them and understand how you can build a relationship with them. The relationship between early years workers and parents is an essential one as parents will be trusting you, in their absence, to care for their children. (Helping children to settle in is covered in Chapter 9, page 205.)

This chapter looks at why parents and carers are important in children's lives and how we can work in partnership with them.

The chapter is split into three sections:

1 The role of parents.

2 How to communicate with parents.

3 Your role in relating to parents.

In this chapter the term 'parents' is used to mean all those people who are the primary carers of children. This may be relatives – for example, grandparents, aunts and cousins – or other carers – for example, foster carers and step parents.

1 The role of parents

Why are parents and primary carers special?

Collections/Sandra Lousada

Even though they might not realise it, most parents are great teachers. Through being with their parents, children learn about their own personal history and their place within the family. They learn about the culture and beliefs of their parents, which gives them a sense of belonging and stays with them for their lives. Every family has its own traditions that are passed on to the children and make each family different and special. In some families the children learn a language from their parents that is different from that in their school or nursery. Families have their own ways of celebrating festivals and most families even have their own jokes. Skills and hobbies are learnt from being with parents. For example, children whose parents are musical will be encouraged to make music and parents who keep animals often give their children pets to care for.

The skills, attitudes and beliefs that parents pass on to their children are just as important as those learnt in educational settings and to work in partnership with parents we must respect and understand this.

Think about it

1 *Does your family have its own jokes?*
2 *Do you remember learning a skill or hobby with a parent or carer?*

Think about it

It is easy for early years workers to forget that by the time children come to be cared for, they have often learnt many skills from their parents. For example, they may know their colours and know how to dress themselves.

Sam is three years old and is just about to start playgroup. He has been cared for at home by his parents. He is a bright, happy child who is quite independent and confident.

Assuming that Sam's development is right for his age, make a list of the skills that Sam will already have learnt from being brought up by his parents. For example, he will have learnt to feed himself.

(You may like to do this task in pairs.)

Different types of parenting style and attitude

Mr and Mrs Goodenough and their family

In the same way that each family is different, every parent has different ways of managing their children. Looking after children and providing them with love and care is a demanding task and parents try hard to do their best for their children. All parents have their own style of parenting which is influenced partly by their own childhood and partly by any pressures they are facing. Some parents are authoritarian in style – tending to limit and control their children – while others are permissive – preferring to allow children more freedom of expression. There are advantages and disadvantages to both approaches and in the main most parents fall somewhere in the middle.

The emotional bond between parent and child is often powerful, making the relationship intense. Parents can feel anger but also great love towards their children. The strong emotions that parents feel makes it hard for them to be perfect all the time. Studies show that they do not need to be perfect for their children to flourish. This is the idea behind 'good enough' parenting. We know that, although most parents are not perfect, they are still the best people for children to be with.

Different types of family structure and arrangement

The way in which people live together as families has changed over the past fifty years. This means that we cannot assume that children are living with a mother and father who are married.

Some children may live in lone-parent households, some children may grow up in communities where care is shared. There may be children who spend three days a week with one parent and four days with the other. Some children may live with other family members other than parents – for example, grandparents, aunts and uncles – who all help to care for them. Understanding and respecting that there are different ways of looking after children helps us to meet the needs of children and their families.

The following diagram shows some of the ways in which children may be brought up.

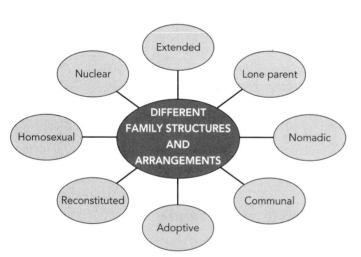

Nuclear family	Mother and father, living together with their children, but separately from other family members. They may be married or cohabiting
Extended family	Family members living together and sharing the care of children.
Lone parent family	Single parent taking care of children either through choice or other reasons – e.g. the death of a partner, divorce or separation.
Homosexual family	Homosexual couple taking care of children – could be gay or lesbian.
Nomadic family	Parents do not have a permanent home and travel from place to place with their children – e.g. gypsies and travellers.
Reconstituted	Children live with one natural parent and a step parent. Families may also include step and half sisters and brothers.
Adoptive families	Children may live with adopted or foster parents.
Communal families	Children may live with their parents in communes where other members are also involved in their care.

Think about it

Jason lives with his father for two weeks of the month and with his mother for the other two weeks. His mother has a new partner who has two children of a similar age. Jason's father has married again and so he also has a step mother.

You are asked to make Mother's Day cards with a group of children that includes Jason. You think that it is likely that he will see both his mother and step mother on this day.

1 *Should Jason be told to make more than one card?*
2 *How would you handle this situation?*
3 *Why is it important that early years settings do not assume that children are living with both parents?*

(You may like to do this activity in pairs.)

Parents as partners in the care and education of their children

Most parents want to be involved in all aspects of their children's lives and are keen to share their views and knowledge of their children. Parents provide long term-care and love which often carries on well past the age of eighteen. They are

important because they are the people to whom children turn in moments of need – for example, when they feel ill, angry or unhappy.

Parents know their children best and can therefore help us to work with them. Both parents and early years workers are important in different ways – we fit together like a jigsaw. By working together closely – sharing knowledge and information – we enable children to learn, feel settled and, most importantly, to be happy.

Parents who do not share the values of the early years setting

Every parent has their own set of values in terms of religion, culture and expectations of children. Some – or all – of these values may be different from the values of the early years setting and we need to appreciate that there are instances when parents have not chosen the child care arrangements. For example, if there is a child protection order that requires parents to take children to a family centre or if no place is available at the parent's first choice of school. Some parents may not feel comfortable in certain educational settings because their own experience these settings was not pleasant.

Even parents who broadly support the early years setting may not always share all of the values. They may not consider all of the work that you do as important – for example, making children aware of different religions or your approach to managing children's behaviour. Some parents may not understand the value of play and would prefer to see more structured activities. Early years settings can use workshops and parents' evenings to explain their approach but we should still remember that parents are entitled to have their own viewpoint and that good relationships are built on respect.

Parents and the Children Act (1989)

The 1989 Children Act gave people who care for children rights and responsibilities.

The act was important because it considered children's needs to be most important. It recognised that most children need to stay with their families and encouraged local authorities and other services to work with parents for the good of the children.

Under the act, people who have legal responsibility for children are given *'parental responsibility'*. This lasts until children are 18 years old – even if the child is no longer living with them.

Parental responsibility means that they have the right and responsibility to:

- name and register the child at birth

- apply for a passport for the child

- maintain and protect the child

- choose the religion in which the child is to be brought up

- decide where the child is to live

- consent to medical treatment for the child

- choose how and where the child is to be educated.

Parental responsibility is automatically given to married parents and unmarried mothers. Where a father is not married to the mother and wants to have parental responsibility, he can apply to the courts or be made a legal guardian by the mother.

Parental responsibility can be given to people who are not the children's natural parents – for example, a court might grant a residence order for children to live with their grandparents which would mean that they would have parental responsibility for the child while the child is with them. Local authorities have parental responsibility where a care order is issued.

Families live in a variety of environments and under different pressures

Parents bring up children in many different environments which means that no one has exactly the same experience of childhood. Some children live in communities where the dominant religion different from their own. Some children live in areas where everyone has cars and lives in large houses. We need to remember that all families have different needs and pressures. Families that are very wealthy still have pressures, although these will not always be the same as for families on low incomes. Illness, problems at work and breakdown in relationships affect all families. Some pressures may be short-term – for example, the upheaval of moving house – while others may be long-term such as the illness of a family member. By learning about the types of pressures families face and trying to understand them, we are more likely to be able to meet the children's needs and build better relationships with their parents.

Some factors that might affect families are:

- low income

- poor housing

- being a minority group in the community – e.g. mixed race, travellers

- working long hours

- long-term illness of a family member

- moving into a new area

- loneliness

- death in the family.

Case Study

Daniella is four years old and is being cared for by her mother. They have just been housed by the local council on a large estate on the outskirts of the town after spending some time in a refuge for battered women and their families. Daniella's mother is finding it quite hard to live alone and misses the support of the refuge. She brings Daniella to the playgroup where you work and often stays to act as a helper.

Questions
1 What are the main pressures on Daniella's mother?
2 Why do you think Daniella's mother enjoys being a helper?
3 Why is it important for early years workers to think about the pressures that families are under?

2 How to communicate with parents

The importance of relationships with parents

It is not many years since parents used to wait for their children by the school gates – they were not seen in early years settings unless it was parents' evening or they had made an appointment.

Attractive reception areas can make parents feel welcome

It is different today. Most early years settings have an 'open door' policy which means that parents are encouraged to come in at anytime, with or without an appointment, and are made to feel welcome. The open door policy also means that parents and childcare workers can talk together, share information and build a strong relationship without waiting for the next parents' evening. They can talk informally about children's progress, mention any concerns they might have, look at their children's work and feel involved in the early years setting. This positive attitude towards parents helps children to feel more settled and secure. They can sense that all the people who care for them are working together and this helps them to talk about what they have been doing more easily – for example, 'I did a painting today that's up on the wall. Come and look at it.'

Knowledge into Action

1 *Find out if your workplace or placement has an open door policy.*
2 *Do parents come into the early years setting often?*
3 *Is there a reception area for parents?*

Ways of relating to parents

Every parent has different needs and each parent relates to us differently. Parents who are leaving their children for the first time are likely to need reassurance while parents who have used the early years setting over many years are likely to enjoy talking to their friends. Relating to parents is an important skill, as relationships need to be built up. When early years settings have good relationships with parents, difficult subjects can be brought up more easily – for example, if parents are not collecting children on time.

Good practice – relating to parents

✔ Find out how parents wish to be addressed. Some parents prefer to be called by their first names and others by a title – e.g. Mr or Mrs.

✔ Never assume that parents share the same family name as their children.

✔ Smile and greet parents, do not ignore them.

✔ Talk to them about their child's achievements.

✔ Make parents feel that you will listen to them. This is particularly important for parents who are feeling under pressure. They may be grateful for a sympathetic ear.

✔ Refer on any queries that you cannot deal with so that parents get accurate information.

Barriers to communication include the layout of the building, time and nervousness of parents and early years workers.

▪ A poor layout of a building may prevent parents from coming in to collect their children because there is not enough room. In some cases, layouts, or the way in which children are handed over, can be changed to allow more opportunities for communication.

▪ Time can be a barrier to good communication. Some parents may need to drop off or collect their children quickly and may not have time to stop. This does not mean that they are not interested in the early years setting or their child. A friendly nod or wave when it is not possible to speak to a parent is a way of showing that we are pleased to see them.

▪ It is important to show parents that we are always prepared to talk and listen to them, even if this means we have to stay on for longer. Early years workers who work at children's homes may need to allow extra time in the morning or evening so that information can be exchanged with parents.

▪ A 'them and us' atmosphere can be created by childcare workers avoiding contact with parents – e.g. through nervousness. This can make parents feel rejected and awkward. The best way to start communicating with parents is by smiling at them to show you are interested in them not only as parents but also as people.

- When there is no shared language – e.g. because a parent is deaf or does not speak the language of the early years setting – you could either arrange for an interpreter or use a book that contains pictures or symbols. Sharing information in writing can be helpful for parents who do not share the language of the early years setting, as they can ask someone to help them write something or ask someone to translate what has been written down for them. It may not always be appropriate for children to be used as interpreters as the information may be sensitive. Good eye contact, patience and smiles generally help in these sort of situations.

Think about it

Steven's mother always waits at the nursery door for him to come out. She never talks to the other parents and seems to keep her eyes down. You find out that she is deaf although she can lip read.

1   *What might be preventing her from coming in?*
2   *How could you approach her in order to build a relationship with her?*
3   *What would you say to her?*
4   *Why is it important for Steven to see that his mother and you are communicating?*

Exchanging routine information

In all early years settings routine information needs exchanging. In a home environment, the early years worker may need to note down that there has been a telephone call. In other settings, parents can tell the early years worker that their child is going to be collected by another parent. This type of information keeps the links between parent and early years worker strong and helps to build positive relationships. Routine information can either be spoken or written down. You will need to know how to pass on both types.

Spoken information is often exchanged at the start or end of a session. Whenever possible, we should use these moments of the day to praise children in front of their parents. It is reassuring for parents to feel their child is happy and has enjoyed the session. Furthermore, seeing that their child is seen as an individual gives them confidence in the early years setting.

The advantages of exchanging information in this way are:

- everyone is sure that the information has been received

- immediate action can be taken if needed – e.g. lost items can be looked for, parents can see work and queries can be answered straight away

- some people feel more at ease when they are talking and find it harder to write things down.

Handling spoken information. We need to record information that we receive or promptly pass it on to the appropriate person. If you think that you may forget what you have been told it may be a good idea to note it down at the time. This shows parents that you value what they are saying and it helps you to pass on the information accurately.

We also need to remember that information we receive may be confidential.

Think about it

Rosie's mum has taken time off work to take her to the dentist. She arrives to pick up Rosie in a taxi only to find that Rosie is not ready to come. She says that she had mentioned this to another member of staff. You are Rosie's key worker and no one had passed on the note to you.

In pairs:

1 *Write down how you think Rosie's mum feels.*
2 *What can you do to make Rosie's mum feel that this will not happen again?*
3 *What would you say to Rosie's mum?*
4 *Who should you talk to in the early years setting about this incident?*

Written information. Communicating in writing helps to maintain contact with parents who are unable to visit an early years setting often. There are many reasons for this and we cannot assume that this is through lack of interest – for example, children who live a long distance from a special needs school may be brought in by taxi or minibus. Some parents may work different hours from those of the early years setting and rely on other people to meet their children. As an early years worker, you will need to be able to write down notes to parents, although more formal letters and reports are often written by managers and supervisors.

Writing information. When we write information down, it needs to be clear, accurate and legible. If spelling is a problem, it is worth using a dictionary or checking with other adults. In some early years settings, there is a policy that all written communications are shown to the manager or supervisor before being sent out. Always keep a copy of any letters that you send in case they are needed in the future. If negative information needs to be shared, remember that most people tend to focus on negative comments and so we must be careful about what we write.

Case Study

Dear Mrs Martin

Just a quick note, to let you know that Simon will need some more nappies in the next few days. He seems much more settled now and he is just starting to make friends with one or two of the others in the toddler room.

I am looking forward to our meeting at the end of the week so that we can discuss his progress. How's the new job going?

Catherine
Nursery Assistant

Dear Mrs Martin

Simon will need some more nappies. After Friday, we will have run out so please make sure that you bring them in soon.

He no longer seems upset when you go, although he is only just making friends.

I will see you when you come in at the end of the week to talk about this.

Yours faithfully

Catherine
Nursery Assistant

1 Which letter would you prefer to receive?
2 Work out why these letters read so differently.

Knowledge into Action

Chris is three years old and can sometimes be aggressive. The early years setting has agreed to let his parents know how he is settling in. His key worker writes a brief note home each day because his parents are unable to bring him into the nursery. Today he has painted a picture, enjoyed playing in the sand with another boy, eaten his lunch and sat quietly at story time. He has also bitten another child who was trying to take a toy from him.

1 *In pairs, write a brief note to his parents which includes both the negative and positive information.*

The disadvantages of written communications. We need to be aware that some people may have difficulties in reading and writing and that they might not feel able to ask for help. We also need to remember that unless sent in the post, some written information may not reach parents as children can forget that they have been asked to pass something on. Some early years settings use noticeboards as a way of passing on information. They may put up a copy of a letter that they have sent out as a reminder for parents.

Types of routine written information

Written information	Why it is used	What is recorded
Letters	These are used to send out a variety of information – e.g. trips, concerts, parents evenings.	Letters can be named to check that each child has taken one. Some early years settings may add on a reply slip to collect responses.
Accident slips	These are sent home when children have had a minor injury or other problem – e.g. wetting themselves.	Basic information about the incident is recorded, including time of incident and any treatment/action taken.
Activity slips	These let parents know what children have done during the day or over a week.	Activity slips may include information about what children have enjoyed doing and how much they have eaten and slept.
Home books	Home books go between the home and early years setting. Both parents and childcare workers make comments in them. They are often used with children who have special needs and may not be able to communicate what they have been doing either at home or at school.	Home books may record what medication children have received, how they have slept as well as comments about what children have enjoyed doing and their behaviour and progress.
Newsletters	These give advance information about forthcoming events in the early years setting.	Newsletters may include dates for diaries and news about the early years setting. Some early years settings use newsletters to let parents know about the topics and themes that they are doing.
Notice boards	These can be put on walls outside or in entrances. They are often seen by parents who are waiting for their children.	Notice boards can act as reminders for parents – e.g. photograph money is due in or general information such as how to recognise head lice.

Portfolio activity

1   *Find out what types of written information are sent out by your early years setting.*
2   *Ask your supervisor if you can have a copy of some of them.*
3   *What is the policy on written information in your early years setting? For example, does the manager look at written notes and slips before they are sent out?*

DAILY ROUTINE

The Nursery opens at 8.00 am, the rooms having been already set out the night before in order to provide an inviting and attractive environment. Breakfast is served from 8.15 am until 9.15 am. This is an optional meal which serves a dual purpose in that it is available for children who have not yet eaten and it is a calm, welcoming start to the day.

9.15 am   While breakfast is cleared away the children are read a story, and the register is taken.

9.30 am   The children are split into two groups and are taken into the playrooms, where activities have been pre-planned and set up to meet all the diverse needs of each child in a freeplay session, and compliment all of the Desirable Learning Outcomes.

10.30 am   Children and staff clear away activities and tidy rooms, ready for milk time.

10.45 am   Drink time – this can be in individual rooms or staff and children can join together in a large group. Children are encouraged to share their news, sing songs and nursery rhymes, which helps promotes their language skills.

11.00 am   Theme time – Staff take their key children and carry out activities linked to our present theme. All these activities are carefully thought through and are age appropriate to each individual child.

11.20 am   Outdoor play (weather permitting), a wide range of transport vehicles are provided, along with climbing frames, slides and various other equipment. These are to help develop fine and gross motor skills and promote spatial awareness.

11.40 am   Bathroom – All children are taken to the bathroom to prepare for lunch.

12.00 pm   Lunch is served sitting in small family groups with their key carer. The children are encouraged to serve themselves (with supervision), from tureens in the centre of the table.

12.30 pm   Children are taken to the bathroom. One member of staff clears away the lunch and prepares the playrooms for the afternoon session whilst another member of staff sings songs and reads stories with the children.

12.45 pm   The morning session children are collected.

1.00 pm   Afternoon session children arrive.

1.15 pm   Register is taken. The children are split into two groups with the children attending school in September going into a pre-school group, whilst the younger children choose from a wide range of toys and activities that are made available using our toy plans, complementing the weekly theme.

2.45 pm   Children and staff clear away activities and tidy rooms.

3.00 pm   Outdoor play (weather permitting).

3.25 pm   Children go to the bathroom and wash hands ready for tea.

3.30 pm   Tea time – tea is served, although it is a lighter meal than lunch it is served in a very similar way although according to the tea it may be served in a tea circle without tables.

4.15 pm   Group time – When the nursery comes together in either one large group or smaller groups for singing, games, musical instruments, and drama. Observations are carried out to make sure children are reaching their full potential. (Parents/carers are welcome to see these at any time.)

5.00 pm   Children start going home so this is a more flexible time where we may put out the large apparatus or simply put out dressing up, puppets or other toys that the children particularly enjoy, these are promoting the Desirable Learning Outcomes and again will be complementing the theme of the week.

5.30 pm   Children and staff tidy up, then the children are taken for stories/musical tapes and computer work as this enables them to wind down for the end of the day.

The Nursery closes at 6.00 pm. Children start going home from approximately 4.00 pm. Although this is a typical daily routine we try to be as flexible as possible according to the individual needs of the children, encouraging positive self-esteem and learning through play.

Portfolio activity

Using a computer, design an activity slip that would give a parent information about their child's day. The slip needs to be attractive and easy to fill in.

Emergency numbers

There are times when parents need to be contacted quickly. For example, if a child needs medical attention, or due to a power failure at the early years setting.

As part of the admissions procedure, parents are asked to leave emergency contact numbers and addresses which can be stored in a central place – for example, an office. In home environments, parents may leave these names and numbers in an agreed place. From time to time, emergency numbers need to be checked to see if they are still accurate.

There are also times when parents may need to contact us so they need the telephone/fax number of the early years setting. Telephones need to be answered promptly in case a parent needs to make urgent contact.

Communicating in an emergency Passing on information over the phone needs to be done in such a way that unnecessary worry is not caused.

- Stay calm.

- Check that you are talking to the correct person.

- State who you are and your role.

- Briefly explain why you are phoning.

- Explain what the early years setting is doing.

- If you have to leave a message, give a contact number so the parent can ring back.

Knowledge into Action

You are caring for a three-year-old child, who has just been sick. He has a high temperature and you need to contact his parents.

In pairs, work out what you would say at each stage of this situation.

Do this as a role play.

1 *You telephone the workplace number, but you are told that the parent's phone is engaged.*
2 *You wait for another five minutes and are told they are in an important meeting.*
3 *You speak to the parent.*

3 Your role in relating to parents

Ways in which early years settings involve parents

Every early years setting develops its own ways of involving parents. These vary according to the differing needs of the community and early years setting. As an early years worker working in an early years setting, you may be involved in some of these events.

Common ways in which early years settings try to make contact with parents include:

- encouraging parents to come into the early years setting as helpers

- open days and afternoons

- working with parents to fundraise

- running workshops on topics such as reading or play

- having parents' evenings or consultations

- holding concerts, children's parties and other events.

Parents as helpers. Most early years settings recognise the benefits that different people can bring into the early years setting. Children benefit from the extra attention and some parents may have skills they can share with children and staff – for example, they may draw, dance or sew.

Parents who do not share the same language or values of the early years setting and who want to be involved with the early years setting are particularly welcome. They can extend the knowledge and awareness of children and staff. They might cook with children or bring in books and objects that the children are not familiar with.

Some parents may help regularly, while others might wish to come in from time to time to help – for example, with a concert or an outing. New parents who come in as helpers can feel reassured to see the early years setting in action and may enjoy meeting other parents who know the early years setting well.

Open days and afternoons. These are times when parents can come in and see what is happening in the early years setting. Children can show their parents around, introduce them to their friends and show them what they have been doing. Parents and staff can often talk to each other without appointments and may use this as an occasion to share information. Open days and afternoons can also be times for parents to meet each other. This is often useful for new parents and those who might be isolated in the community – for example, parents who do not share the language or culture of the area.

Parents as fundraisers. Many early years settings have committees that try to raise money for equipment and materials. It is a chance for parents and staff to

Think about it

A new parent is coming into the nursery to help for the first time today. She is new to the area and has just started bringing her child to the early years setting. She says that she doesn't mind what she is asked to do.

Mckenzie heritage picture archive/Jeni Mckenzie

Choose one task from the list for this parent to do and write why you think that it is suitable.

- Wash the cups in the kitchen.
- Play lotto with a group of four children.
- Supervise the painting area with another parent.
- Accompany children to the toilet.
- Read a story to a small group.
- Tidy the book corner and repair books.

work together and helps parents feel they are contributing and are part of the early years setting. Some parents find that helping to raise money is also a way of making new friends among other parents.

Workshops. Many early years settings run workshops on such topics as reading, play or maths. These can be held in the evening to allow those parents who cannot visit the early years setting during the day to attend. The workshops help the early years setting to explain the work they are doing with the children.

Parents consultations/parents' evenings. All schools and most early years settings have times when parents are invited to talk to the staff about the progress of their children. Sometimes these are held early in a school year to allow parents and staff to discuss how their children are settling in. Some parents feel nervous about coming to parents' evenings. We must be sensitive to how they are feeling and look for ways to reassure them about their child. The aim of these sessions should be to look for ways to work together in helping the child.

Concerts, children's parties and other events. Most early years settings hold events where parents are invited to watch their children or be with them. Concerts help bring people together – staff, children and parents – in a pleasant and fun way.

Admission procedures

Starting or changing a new early years setting is a big step for children and parents. The aim of admission procedures is to ensure that this happens as smoothly as possible. Admission procedures vary from early years setting to early years setting but most early years settings do some or all of the things in the table below.

Leaflet or brochure	Sent or given to parents before their child starts. Gives written information – e.g. session times, policies on behaviour.
Initial visits	Parents, with or without children, look around the early years setting, meet staff and have the opportunity to ask questions.
Admission forms	These ask for children' addresses, emergency contact numbers and any other information that can help the early years setting to meet children's needs – e.g. medication, diet.
New parents' evening or afternoon	At these sessions parents can find out more about the aims and values of the early years setting as well as meet other new parents.
Home visits	Early years workers visit children and parents at home before they start. Having met the early years worker in the children's home can help them to settle in more quickly. Parents may feel more at ease to ask questions.
Contract	Some early years settings have contracts that set out the fees, arrangements and responsibilities – e.g. who is responsible for providing food, drink and nappies.
Individual discussion/interview	These are often held between the parent and the supervisor. Plans for settling in children are discussed and parents can pass on any information they think may be useful.

Sharing information with parents is particularly important when children first start in an early years setting. Parents need to find out how their children are settling in and they may also need to find out more about the routine of the day or about what their child has been doing. In many early years settings the child's key worker or the supervisor will talk to parents, as they are responsible for that child. If you are a key worker for a child, you will need to keep a note of how that child is settling in and make sure that you can give accurate information to parents.

Case Study

Anya has started in the nursery and you are her key worker. Anya is quiet, but is joining in the activities, although she likes to keep close to you. She loves the sand and water areas of the nursery. At meal times, she eats nearly all of her food and this week she has started to join in more with the other children. You are seeing her mother to discuss how she is settling in.

Questions

1 *Why is it important to ask Anya's mother how she thinks Anya is settling in?*
2 *What would you say to Anya's mother about her progress?*
3 *Why is it important that key workers are honest about how children are settling in?*

(You may do this activity in pairs.)

Other types of information requested by parents

There are times when parents may ask for other information they need – for example, benefits, health topics. A mother might be expecting twins and might ask if there is a support group. Helping parents to get the information they need is one way of showing them we value them and wish to support them. It is important that any information we give is as accurate as possible. Sometimes we may have to say that we are unsure and offer to ask someone else in the early years setting.

Portfolio activity

Choose one of the following topics and collect together as much written information about it.

Lone-parent benefit   Council tax

Asthma   Giving up smoking

Sources of information

Every area has its own sources of information – for example, local radio and newspapers – and where possible it is a good idea to find out what sort of advice is available in your area. The table below shows some common places to find information.

Sources of information	Type of information available
Telephone book	Most telephone books have a section called 'Useful Numbers' at the front. This includes the numbers of the social security offices, hospitals and advice lines.
Library	Libraries have a range of leaflets from government departments as well as charities.
Citizen's Advice Bureau	These are centres where people can see someone to get advice about many topics – e.g. housing, benefits, debt and divorce. The advice is confidential and free. Appointments are not always necessary to get advice.
Health centres, clinics and doctors surgeries	Most of the leaflets available are about medical conditions or support groups. Appointments to see a doctor or nurse are generally necessary to get advice.
Chemists	Local community information is often available.
Help lines	Help lines are run by many organisations – e.g. charities and health authorities. The help lines are meant to give immediate advice or information to the caller – e.g. Crysis, a help line for parents whose babies keep crying. Some numbers are free and some are charged at local rate.

Understanding the role of early years workers in relation to parents

In order to relate well to parents, it is important for early years workers to understand their exact role where parents are concerned. The key point when working in an early years setting is always to ask if you are unsure.

MAPLEHURST NURSERY
Confidentiality Policy

The nursery's work with children and families will sometimes bring us into contact with confidential information.

To ensure that all those using and working in the nursery can do so with confidence, we will respect confidentiality in the following ways.

- Parents will have ready access to the files and records of their own children, but will not have access to information about any other child.
- Staff will not discuss individual children, other than for purposes of curriculum planning/group management, with people other than the parents/carers of that child.
- Information given to the nursery manager or key worker by the parents/carers will not be passes on to other adults without permission.
- Issues to do with the employment of staff, whether paid or unpaid, will remain confidential to the people directly involved with making personal decisions.
- Any anxieties/evidence relating to a child's personal safety will be kept in a confidential file and will not be shared within the group except with the child's keyworker/manager and the nursery director.
- Students on any recognised courses observing in the nursery will be advised of our confidentiality policy and required to respect it.

All the undertakings above are subject to the paramount commitment of the nursery which is to the safety and well-being of the child.

Confidentiality. For any good relationship to work there needs to be some trust. To trust somebody is to expect them to keep things they have seen or been told confidential. Learning how much you are allowed to repeat and who to repeat it to is an important part of being a professional. As an early years worker you will learn a lot about children's home life, their achievements, parents etc. This information will be shared with you because you are expected to keep it confidential, discussing it only with people who are permitted to know. Years of work in building good parent relationships can be put at risk if, through thoughtlessness or temptation, an early years worker repeats information to inappropriate people.

As confidentiality is a complex, yet important, area most early years settings have a policy and in some cases it may be part of a written contract.

Good practice – confidentiality

✔ Regard all information learnt about children, parents and staff in the workplace as confidential.

✔ Understand and refer to the early years setting's policy on confidentiality.

✔ If you are unsure whether you can repeat something ask a more experienced worker.

✔ Think before you speak! Most breaches of confidentiality happen because of thoughtlessness.

✔ Never make a promise to keep something confidential if the information will affect the well-being of children. Your first duty is the welfare of children.

Being friendly is not the same as being friends. However often we see a parent, we must not confuse being friendly with being friends. We work with parents in the interests of children. To do this we need to show respect for parents and aim to provide them with as much support as possible. Our relationship is a professional one.

There may be times when you already know a parent of a child who attends the early years setting where you work. We must remember that while we are in the workplace we must treat all the parents with equal respect and fairness. This professional approach avoids possible comments about favouritism from other staff or parents.

Finding the right balance can be difficult for nannies who live with the parents of the children they care for as when they are 'off duty' they are sharing the family home.

Think about it

You have started working as a daily nanny for a lone-parent family. One day the parent returns from work with some flowers and he asks you if you would like to go out for a friendly drink some time as a thank you for your hard work.

1 *Why might it make your job harder if you accept the offer?*
2 *How can you handle this situation without appearing rude?*

Understanding your role in relation to parents in the early years setting

How much information you should receive or give out will depend on your position in the workplace. In most early years settings there is a line of management. This means that there are rules in place to make sure that the confidentiality of either the parents or the early years setting is not broken. The table below outlines the roles of different people who work in early years settings. If you are unsure about your role, you should ask advice from your supervisor or tutor.

Job	Role in relation to parents
Student	Students are not members of staff and they must not give this impression to parents. If parents ask them for information they must refer them to a staff member. They need to be friendly, yet understand the early years settings' code of confidentiality. They need to work under the direction of their supervisor.
New member of staff	New members of staff need to form relationships with existing parents. They need to appear confident and friendly. New members of staff need to learn about the general routine of the day quickly and to work under the direction of senior members of staff. At times they may need to refer to other members of staff to check that the information they are giving is correct or appropriate. They must know when to refer parents to children's key workers or their supervisors – e.g. if a parent wishes to find out more about their child's progress.
Key worker	Key workers need to form close relationships with the children they are responsible for and with their parents. They must make sure they are keeping up-to-date records and can show a good knowledge of the children when discussing them with parents. The information they keep about the children is confidential and is likely to be discussed only with parents and their manager. They need to work closely with their manager/supervisor.
Supervisor/manager	The supervisor or manager of the early years setting needs to know all the children and their parents well. Because they are responsible for all that happens in the early years setting, they need to be kept up-to-date with any incidents that happen during the day. This means they can discuss them with knowledge to parents if necessary – e.g. if a child is feeling unwell or has fallen over. They will also have access to all information available about the children, including emergency contact numbers.

Portfolio activity

Think of a time when you were approached by parents in your workplace and you referred them to a member of staff.

1   *Write about how you addressed them and made them feel valued.*
2   *Why did you decide that they should be referred to a member of staff?*

Make sure that when you write about this that you do not breach any confidential information.

Unit test

Quick quiz

1   A mother asks if she could have the address of another parent. The early years worker should:
    a   give the parent the address
    b   ask the parent why she wants the address
    c   ask the other parent if she wants her address given out
    d   give the parent the phone number instead of the address.

2 A parent ask an early years worker if they could look after the child after the session finishes. The early years worker should:
    a refer the parent to the supervisor
    b agree to the request
    c ask the parent why they need the extra time
    d politely tell the parent that this is not possible.

3 A child lives with her mother, step father and his children. This is an example of:
    a a nuclear family
    b a reconstituted family
    c a lone-parent family
    d an extended family.

4 Parental responsibility is automatically given to:
    a all fathers
    b parents who are married at the time of the birth
    c parents who are living together
    d anyone who is caring for children.

5 Before sending out a letter to a parent, an early years worker should always:
    a check spellings
    b show the letter to lots of other people
    c keep a copy of the letter
    d make sure that the information given is accurate.

6 Parents are encouraged to help in early years settings because:
    a they can do some of the clearing away
    b fewer staff are then needed
    c children enjoy meeting other children's mothers
    d staff and parents can get to know each other.

Short answer questions

1 Why should you find out how parents wish to be addressed?

2 Give three examples of family structures.

3 What is meant by the term 'open door' policy?

4 Give two example of barriers to communication.

5 Name three sources of information on health topics.

Understanding Children's Behaviour

In the first years of their lives, children have a lot to learn. They become mobile, learn physical skills and start to communicate. At the same time, children have to learn behaviour that is acceptable way to the society that they live in. This is a gradual learning process because we are not born with self-control and consideration for others. It is also an essential process because acceptance by others is linked to behaviour.

An important part of your role as an early years worker will be promoting what is, in our society, seen as desirable behaviour.

This chapter is divided into three sections: the first section looks at how children learn behaviour and your role in promoting acceptable behaviour; the second section looks at ways of managing unwanted behaviour; the third section looks at reasons why children might show inappropriate behaviour and ways of recording and assessing this behaviour.

Expectations

Expectations of behaviour vary between countries and also change over time. For example, thirty years ago it was considered rude to eat in the street, whereas today, people often eat burgers or crisps while walking along. There are also cultural variations – for example, in some cultures food is eaten with the fingers while in others this is considered bad manners.

A good starting point when thinking about promoting children's behaviour is to consider our own expectations of behaviour. We all have different opinions about what is acceptable behaviour in children. Most of our ideas about what is and is not acceptable come from our own experiences and culture.

Think about it

Decide whether you agree or disagree with the following statements.

1   *Children under eight years old should not answer the telephone.*
2   *At about six years old children should choose what to wear.*
3   *Children should ask if they wish to leave the table during a meal.*
4   *Children should give up their seats on buses to let adults sit down.*
5   *If a three-year-old child does not eat up a meal they should not be given pudding.*

You may like to do this activity with some other people and see if their answers are the same as yours.

As views on behaviour can vary, you need to understand the expectations in the early years setting where you work. Many group settings have policies relating to behaviour but if you are looking after children in a home environment you should talk to the parents about the types of behaviour they consider acceptable. There will be many differences in expected behaviour between group settings and the home environment. For example, some children at home may be allowed to leave the table as soon as they have finished eating, whereas in a busy nursery staff may not be free to supervise children in another room so the children would have to wait until everyone had finished the meal.

What is good behaviour?

Learning to respect other people is the key to good behaviour in our society. To do this children need to learn some self-control as good behaviour stems from thinking of others and their needs as well as our own. This means that children need to be able to share, take turns, listen to others and be courteous and helpful.

How children learn behaviour

Chapter 7 (pages 134–7) looked at how children learn. Some of the theories about how children learn can also explain how they learn to behave.

Social learning theory suggests that children copy the behaviour of adults and later of other children.

This theory is widely accepted and is extremely important in understanding children's behaviour. It means that children learn desirable and undesirable behaviour from watching adults. For example, children who hear adults swearing may try out swear words while children who see an adult open a door for another adult may copy this behaviour.

Linking theory to practice

- You can teach children about desirable behaviour through your actions. For example, if children hear you saying please and thank you, they are likely to copy this. Children can learn how to be thoughtful by seeing you act in a kind, caring way towards other children, staff and parents.

- If children see adults who have an aggressive manner, they think this is acceptable. This means that you should not shout at children, as they will learn that being aggressive is a good way to get what you want. In order to help children settle their disputes you need to show them how adults co-operate with each other.

Think about it

Is this child learning how to help others?

Are you a good role model for children?

Think about the following statements.

1 *I always say hello or good morning to the people around me.*
2 *I offer to help other staff members set up or tidy away.*
3 *I always share sweets or other such food.*
4 *I always say please and thank you.*
5 *I am patient.*
6 *I like to help people.*
7 *I listen to other people's points of view.*
8 *I am tidy and organised.*

How many of them are true for you?

Behaviourist theory suggests that behaviour is repeated if children get some type of reward. Psychologists call rewards **positive reinforcement**. These can be in the form of enjoyment, praise, money or food but they can also be in the form of attention. Getting the attention of adults is often important for children. A child who receives praise from an adult while helping another child to pick up toys is more likely to repeat this behaviour. Unfortunately, children also show undesirable behaviour to get adult's attention. If they are successful in gaining the attention, they will repeat the behaviour.

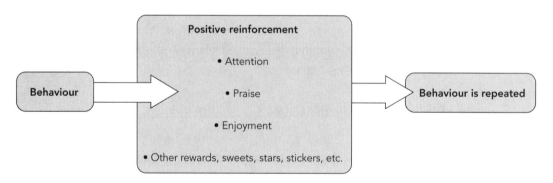

Linking theory to practice

■ Using 'rewards' to help children show desirable behaviour is extremely effective. One of the strongest rewards is praise and encouragement. This means that in our day-to-day practice, we should praise children often, making it clear why we are praising them. For example, saying 'Well done, that is kind of you to share the dough.' is better than simply saying 'Well done.'

■ We can also prevent undesirable behaviour from becoming a habit by not giving attention for it. For example, a toddler might squeal at a high pitch. If the squeal attracts attention then it is more likely to be repeated.

ALL SAINTS JUNIOR SCHOOL
(Church of England Aided)

𝕬chievement 𝕬ward

presented to

Anne-Marie Tassoni

for

excellent vocabulary work

8/11/96
Date

Claire M. Ockwell

*Certificates like this encourage
children to repeat behaviour or actions*

Consistency is important. If children learn that *sometimes* they can get adult attention or other 'rewards' for inappropriate behaviour, it is still worthwhile to them to behave this way as there is a possibility that they will get what they want. On the other hand, if children never get the attention or reward, they will learn that there is no point in showing this behaviour.

Case Study

In the quiet corner there are a few cushions. The children take turns to sit on the cushions. Michael is sitting on the cushion when it is not his turn. The adult decides not to say anything this time, although Michael has been told before that he should wait his turn.

Questions

1   *What has Michael learnt by nothing being said?*
2   *What have the other children in the group learnt by seeing Michael on the cushions?*
3   *Why is it important that all members of a team expect the same behaviour?*

Self-fulfilling prophecy theory suggests that the way adults think about children will influence how the children behave. An adult who believes a child is 'good' will influence the behaviour of that child and the child is likely to show 'appropriate' behaviour. On the other hand, if an adult believes a child is 'naughty and difficult' the child is more likely to behave that way.

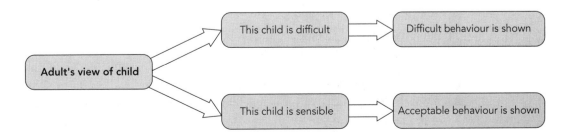

Theory into practice

- The self-fulfilling prophecy theory means that in our day-to-day practice, we should be extremely positive towards children. Children who feel they can meet our expectations are more likely to show appropriate behaviour. This needs to be shown in our comments and body language. Smiling and praise are good ways of showing children that we value them.

- When we need to discipline children, we should make it clear that it is their actions that we are unhappy about, not themselves. Words such as 'naughty' do not help children to believe they can be 'good'.

- We should also not judge children before we get to know them as this can influence the way we think about them. This is why stereotyping families and labelling children can be so damaging. It can mean that adults are looking for problems when they should be making children feel positive about themselves.

Think about it

You have just started working in a nursery. One of the other assistants says to you:

'Keep an eye out for Luke. He's bags of trouble and you'll need to be firm with him.'

1 *Why could this remark change your attitude towards this boy?*
2 *How should you act when you meet him?*

Collections/Anthea Sieveking

Tantrums – often a result of frustration

How age and stage of development affects behaviour

Learning desirable behaviour is a gradual process for children. Being able to share and think of other people cannot happen until children have some communication and cognitive skills. Children also find it hard to share and play well with children until they are able to control their feelings.

As early years workers we need to judge what level of behaviour is appropriate for the children we work with – for example, children under the age of three find it difficult to share toys without adult help. Expecting too much of children can mean they fail and

Age	Stage of development	Goals for behaviour	Role of adult
1–2 years	• Actively explores environment • Imitates adults in simple tasks • Repeats actions that gain attention • Alternates between clinginess and independence • No understanding that toys or other objects may belong to others	• To play alongside other children (parallel play) • To carry out simple instructions such as 'Can you find your coat?'	**Good supervision** is necessary as children of this age do not understand the dangers around them. **Distraction** works well in stopping unwanted behaviour as children often forget what they were doing – e.g. if a child wants another child's toy, offer them a different one instead. **Praise** is needed for children to understand how to get adult's attention in positive ways and to develop good self-esteem. Being a good role model is important as children learn behaviour through imitating those around them.
2–3 years	• Easily frustrated and may have tantrums • Dislikes adult attention being given to other children • No understanding for the need to wait • Finds sharing difficult • Rapid physical and emotional learning • Tries to be independent	• To wait for needs to be met – e.g. at meal times • To share toys or food with one other child with adult help • To play alongside other children • To sit and share a story for five minutes • To say please and thank you if reminded • To follow simple instructions with help such as 'Wash your hands.'	**Good supervision** and anticipation are the keys to working with this age range. Children are trying to be independent, but lack some of the physical and cognitive skills they need. This makes them frustrated and angry. Adults need to anticipate possible sources of frustration and support children either by offering help or by distracting them – e.g. a child who is trying to put their coat on may need an adult to make a game of it so the child does not become frustrated. **Praise and encouragement** are needed for children to learn what behaviour adults expect from them. Some unwanted behaviour that is not dangerous should be ignored so that children do not learn to use it as a way of getting adult attention. **Consistency** is needed as children will try to work out what the limits are on their behaviour. **Being a good role model** helps children as they model their behaviour on others around them. This is especially important at this age as children act out their experiences through play.
3–4 years	• Follows simple rules by imitating other children – e.g. collects aprons before painting • Able to communicate wishes • Enjoys activities such as painting • Enjoys being with other children • Can play co-operatively • Enjoys helping adults	• To follow rules in games when helped by adult – e.g. playing lotto • To say please and thank you often without reminder • To take turns and share equipment • To follow adults' instructions most of the time – e.g. 'Let Simon have a turn.' • To help tidy away	**Praise and encouragement** builds children's confidence and makes them more likely to show desirable behaviour. **Explanation** of rules should be given as children are more likely to remember and understand them. **Good supervision** is still needed as, although children are able to do many things for themselves, they are still unaware of the dangers around them. Most of the time children will be able to play well together, but squabbles will still break out. **Being a good role model** will help children learn the social skills they need to resolve arguments and express their feelings.

Age	Stage of development	Goals for behaviour	Role of adult
4–5 years	• Plays with other children without help from adults • Is able to communicate feelings and wishes • Understands the needs for rules	• To ask permission to use other children's toys • To comfort playmates in distress • To say please and thank you without a reminder • To tidy up after activities	**Providing activities and tasks** that are stimulating and allow children to develop confidence is important. Children of this age are keen to help adults and enjoy being busy. Tasks such as laying the table or getting objects allow children to feel independent. **Praise and encouragement** help children feel good about themselves. This is important because they are often starting school at this time. Children need to feel that they can be 'good'. **Explanation** helps children to remember and understand the need for rules or decisions. Being a good role model helps children to learn social skills they will copy what they see.
5–8 years	• Has strong friendships • Can argue back • Copies behaviour of other children – e.g. may swear or spit • Understands the needs for rules and plays games that have rules • Understands the difference between right and wrong • Has many self-help skills – e.g. getting dressed, wiping up spills	• To follow instructions from adults • To apologise to others • To listen to others **From six years onwards:** • To work independently and quietly in educational settings • To be helpful and thoughtful	**Praise and encouragement** means that children do not look for other ways of gaining attention. Praise is needed as children become more aware of others and compare themselves critically. **Explanation** helps children to understand the reasons for rules and decisions. Children should also be made to consider the effect of their actions on others. As children become older they are likely to argue back and so clear boundaries are needed and must be enforced. **Being a good role model** is still important as children will try to understand more about the adults they are with. Speech and actions are modelled increasingly on adults that children admire. **Providing activities and responsibilities** can help children 'mature' as they learn more about their capabilities. Small responsibilities help children to become independent as well as giving them confidence – e.g. they may be asked to tidy areas of an early years setting or pour out drinks for other children.

therefore come to believe they are not 'good'. In the same way, if expectations are too low children will not develop appropriate behaviour.

The chart above outlines the behaviour of children in relation to their development; it also shows the role of the adult in promoting such behaviour. However, as with any developmental chart, it must be seen as a guide as children vary enormously in their development.

Think about it

Look at these examples and consider whether these types of behaviour are usual for these ages of the children.

1 *A four-year-old pushes another child down the slide.*
2 *A five-year-old has a temper tantrum because she wants the red crayon and another child has it.*
3 *A two-year-old snatches a biscuit from another child.*
4 *A three-year-old refuses to help tidy up.*
5 *A three-year-old cannot sit still and listen to a short story.*
6 *An eight-year-old takes another child's toy home deliberately.*

Knowledge into Action

Ask your supervisor if you can observe a child in your workplace.

1 *Record the age of the child.*
2 *Make notes about the behaviour that you see.*
3 *How does this child's behaviour compare to the chart above?*

Children with particular needs

When children's development is delayed in one or more areas, they may find it harder to meet some of the goals in the chart. Some children may not have the cognitive or language skills necessary to show social skills such as sharing and turntaking.

Sometimes children with particular needs are aggressive – for example, they might bite, throw toys or hit others. Aggressive behaviour is often linked to frustration as children either cannot express their needs or are dependent on others to meet these needs. This means that early years workers need to get to know the children they work with well and supervise them carefully. By doing this, early years workers can often prevent inappropriate behaviour.

Case Study

Peter is six years old and has a speech impairment that means he cannot always make himself understood. He is able to understand other people.

He is standing by the slide when another boy pushes in. He tries to tell him that it is his turn, but the other child does not move. He kicks the other child.

Questions
1 *Is this a normal reaction for a six-year-old?*
2 *Why did Peter react in this way?*
3 *Why might Peter need an adult to be with him at play times?*

Setting goals and boundaries

To be able to show appropriate behaviour, children need to understand what is expected of them. Adults can do this by setting goals and boundaries for them. Goals are targets for behaviour – for example, saying please when something is wanted. Early years workers can show that this is a goal by reminding children to say please and then praising them.

Boundaries are limits on behaviour. They are often simple rules that children know must not be broken. Boundaries must be clearly set so children understand what they can and cannot do. For example, an adult might say 'You may play in the sand, but you must not throw it'. Most boundaries are there to protect children – for example, doors should never be slammed because someone might get hurt.

Ways of setting goals and boundaries include:

FIVE CHILDREN CAN PLAY IN THE HOME CORNER

- Telling children – in a positive way – what is expected of them before they begin an activity – e.g. 'When you have finished feeding the guinea pig, you will need to wash your hands.'

- Writing rules down – e.g. 'No more than four children at the water tray.'

- Reminding children – e.g. 'What must we do when we have finished our paintings?'

Policies in the workplace

Boundary and goal setting work best when everyone involved with the children is in agreement. This is because children are quick to discover any differences in expectations – for example, 'Mrs James said I can . . .!' It is important for children to see that boundaries and goals do not change from day to day. The expectations of adults need to be consistent so children do not feel they must keep testing them.

It is for this reason that most workplaces have a policy on managing children's behaviour. Most policies outline the strategies to be adopted by members of staff and give direction as to what a staff member should do if a child becomes disruptive. This can vary from setting to setting depending on the age of the children, although physical punishment and restraints must never be used and are often expressly forbidden in policy documents.

Good supervision is also an essential tool in promoting children's behaviour. Incidents are more likely to occur when children are unsupervised or bored with activities. For example, a child throwing sand might encourage other children to start doing the same, unless an adult intervenes.

MAPLEHURST NURSERY

DISCIPLINE POLICY

Maplehurst Nursery's discipline policy is based on the National Children's Homes principles. Following staff discussions about discipline it was felt these principles reflected our views and stated them in a clear and concise manner. As a staff body we are trying to create an environment where children, parents and staff all value, respect and care for each other. We believe the principles listed below i.e.:

> set boundaries, consistency, a need for security, praise and sensitivity

will help build a happy and relaxed atmosphere.

This nursery does not use corporal punishment.

Appendix to Principle. No.8.

It was felt after discussion, that the need to say 'sorry' was important but only if the child was capable of understanding what 'being sorry' means.

1. Always reject the behaviour, not the child. Never label a child as bad or naughty either to her or him or to someone else in their hearing – they will live up to it!

2. Give direction and correction to children in a positive way, e.g. – 'keep the sand in the sand tray' not 'don't drop sand on the floor.'

3. Give praise as often as possible – notice behaviour you like and remark on it.

4. Set limits. Children need to be secure in knowing you will not let either their behaviour or their feelings get out of control. You will neither let them hurt or be hurt.

MAPLEHURST NURSERY

DISCIPLINE POLICY CONTD.

5. Be consistent. The same reaction to the same situation each time gives children a feeling of security. You give them the power to predict the future and an ability to avoid unhappy situations.

6. Do what you have said.
   Do not threaten what you can't do.
   Build up trust.

7. When talking to children about their behaviour be close, calm and at their level.

8. Never make a child say 'sorry'

   (a) It's an excellent excuse for not getting into trouble.

   (b) You may just be teaching them to lie.

   (c) You may get yourself into a no win situation – you can't force a child to talk.

9. Make children sensitive to their own feelings and other people's. Feed back how they are feeling e.g. 'You look angry to me'. Give them different options of how to express it or deal with it. Get them to be aware that other people have feelings. Point out physical signs – tears, smiles and ask them to remember how they felt when they did the same.

10. Sometimes there isn't time for reasoning. Children need to recognise an adult's authority and respond to a 'No'.

Portfolio activity

Give a written example of how you have promoted children's behaviour by using praise.

1 *What was the situation?*
2 *What did you say to the child?*
3 *How did the child react?*

Intervening when children show unwanted behaviour

There are times when unwanted behaviour must be stopped, although early years workers should aim to create a positive atmosphere so that unwanted behaviour is rare. Distraction, praise and good supervision are, in the long term, the best ways of managing children's behaviour.

You should always intervene when:

- children are putting themselves in danger

- children are putting others in danger

- children are making racial or other offensive remarks.

There are many ways in which we can show children that their behaviour is unwanted.

Strategies for managing unwanted behaviour

Eye contact and facial expression are good ways of clearly showing that behaviour is not appropriate. Eye contact needs to be held with the child. Use praise once the act has stopped.

No! This one word can be effective, providing it is not over used. Children must also learn that 'no' means 'no' – if they have heard the word and then been able to carry on with their behaviour, it will have no value. Use praise once the act has stopped and explain why the behaviour was unacceptable.

Explaining the consequences of actions helps children to understand why they must not carry on with their behaviour and what will happen if they do. For example, children who are throwing balls at a window must be told that the window might break and if they carry on the balls will be taken away from them. It is important that if a sanction has been threatened it is carried out. Do not impose sanctions that you cannot justify or carry out.

Removal of equipment is a final measure, and may be used when children are putting themselves or others in danger – for example, if a child is hitting another with a bat. Children should be told why the equipment is being removed and when they are likely to be able to use it again.

Time out is often used with older children who are not coping with a situation. The idea is that children are given some time to calm down before returning to the situation. This technique can work quite well, although it should not be used as a punishment as once children feel they are 'naughty' and excluded, they are less likely to show appropriate behaviour. Remember that children with good self-esteem are more likely to show desirable behaviour.

Case Study

Aklim and George are four years old and are playing with the sand. George starts tipping it over the side and onto the floor. Aklim starts to copy him, but also throws it in the air. The adult walks over to them and asks them to stop it explaining that sand can get in eyes and be painful. A moment later they start throwing the sand again.

Questions

1 *Why is it important for the adult to intervene again?*
2 *How should the adult intervene this time?*

Attention-seeking behaviour

Specific types of unwanted behaviour

There are some specific types of behaviour that early years workers may need to deal with. If children are showing behaviour that is of concern – for example, self-destructive behaviour such as head-banging – you should always talk to your supervisor (or parents if you are working in a home environment).

Unwanted behaviour in children

Attention seeking	Many children show attention-seeking behaviour at times. It can be a sign of insecurity or in some cases mean that children have become used to having a lot of adult attention. There are many ways in which children show this type of behaviour – e.g. answering back, making noises, challenging instructions.	• It is often best to ignore attention-seeking behaviour unless it is dangerous, as by challenging it you may be teaching children that they can get attention this way. • Plenty of praise when children are showing appropriate behaviour can teach them the right way to get your attention.
Destructive behaviour	Some children may show aggressive behaviour towards their surroundings and others. This can be a sign of frustration or unhappiness, but it is important that children are not allowed to become out of control, as this is very frightening for them and teaches them that there are no limits on behaviour.	• You should stay calm when dealing with children who are aggressive. It is important that they can see that you are in control of the situation. • Talk quietly, but firmly to them. It is often best to take them to a quiet place where they can calm down. (If you are in a large setting you may need to ask another member of staff for help.) • Once children have calmed down, it is important to find out what has upset them and also to make sure that they understand that their behaviour is unacceptable.
Name calling, swearing and other offensive remarks	Children who call names and make offensive remarks are often repeating comments that they have heard. Remarks such as 'fatty' or 'stupid' need to be challenged, but in such a way that children are not blamed for what they have said.	• You should ask children where they have heard the remark. • Explain that it is hurtful and why. • Tell children that these comments are not to be made in the setting.

Portfolio activity

When managing unwanted behaviour, you must make sure that you are following the early years setting's policy.

1   *Give an example of how you have intervened when children have shown unwanted behaviour.*
2   *Write about the circumstances and why you decided to intervene.*
3   *How did you handle the situation?*

Factors affecting children's behaviour

There are many factors that affect children's behaviour. It is important for early years workers to recognise these factors so that expectations of behaviour and ways of managing behaviour are appropriate for the circumstances of the children.

How changes in children's lives can affect their behaviour

Children tend to react to such changes in different ways depending on their age and their understanding of the situation. In some situations – for example, when a new baby arrives – children need reassurance that they are still loved. In other situations – for example, when there is a change of carer – children may try to test out the boundaries and see whether the limits are still the same.

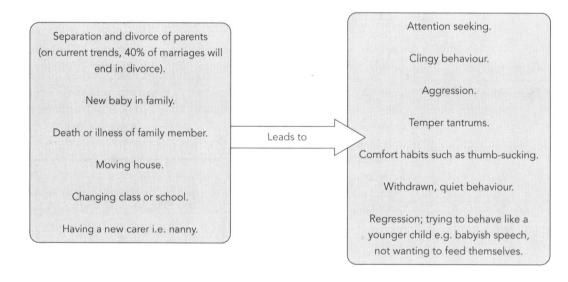

Separation and divorce of parents (on current trends, 40% of marriages will end in divorce).

New baby in family.

Death or illness of family member.

Moving house.

Changing class or school.

Having a new carer i.e. nanny.

Leads to

Attention seeking.

Clingy behaviour.

Aggression.

Temper tantrums.

Comfort habits such as thumb-sucking.

Withdrawn, quiet behaviour.

Regression; trying to behave like a younger child e.g. babyish speech, not wanting to feed themselves.

Knowledge into Action

Children are more likely to show unwanted behaviour when they are hungry, tired or have been unable to run around because of the weather.

In your workplace are there any points in the day or week when children are more likely to show unwanted behaviour?

Reporting and recording incidents

When serious unwanted behaviour occurs – for example, if a child bites another – a record must be kept. The date and time of the incident, names of those involved and the action taken need to be noted. If there were any injuries as a result of the behaviour, these must be recorded in an accident book (see Chapter 3, page 67). Any written records are confidential and should be stored safely. It is often useful to ask children what made them behave in the way they did. There may be reasons that we are not aware of – for example, another incident earlier in the day that has made the child react.

Assessing children's behaviour

If a child persistently behaves in a way that is unusual and problematic we need to find out as much information as possible about why it is happening. There may be a trigger to the behaviour – for example, something may be happening at home and we are seeing a reaction to it. The two key ways to assess children's behaviour are:

1   to record behaviour

2   to talk to parents and other professionals.

Once information has been collected, an action plan can be drawn up.

Recording children's behaviour

Where children's behaviour is a cause for concern, you may be asked to carry out an observation and keep a diary of a child's behaviour. These records may be used to form an assessment on a child and this means that you must be accurate in your recording. One method of recording children's behaviour is called an event sample.

The aim of an event sample is to record each occurrence of the type of behaviour that is causing concern. For example, if a child is biting other children, you may be asked to note it down each time. The record shows *what* happened, *who* the child was with at the time and *how* the incident was handled.

Event samples allow early years workers and other professionals to build up a picture of a child's behaviour as sometimes there may be a pattern emerging.

Working with parents and other professionals

There are many professionals who may be involved in helping children whose behaviour is not appropriate. Children are often referred to these professionals by their family doctor or by their parents after concerns have been raised.

Where parents and other professionals are involved in assessing children's behaviour, a team meeting may be called. This allows everyone to contribute so that a picture of the behaviour can be built up. Early years workers may be asked

Case Study

The staff at the nursery were concerned that Jo was aggressive towards other children. Jo is nearly five years old. The staff completed an event sample for Jo.

Event	Date Time	Social group	Incident	Outcome
1	14/5/98 9.25am	Jo, Simon. Rajeet	Jo. Simon and Rajeet were playing with the Lego bricks. Jo was making a yellow tower and asked Simon for some of his bricks. Simon said no because he wanted them. Jo picked up Simon's model and broke it up.	Jo was told to go and pick up the pieces and a staff member stayed with the group to make sure that Jo had calmed down.
2	14/5/98 11.30am	Jo, Simon	Jo and Simon were at the painting table. Simon told Jo that his painting was stupid. Jo thumped Simon on the back.	Jo was given time to calm down – 'time out' – and a staff member talked with Jo about how he could have expressed himself. Simon's back was checked over and he was told that he should not tease Jo.

Questions

1   Can you see any patterns emerging?
2   Why is it important to record what lead up to the incident as well as the incident itself?
3   Why might Jo's behaviour need to be monitored over several days?

to provide information about behaviour patterns. This is why it is important to keep accurate records of any serious unwanted behaviour. Records need to have dates, times and detailed accounts of the behaviour. Any information passed at these meetings is always confidential and you must never break the trust that has been given to you. As a result of the meeting, early years workers and parents may be asked to keep a further record or to try out an agreed action plan with the child.

Paediatrician
Specialises in the health and development of children.

Play therapist
Helps children to express trauma or emotions through play.

Educational psychologist
A specialist in children's learning and behaviour.

Physiotherapist
Helps to improve body function.

Child psychiatrist
Works well with children and family to discover what children are thinking and feeling.

Health visitor
Monitors and gives advice on children's development under the age of five.

Speech therapist
Helps improve speech and language.

Good Dragon Star Chart

1. When you do a good thing, your teacher or parent will let you colour in a spot on the dragon.
2. When you have coloured all his spots in you will be given a present

Action plan

Where children's behaviour is inappropriate, an action plan may be drawn up. The idea is to set some small goals for children to achieve and work towards. For example, as a first step a child who has difficulty in sharing could be encouraged to hand out drinks at snack time. Action plans help everyone working with a child to know what they should be aiming for and the strategies they should be using.

A common strategy when helping children to change their behaviour is called **behaviour modification**. It is based on the behaviourist theory that desirable behaviour will be repeated when children receive some reward. Many early years settings use a system of behaviour modification called **star charts**. Children are told that each time they meet the behaviour that is expected of them, they can have a star to put on a chart. After a certain number of stars have been collected they are given a reward such as a book or a longer breaktime. Look at the example below.

Case Study

Paul is five years old. He finds it difficult to share with other children yet at the same time becomes frustrated when they will not play with him. He has been increasingly aggressive towards them.

After talking to his parents, the staff have decided to use a star chart with him and at the same time plan activities that will help him to work with other children.

Paul is shown the chart and is told that every time he can share he will get a star to put on his special chart. His mother has agreed to come into the early years setting and praise him as he gets stars.

Day One – as Paul arrives he is asked if he will help by handing out the paper for the activity. He is immediately given a star to put on his chart.

During the activity an adult sits with Paul to make sure that he can't get himself into trouble. He plays a game with the adult and another child. He gets a star.
By the end of the day Paul has five stars.

Questions

1 *How might he feel at the end of the day?*
2 *Why is it important to involve Paul's parents?*
3 *Why should the staff continue to carry out this programme over several weeks?*
4 *Can you think of four activities that will help Paul to share and mix with the other children?*

Legal issues involved in physical punishment

Until fairly recently physical punishment was considered an effective way of disciplining children. Today attitudes have changed and so has the law. Schools and early years workers *must not* use physical punishments – for example, smacking or hitting – as a way of disciplining children.

Although parents are still legally allowed to smack their children, it is not an effective method in the long term for four main reasons:

1   Children learn that in some situations you are allowed to hit people.

2   Children do not learn how to manage conflict and feelings of anger.

3   Children are less likely to tell the truth if they think they may be smacked.

4   Smacking does not teach children why what they have done is wrong.

There is also a danger of serious injury to children, as parents often smack when they are angry and can therefore misjudge their strength. Smacking also creates a negative atmosphere and the key to good behaviour is to create a positive environment where children are guided towards appropriate behaviour.

Think about it

You are looking after two children aged three and five years. One day, you mention to their mother that they have had a squabble over a toy, but that you helped them to sort it out. The mother says that next time, you should give each a smack and take the toy away.

In pairs, work out a role play showing how you would handle this situation.

Good practice – promoting positive behaviour

✔   Be a good role model for children at all times. This means being courteous, calm and letting children see you sharing and turntaking.

✔   Praise and encourage children when they show desirable behaviour.

✔   Remember that giving attention to children showing undesirable behaviour may lead them to repeat it.

✔   Make sure that children feel you believe in them.

✔   Do not make any negative remarks in the presence of children.

✔   Make sure that activities and play opportunities are stimulating and fun.

✔   Give clear instructions so that children understand what they can and cannot do.

✔   Make sure that your expectations of children's behaviour are appropriate for their age and stage of development.

Unit test

Quick quiz

1 What is the earliest age at which most children are able to share?
   a 12 months
   b 2 years
   c 3 years
   d 4 years.

2 An 18-month-old tries to take another child's toy. The early years worker should:
   a tell the child to stop
   b show the child another toy
   c make the child sit away from the others
   d ignore the behaviour.

3 Tantrums are often the result of children feeling frustrated. With what age group are they commonly associated?
   a 12–18 months
   b 2–3 years
   c 3–4 years
   d Any age up to 8 years.

4 A six year old uses a swear word in the playground. The adult should:
   a tell the child to go inside
   b ignore the behaviour
   c explain to the child why they must not use this word
   d write a letter to the parents asking them not to swear.

5 At what age should children be starting to say please and thank you without a reminder?
   a 2–3 years
   b 3–4 years
   c 4–5 years
   d 5–6 years.

Short answer questions

1 What is a star chart?

2 Why is it important for adults to act as good role models?

3 Name two factors that might change a child's behaviour pattern.

4 What should be noted when recording an incident of behaviour?

5 Why is it sometimes best to ignore attention-seeking behaviour?

Early Years Services

This chapter looks at the services that are currently available for families and children, although it is important to understand that services and ways of delivering them are reviewed regularly.

In the UK there is a general belief that vulnerable groups – for example, children, the elderly, the sick – should be supported by the state.

The present framework has been changed considerably since the publication of its design in 1942 by a committee headed by William Beveridge. Until then many services that we now think of as essential had to be paid for by the people using them. Doctors charged their patients; there was no state pension; help with housing and for the unemployed was limited. Private charities and voluntary organisations – for example, the Salvation Army – provided what help they could.

This changed in the years following the 1942 Beveridge Report, which looked at ways of supporting people in need of help. A scheme was suggested in which people paid in contributions when they were working and in return received free medical treatment whenever they needed it as well as benefits when they were unable to work. The idea of the Welfare State (as it is often called) was to make sure that everyone who needed help received it. This principle remains today, although the way the system works has changed considerably.

What does the term 'statutory services' mean?

Over the years, various laws have been passed by Parliament that make central and local authorities responsible for a wide range of services. These are sometimes known as **statutory services** because they are provided by the state (often through local authorities). These services are aimed at meeting the needs of communities. For example, it is in the country's interest that children are given education and training, and so by law these services must be provided.

The main services that are used and needed by children and their families are education, health and social services. These are paid for by all citizens through a range of taxes.

Services and support are provided either directly through central government – for example, social security is directly under government control – or through local authorities.

The role of central government in providing services

Central government is divided into departments. Each department is headed by a secretary of state who is responsible to Parliament. The Prime Minister appoints

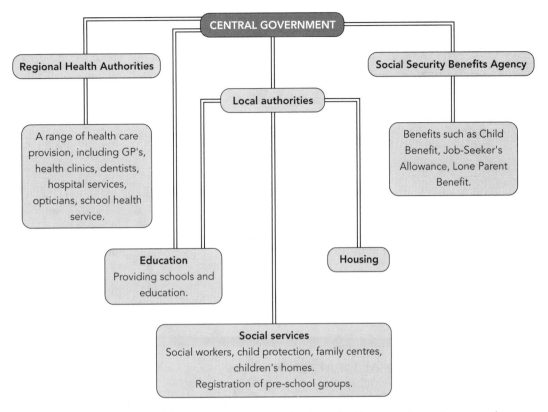

Note: This was the structure of the statutory services at the time of writing. Benefits and systems of delivering services are often changed.

You may need to check this chart with your supervisor or tutor.

secretaries of state from among members of Parliament. They must make sure that their department provides the statutory services effectively. In many cases the department may do this by overseeing the work of local authorities which are responsible for the day-to-day running of many services. For example, local authorities are responsible for the homeless in their area but follow the guidelines set out by the Department of the Environment.

Think about it

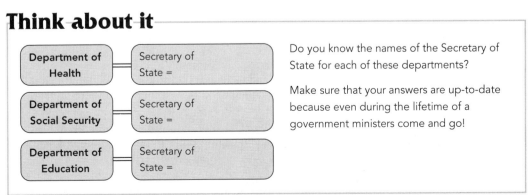

Department of Health	Secretary of State =
Department of Social Security	Secretary of State =
Department of Education	Secretary of State =

Do you know the names of the Secretary of State for each of these departments?

Make sure that your answers are up-to-date because even during the lifetime of a government ministers come and go!

There are several government departments. The most powerful department is probably the Treasury as it controls the amount of money available for spending by other departments. The Treasury collects money from taxes, for example, on business and working people. Every year the other government departments bid for money and the Treasury decides how much money each department can have. This affects the services that are available.

Below is a chart that shows which services are provided by each of the key government departments.

Department for Education and Employment	Responsible for schooling and standards in education
Department of the Environment	Responsible for housing policy
Department of Social Security	Responsible for benefits – e.g. Jobseekers' Allowance, Child Benefit
Department of Health	National Health Service

The role of local authorities

Local authorities provide many of the everyday services that we take for granted – for example, maintaining the roads, collecting refuse and lighting the streets. It is through local authorities that many of the statutory services are provided – for example, education, social services and housing. Spending decisions in local authorities are made by councillors – who are elected by local people.

Local authorities get the money needed to run services in three main ways:

- from central government

- from householders paying council tax

- from local businesses paying business rates on properties.

Most local authorities have to make difficult choices each year as they decide how much money to spend on each of the services they provide. Most local authorities also provide services that are not statutory, but are still desirable. For example, they may give grants to local festivals or build play areas for local children.

Portfolio activity

Find out about the services that the local authority in your area provides.

Write down the telephone numbers for the following services:

Library Service   Highways   Sports and leisure   Trading standards

DEPARTMENTS OF A BOROUGH COUNCIL

Chief Executive's Department
Personnel Department
Secretary's Department
Economic Development and Estates

Management
Treasurer's Department
Technical Services Department
Housing Department

Rent and Repairs Office
Lifeline
Tourism and Leisure Department
Environmental Services Department

ALPHABETICAL LISTING OF SERVICES IN A BOROUGH COUNCIL

Abandoned Vehicles
Access Officer
Adoption of Roads
Advertisement Control
Allotments
Animal Welfare/Licences
Architectural Grants
Arts Development
Bandstands
Banners and Posters over the
   Highway
Beach Foreshore/Bandstands
Beach Office
Building Conservation
Building Control
Business Rates
Buss Passes and County Cards
Bus Stops and Shelters
Car Parks
Catering (In Style)
Cemetery and Crematorium
Children's Play Areas
Cleansing Services
Coast Protection
Community Charge
Complaints
Conference Promotion
Conservation Areas
Conservation Area Partnership Scheme
Council Tax
Council and Committee Meetings
Country Park
Creditor Enquiries
Dangerous Structure Inspections
Debtor Enquiries
Demolition Notices
Development Control
Divisional Highway Engineer
Dog Control
Drainage – Private Sewers

Ecology Enquiries
Economic Development
Electoral Registration and Elections
Enforcement of Planning Control
Environmental (Green) Information
Estate Management
Fitness Centre
Food Hygiene and Safety
Footpaths
Golf Course
Graffiti
Grants
Grass Mowing
Harassment and Illegal Eviction
Health and Safety
Highway Defects
Highway Drains
Highway Licences
Homelessness
Housing Benefit
Housing Conditions/Grants
Housing – Council
Industrial Estates
Land Charges
Land Drainage
Landslip Inspections
Legal Services
Leisure
Licensing
Lifeline
Listed Buildings
Litter Line
Local Government Review
Marketing (Tourism and Leisure)
Mayoral Services
Museum and Art Gallery
Museum, Old Town
Noise Nuisance
Parking (On Street)
Parks and Recreation

Pest Control
Planning
Pollution Control
Private Tenants Advice
Promotion of Hastings to Visitors
Public Conveniences
Public Entertainment Licences
Recruitment
Recycling Information
Recycling Project – HARP
Refuse Collection
Right to buy Council Houses and Flats
Roads
Scaffolding on Highways
Seafront
Seafront Concessions
Sheltered Housing – Council
   Properties
Skips on Highways
Sports Centres
Sports Facilities
Street Lighting
Street Naming, Numbering and
   Nameplates
Street Works Supervision
Taxi/Private Hire Licences
Tourism
Tourist Information Centres
Town Centre Development
Trade Waste
Traffic Calming
Traffic Problems
Traffic Signal Faults
Traffic Signs and Road Markings
Trees
Twinning with Other Towns
Vehicular Footway Crossings
Watercourses
Weather (Local Statistics)
Woodland Management

The legal and political framework of statutory services

Although most people in the UK accept that there must be some statutory services such as education, there is often a difference of opinion as to how these services should be provided.

It is important to remember that, although services such as the police and fire brigade seem free, we pay towards them in different ways. The money for services comes from us through taxes. The main taxes are Income Tax, Council Tax, VAT and National Insurance.

As people pay for services through taxes, there is always a balance between what can be provided and how much tax people are prepared to pay. When asked, most people are prepared to pay more money for education and for old-age pension, but at the same time they do not want to see taxes rise!

Think about it

Here are some of the arguments that politicians need to consider. In groups, discuss and report back with your views.

1   *If you give more money to the unemployed they won't bother looking for work.*
2   *Child Benefit should be means tested because at the moment every family gets it – even if they are millionaires.*
3   *Paying benefit to lone parents makes it easier for people to get divorced and encourages young women to get pregnant.*
4   *Class sizes in schools are too big and more teachers are needed.*
5   *There are lots of people who are paying taxes and not getting anything out of the system.*
6   *No one should pay prescription charges even if they are well off because they have already paid income tax.*

In the same way that many individuals have different opinions as to what services and benefits need to be provided, political parties also have different approaches.

The high and rising costs of providing a National Health Service as well as social security payments has meant that all political parties are looking for ways to save money.

The period from 1979–1997 saw a great change in the ways services were provided. The emphasis was on getting better value for money. The Conservative government at the time thought that services, which had previously been provided by central or local government, might be run more efficiently by private firms. This meant that the opportunity to offer services – for example, cleaning schools or collecting refuse – was given to private firms. If a private company could do the same work more cheaply than the local authority, the company was asked to run the service.

Legal framework

In order to make any major changes to the provision of statutory services governments need to pass Acts of Parliament. For example, in 1944 an education act was passed that made attendance at school compulsory for all children over five.

The 1989 Children Act is considered to be one of the most important acts to affect children and their families. It has been widely welcomed by most professionals who work with children. It is a wide-ranging piece of legislation that covers issues such as family breakdown and child protection, and it aims to make professionals involved with children think about their needs.

Some of its main principles are below are set out below.

1 Support services for children and families

The act recognised that children need their families and local authorities now have a duty to help families bring up 'children in need'. For example, if children under five and not at school have been assessed as being 'in need' local authorities must provide daycare services for them.

2 Care and protection of children

A wide range of court orders was introduced to help protect children. The social service departments of local authorities have a duty to work with parents and they can only take a child into care if they have exhausted all other possibilities or if a child is in extreme danger.

The act provides guardians to give children a voice in court proceedings and to make sure that their best interests are being considered. The guardians are often trained family experts and are independent of the parents and the local authority.

Local authorities must also have a complaint procedure for children to use if they are taken into care. While children are in care, parents share parental responsibility with the local authority.

3 Inspection and registration of daycare services, childminders and residential accommodation

The local authority has a duty to inspect and register daycare settings where children under eight years old are being looked after for more than two hours.

This covers playgroups, nurseries, crèches and childminders. Registration with a local authority lasts for one year and it is an offence to look after children in daycare settings that are not registered.

The local authority also has a duty to inspect and register residential accommodation – for example, voluntary children's homes and residential schools.

The aim of the inspection procedures is to check that children are well cared for and to make sure that staff are well trained and appropriate.

Knowledge into Action

Ask your supervisor when your workplace was last inspected.

1   *How long did the inspection last?*
2   *What did the inspectors look at?*
3   *Did the fire officer also check the premises?*
4   *How many children is your workplace registered for?*

The amount of help children and their families receive can vary from one local authority to another depending on the authority's interpretation of some of the acts of parliament. A good example of this is the interpretation of the phrase 'in need.' If cash is short, local authorities may do the minimum possible to help families. Services that are nationally provided – for example, benefits – do not vary in this way.

Health services

A wide range of health services is available to children and their families. There is no charge for any of the health services for children. This means that medical prescriptions and dental and eye checks are free. This has always been an important principle for all political parties as they recognise that introducing charges may harm the health of some groups of children. During pregnancy, and for 12 months afterwards, mothers also receive free prescriptions and dental treatment. Free milk and vitamins are provided for children under five if parents are receiving some type of benefit.

Think about it

1   *Why might groups of children be put at risk if prescription charges were made?*
2   *Why do you think that free milk and vitamins are given to children under the age of five when parents are on some form of benefit?*

Community health services

Most children and families use the community health services that are organised by their regional health authority. Over the last few years the trend has been for services to link together. This means that health visitors and community midwives are attached to GPs so that children and families are likely to see the same people. It is thought that this may encourage families who are having difficulties to seek help.

Sally & Richard Greenhill

The team of health visitor, midwife and family doctor is often referred to as the **primary health care team**. They have a strong role in advising families on preventing illness and disease. For children over the age of five, the school health service takes on the role of the health visitor and developmental checks – for example, on hearing and vision – are carried out at school. School nurses may also advise parents on issues such as head lice and bedwetting.

Health visitor weighing a baby

Community health services

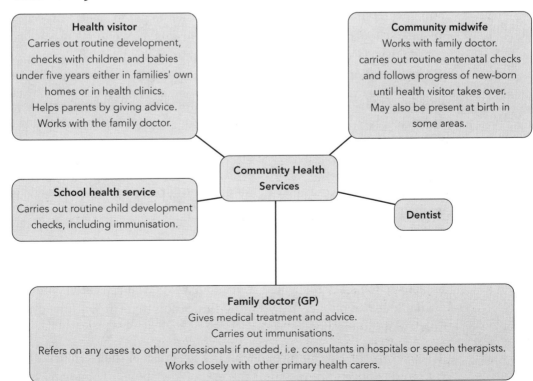

Health visitor
Carries out routine development, checks with children and babies under five years either in families' own homes or in health clinics.
Helps parents by giving advice.
Works with the family doctor.

Community midwife
Works with family doctor.
carries out routine antenatal checks and follows progress of new-born until health visitor takes over.
May also be present at birth in some areas.

School health service
Carries out routine child development checks, including immunisation.

Community Health Services

Dentist

Family doctor (GP)
Gives medical treatment and advice.
Carries out immunisations.
Refers on any cases to other professionals if needed, i.e. consultants in hospitals or speech therapists.
Works closely with other primary health carers.

Children and education

The 1944 Education Act made full-time education for children between the ages of 5 and 15 compulsory (it was raised to 16 in 1972). Parents have a duty to make sure that their children are receiving education. Local authorities employ Education Welfare Officers who make sure that children are attending school.

State schools and schools receiving public money such as church-aided schools do not charge fees. They are run either by the local education authority or they receive a grant from central government.

By law, children whose parents are receiving certain types of benefit are entitled to a free school dinner at lunchtime.

Think about it

Some parents do not want their children to have free school meals even though they are entitled to them.

1 *Why do you think that this might happen?*
2 *If you are working in a school, find out how many children have free school dinners.*

Types of school

There are a number of different types of school and the system of education can vary between areas – for example, in some areas secondary schools are selective. This means that children have to pass a test to get in to certain schools. Education in state schools is free, although some parents may choose private schools, which charge fees. Occasionally, if a child has particular needs – for example, dyslexia – the local authority may pay the fees of a specialist private school.

In some areas of the country the local education authorities also provide free nurseries.

Schools are also provided for some children with special needs. These are often known as special schools, although since the 1980 Education Act local education authorities are encouraged to integrate children with special needs into mainstream schools.

Quality of education

Politicians are always concerned with the quality of education in schools. At present schools are inspected every four years and a written report is made available to the public. In 1988, the Education Reform Act introduced the National Curriculum into schools.

Parents receive a written report on the progress of their children at least once a year and children are tested at the end of key stages. The test results of schools

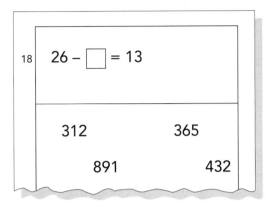

18 | $26 - \boxed{} = 13$

312   365

891   432

Example of a question from a maths test at Key Stage 1

Key Stage 1	5–7 years
Key Stage 2	7–11 years
Key Stage 3	11–14 years

are made public so parents can see how their local schools have performed.

In order to see how much progress children have made in Key Stage 1, they are also assessed when they start full-time education. This assessment is called Base Line Assessment and is linked to the outcomes in the Early Years document called 'Desirable Outcomes'.

Nursery places

There is an increasing trend towards providing pre-school education. In 1997, Nursery Vouchers were given to all parents of four-years-olds. This allowed parents to send their children to playgroups, nurseries and other pre-school settings with fees to the value of the voucher waived. Although the voucher system is ending, the government is asking each local authority to draw up an Early Years Development plan and pre-school education is likely to be increased in future years.

An early years curriculum has been designed to support the National Curriculum. There are six areas of development for pre-schools settings to work towards with four-year-olds in their settings:

- Personal and social development
- Knowledge and understanding of the world
- Mathematics
- Language and literacy
- Creative development
- Physical development

Social services

There is a split between local and central government in providing personal social service to children and their families.

Central government controls the Benefits Agency and the Child Support Agency, whereas local authorities provide other social services.

There are two main types of benefit for children and families:

Contributory benefits can only be paid out if the person has paid enough National Insurance contributions. Examples at the time of writing include: Statutory Maternity Pay; Widowed Mothers Allowance and Job Seekers Allowance.

İŞ GÖRÜŞMESİ GARANTİSİ, işsiz kişilerin işverenlerle ilişki kurmasını sağlayarak iş bulmalarına yardımcı olan bir programdır. Bu programa katılmadan önce, sizin geçmişte ne tür iş yaptığınızı, niteliklerinizi ve yeteneklerinizi öğrenmemiz ve ne gibi bir işte çalışmak istediğinizi bilmemiz gerekmektedir. Daha sonra, sizinle bir görüşme yapacak ve eğer yardımcı olabilirsek size uygun ve açık olan kadroları bildireceğiz. İşverenlerin boş kadroları bulunduğu ve çalışacak kişilere gereksinimleri olduğunda, iş öncesi kısa eğitim kursları da vermekteyiz. Bu kurslar sizi iş görüşmelerine hazırlayacak şekilde tasarımlanmıştır. Bu eğitim paketleri, sizin ve işverenin gereksinimlerini karşılayabilmek için hazırlanmıştır. İş Görüşmesi Garantisi'ne katılabilmek için altı ay ya da daha fazla bir süreyle işsiz kalmış olmanız gerekir. (Ancak bu kural, özürlü kişiler, hükümetçe desteklenen eğitim programlarından ayrılan kişiler ve eski tutuklular için daha esnek olarak uygulanmaktadır.

[Text in Bengali script]

[Text in Urdu script]

[Text in Punjabi/Gurmukhi script]

Non-contributory benefits are paid to anyone who meets the criteria and is entitled to receive the benefit. Examples at the time of writing include: Lone-Parent Benefit; Child Benefit and Housing Benefit.

Many of the non-contributory benefits are **means tested**. People have to show how much savings they have or how much they earn and the amount they receive is adjusted accordingly. At present, Child Benefit is given to all families with children regardless of how much they are earning.

Why some families do not claim benefits. Some groups of people find it hard to claim benefits, either because they are not sure what they are allowed to claim or because they find the forms difficult to manage. Efforts have been made to make the forms easier to complete and they are often available in different languages (see left).

Knowledge into Action

1. *What does a parent have to do in order to claim child benefit?*
2. *Find out how much Child Benefit a family would receive if they had three children.*
3. *How is child benefit paid – e.g. cheque, cash?*
4. *How often is child benefit paid?*
5. *How long is child benefit paid for?*

Child Support Agency

The 1991 Child Support Act was designed to ensure that absent parents – usually fathers – pay for the upkeep and maintenance of their children. The Child Support Agency calculates the amount that the absent parent should pay and then makes arrangements for its collection.

Other services provided by the local authority

There is a large range of services provided by the local authority to help children and their families:

Housing. The local authority has a duty to help homeless people in its area. Children and their families are considered a priority. The quality of housing varies from authority to authority – for example, some families find that they are housed in bed and breakfast accommodation, whereas in other areas they might be offered council housing. In some areas the reasons for a family becoming homeless are also taken into account if housing supply is short.

Rent officers are employed by local authorities to help tenants and landlords. They assess fair rents and can be asked to sort out difficulties between landlord and tenant. In cases where Housing Benefit is to be paid, rent officers check that the rent is reasonable.

Social workers. Social workers work with families where children have been assessed as being 'in need'. Children may be assessed as being in need if they have special needs or if they are on a protection register because they are considered to be at risk from abuse or neglect. Social workers help families in many ways – for example, they help families with claiming benefits or they may arrange child care.

Child care. When children are assessed as being 'in need' local authorities have a duty to provide some child care. Children under five and not in school have to be provided with daycare while older children may be provided with out-of-school activities and care during the holidays. Families with children who have special needs may be offered respite care. This means that the children go, for a time, to a centre or residential home. This allows the family to have a holiday or rest. The length of respite care can vary from a few hours to a week.

Case Study

Harry is seven years old and has severe learning difficulties. He needs constant supervision, as he cannot be left alone. In many ways his developmental level is that of a two-year-old. He wakes up most nights and although his parents love him dearly, they find caring for him quite a strain. There are two other children in the family, Emma, aged four, and Michael, aged eight. Once a month Harry goes to a residential home for a weekend for respite care. This service is paid for by Social Services and helps to take the pressure off Harry's parents. It also means that Emma and Michael are able to spend this time with their parents, as at times they feel 'pushed out'.

Questions
1 *What sort of activities will the family be able to do while Harry is having respite care?*
2 *Why do Emma and Michael need some time alone with their parents?*
3 *Find out what types of respite care are available in your area.*

The role of voluntary organisations and the private sector in providing services

Although the local authority is responsible for providing many services, in some cases it may pay other organisations to carry out the work. This is called **contracting out**. There are two main reasons why a local authority might do this:

1 The local authority is required to do so by law. (The Local Government Act 1988 named services that had to be put out to tender. Further services were added in the following years.)

2 The local authority feels that the work might be done better or more cheaply by another organisation.

If local authorities contract out work, they are still responsible for making sure that it is carried out well. The advantage to local authorities of using the private sector and voluntary organisations is that they pay only for the services they need rather than having to employ people permanently.

Case Study

Gary is three years old and has been put on the 'at risk' register by Social Services. As part of the support offered to the family, the local authority is to provide Gary with a nursery place. The local authority does not have a nursery of its own and so it pays for a place at a suitable private nursery.

Questions

1 *In this case, which other organisation is the local authority working with?*
2 *Why might this be an advantage to the local authority?*

Voluntary organisations

Voluntary organisations raise money from the public and businesses, and are non-profit making. They are often run by teams of paid staff and unpaid volunteers. There are many voluntary organisations providing services, help and advice to children and their families. Some organisations also campaign to raise awareness of issues that they think are important. Local authorities often work with the voluntary sector, as they are able to identify and meet particular needs. Families of children with special needs often find that voluntary organisations are able to give them excellent support. There is a voluntary organisation for most of the major disabilities.

The table opposite shows the type of work that some of the major children's voluntary organisations cover.

The National Childbirth Trust

Forth Valley South Branch

Name of organisation	Type of work	Contact address
Barnado's	Working for children in the community. Runs residential accommodation for children with severe learning disabilities.	Tanners Lane, Barkingside, Ilford Essex IG6 1QG
Children's Society	Works on many aspects of early years care – including fostering and adoption work and community-based projects.	Edward Rudolf House Margery Street London WC1X OJL
NCH (National Children's Home) Action for Children	Provides residential and community care. Runs family centres and other community childcare projects.	85 Highbury Park London N5 1UD
NCT (National Childbirth Trust)	Helps give support and information to parents and parents to be. There are 400 branches in the UK.	Alexander House Oldham Terrace Acton London W3 6NH
NSPCC (National Society for the Prevention of Cruelty to Children)	Works to prevent abuse of children. It runs over 100 child protection teams. Offers training to early years professionals.	National Centre 42 Curtain Road London EC2A 3NH
Parentline	Provides support through help lines for parents having any kind of problem with their child. There are also local groups.	Endway House The Endway Hadleigh Essex SS7 2ANN
Save the Children Fund	The aim of this organisation is to work for the rights of children in the UK and overseas.	Mary Datchelor House 17 Grove Lane London SE5 8RD
National Council for One Parent Families	Gives advice on housing, financial and legal issues. The organisation campaigns to improve the social and financial position of lone parents.	255 Kentish Town Road London NW4 2LX

When the Welfare State was established between 1945–6, it was hoped that the need for voluntary organisations would disappear as the state would be able to provide help for the most needy. But it is now realised that voluntary organisations can provide expertise, advice and practical support. This is done in many ways – for example, they buy and lend out equipment and organise projects.

Voluntary organisations and child care. A range of child care and support is provided by voluntary organisations. They may run play schemes in the holidays, playgroups or toy libraries. Sometimes the local authority helps towards the costs of running these services but quite often they rely on volunteer help and the fees that are charged to parents. Some local services such as playgroups are run independently, but are members of a larger association – for example, the Pre-school Play Learning Alliance.

Voluntary organisations also provide leisure activities for children – for example, Beavers, Rainbows, Brownies etc.

Haddon Davies

The need for after-school care has been recognised by government and a number of clubs are being set up to meet local needs using voluntary organisations. Money is being made available to help with initial set up costs. The aim is to provide 30 000 after-school clubs in the next few years. At present there are around 3000.

Housing Associations Voluntary organisations are also involved in providing low-cost housing for people on low incomes. There are now over a million people who are housed through

Playgroups are examples of voluntary organisations

housing associations. Some housing associations specialise in providing housing for the disabled or for families with special needs.

Knowledge into Action

Find out about one voluntary organisation in your area that supports disabled children and their families

The role of the private sector

Organisations in the private sector carry out the same sort of work as voluntary organisations, but they aim to make a profit. Examples of private sector services for children include nurseries and crèches. Local authorities may use the private sector to provide some of the statutory services – for example, paying for a place in a day nursery or using a private firm to provide school meals.

Finding out about services for children and their families

Every year thousands of benefits go unclaimed. This is often because people do not know what is available or how to make a claim. The Benefits Agency produces leaflets in several languages and has made attempts to publicise benefits. When families need advice they often have to go to several places in order to find out about the support and help they can receive. This can be time-consuming and expensive. Some nurseries and schools display information that might be useful to parents. If information is provided it is important to make sure that it is up-to-date.

As professional early years workers, it is important that we have some understanding of the range of services that might help them.

Useful sources of information and help that can be found locally

Citizens Advice Bureau. Offers independent advice in legal, social and financial matters.

Public library. Reference sections contain guides to social services and the law that can be helpful. Local voluntary groups often display information in libraries.

Benefit Agency Offices. A range of leaflets is available and face-to-face advice can be offered.

Law centres. These are found in most cities and are funded by local authorities. They offer free legal advice.

Housing Advice centres. These are funded by local authorities and can help with housing difficulties.

Local councillors. A list of local councillors is available from town halls or county halls. Councillors are usually aware of services in the area and can be effective in getting help.

Members of Parliament (MPs). Writing to MPs or seeing them at 'surgeries' can be a good way of getting help when bureaucracy seems to be getting in the way. A letter from the local MP often has a way of making things happen!

Useful books

- *Guide to Social Services* published by the Family Welfare Association. This reference book is published each year and can be found in the reference sections of local libraries.

- *National Welfare Benefits Handbook* published by the Child Poverty Action group. This is published each year and explains the benefits that are available.

Portfolio activity

1 *Find out the name of your local MP.*
2 *Find out where your local authority is based.*
3 *Find out the address and telephone number of your local Benefits Office.*
4 *Find out where the nearest Citizen's Advice Bureau is.*
5 *Write down how you went about finding this information.*

Knowledge into Action

You have been asked to find out some information for one of the families that you work with. The mother is expecting twins and her partner has just left her. She has two other children aged two and four and has not worked for a number of years. They live in a rented flat and have no savings.

In pairs

1   *Find out what benefits the mother will be entitled to.*
2   *Find out what support organisations exist in your area for lone parents and also for parents who have twin or multiple births.*

Unit test

Quick quiz

1   Which of one of these is a voluntary organisation?
    a   Barnado's
    b   Benefits Agency
    c   Department of the Environment
    d   Child Support Agency.

2   Which of these could be described as a statutory service?
    a   Girl Guides and Boy Scouts
    b   Health clinic
    c   After-school club
    d   Playgroup.

3   Which of these taxes are collected by local government?
    a   VAT
    b   Income Tax
    c   Council Tax
    d   Road Tax.

4   Under the 1989 Children Act, early years settings that care for children under eight and for more than two hours have to be registered and inspected. Registration lasts for:
    a   6 months
    b   1 year
    c   2 years
    d   5 years.

5 One of the roles of the Education Welfare Officer is to:
- **a** decide who should have free school meals
- **b** check the standards of teaching in schools
- **c** advise on First Aid matters
- **d** check the attendance of children of school age.

Short answer questions

1 Give two reasons why some families do not always claim the benefits they are entitled to.

2 Which government department is responsible for housing policy?

3 Name three places where families can get information about services and benefits.

4 Name three members of a primary health team.

5 Which government department is responsible for paying benefits to families?

Work with Babies   13

Looking after babies is a skilled job. A parent leaving a baby with an early years worker needs to be sure that the baby is going to be kept safe and be well cared for. Caring for babies means thinking about many aspects of their development as well as making sure that their physical needs of being kept warm and fed are met. The first part of this chapter looks at some of the basic principles of caring for babies. The second part covers feeding babies.

1 Caring for babies

Encouraging the growth and development of babies

Watching babies in their first year of life is exciting and rewarding. During their first year, babies grow and develop rapidly. By the end of the year, they are mobile and can smile and communicate with their carers.

Babies need to have their basic needs met in order to grow and develop. Babies are vulnerable in many ways so when we are looking after them we need to understand the importance of their needs and provide an environment that can meet these needs.

Basic needs of babies

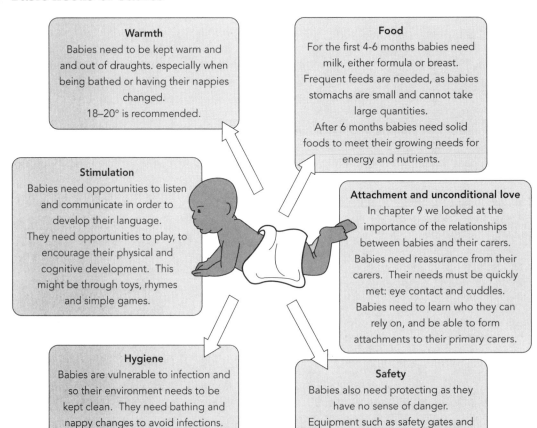

Warmth
Babies need to be kept warm and and out of draughts. especially when being bathed or having their nappies changed.
18–20° is recommended.

Food
For the first 4-6 months babies need milk, either formula or breast. Frequent feeds are needed, as babies stomachs are small and cannot take large quantities.
After 6 months babies need solid foods to meet their growing needs for energy and nutrients.

Stimulation
Babies need opportunities to listen and communicate in order to develop their language.
They need opportunities to play, to encourage their physical and cognitive development. This might be through toys, rhymes and simple games.

Attachment and unconditional love
In chapter 9 we looked at the importance of the relationships between babies and their carers. Babies need reassurance from their carers. Their needs must be quickly met: eye contact and cuddles. Babies need to learn who they can rely on, and be able to form attachments to their primary carers.

Hygiene
Babies are vulnerable to infection and so their environment needs to be kept clean. They need bathing and nappy changes to avoid infections. Equipment that is used for feeding or items that are put in the mouth, such as plastic rattles, need sterilising.

Safety
Babies also need protecting as they have no sense of danger. Equipment such as safety gates and reins need to be used, as well as making sure that such objects as plants are removed from their reach.

As babies grow and develop, their needs change. At first babies spend most of their time sleeping, but by the end of their first year they are able to move, pick up objects and understand simple instructions. As early years workers, it is important that we have an understanding of how babies are likely to develop in their first year so that we can meet these changing needs. If babies do not have a secure, happy environment they will fail to thrive.

The chart below shows the pattern of development that most babies follow during their first year.

Age	Developmental pattern	Role of the adult	Toys and equipment
New born	A new-born baby has many developmental reflexes that are designed to help it survive – e.g. being able to cry and suck. These gradually disappear as the baby gains voluntary control of its body. **Rooting reflex** – moves mouth if face is touched to look for food. **Startle reflex** –throws out hands and legs as if trying to catch something if it hears a sudden sound. **Grasp reflex** – fingers automatically tighten around anything put in the palm of hand. Grasp is so tight that baby can be lifted up. **Crawling reflex** – when placed on front, knees are tucked up underneath as a result of being curled up in the womb.	Babies are physically vulnerable and they need to be kept warm and fed regularly. Babies are very sensitive and react to sounds and sudden movements. Adults looking after new-borns need to be calm and quiet. In the first few weeks after birth, babies and their parents need time together to get to know each other.	• Cradle or warm place to sleep • Nappy changing and bathing equipment including mat, wipes (see nappy changing page 00) • Clothes and blankets • Feeding and sterilising equipment if not breast fed • Soothing music
6 weeks	Starting to have more periods of alertness. Looks at carer, stares at bright lights. Is soothed by carer's voice. Follows objects and faces at close range. Arm and leg movements are jerky.	Meet the primary needs of the baby – milk, warmth, cleanliness. Provide reassurance and build a relationship by talking, singing and cuddling the baby. The baby's head must be supported when being carried or lifted.	• Brightly coloured mobiles within close range of the baby. These must be securely fastened to make sure they cannot fall on to the baby • Pushchair • Car seat • Bouncing chairs are good as they allow the baby to see more of what is happening around them, (never leave on raised surfaces)

Age	Developmental pattern	Role of the adult	Toys and equipment
3 months	Smiles and coos. Kicks legs strongly and moves arms. Movements are less jerky, although still not co-ordinated. Can find hands and bring them to the mouth. Looks at and plays with fingers. Is alert and looks around. Can lift and turn head from side to side when lying on front. Can hold a rattle for a short time, although cannot co-ordinate arms to bring it to mouth.	Meet baby's basic needs. Talk and sing to baby. Respond to baby's smiles and coos. Show baby rattles and brightly coloured toys. Allow baby time to lie on floor and kick. Encourage baby to lie on front for short periods to help back and neck muscles to develop. Allow baby to explore and kick at bathtime. **Safety** Make sure that any toys or items within reach of baby are safe – e.g.avoid clothing with ribbons that can get caught around a baby's neck. At four months the baby may need solid food.	• Baby gyms or pram toys that encourage babies to focus and try to reach out • Rattles and other toys that make a sound can be shown to the baby
6 months	Smiles, laughs and makes sounds. Follows adults' movements. Grasps objects. Beginning to roll over. Pulls up legs with hands when on back. May put foot in mouth. Sits up with support, although some babies are starting to sit up for short periods without support. Pushes head, neck and chest off floor when on front.	Plenty of attention and cuddles. Play games such a peek-a-boo and Humpty Dumpty. Sing nursery rhymes. Provide toys to explore with mouth and to help teething. Build towers of bricks for babies to knock down. **Safety** The baby can now roll. This means that nappy changing may be safer on the floor. Do not leave babies on any high surfaces. In the next few weeks the baby will be mobile. The environment *must* be made safe by using safety gates, plug covers etc. (see Chapter 3, page 49)	• Fabric books, rattles, beakers, toys that make sounds and music. • Activity quilts • Highchairs to allow baby to be fed as part of a family or group – use straps and harnesses • Playpens may be needed from this time on, to keep baby safe – e.g. in the kitchen in a home environment

Age	Developmental pattern	Role of the adult	Toys and equipment
9 Months	Sits up well without support. Can reach out for toys from sitting. May be crawling or shuffling on bottom. Uses fingers and thumb to pick up objects. Can bang objects together. Babbles and starts to understand words such as bye-bye and no.	Respond and encourage baby's language by smiling, talking to the baby and praising attempts to communicate. Play simple games and nursery rhymes with baby. Point to objects when carrying baby, use books. Allow time for baby to play on floor and explore toys by putting several toys out. **Safety** Babies are starting to notice small items on the floor and can pick them up to put in their mouth – e.g. pins or parts of small toys.	• Balls, pop up toys, rattles, beakers, cubes, stacking rings • Babies are also starting to enjoy picture books and images • Bath time toys – e.g. buckets, sponges, boats and ducks
12 months	Most babies are mobile – either crawling, rolling or bottom shuffling. Starting to walk by holding onto furniture – this is often called cruising. May stand alone for a few seconds. Points to objects using index fingers to show adult. Understands name and simple instructions. Drinks from cup; tries to feed using spoon and fingers.	Encourage physical development by making sure that the baby has time and space to explore. Give baby opportunities to feed themselves Play with the baby – games such as stacking beakers, dropping toys into shape sorters, pulling toys along. Encourage language by singing, making the baby part of the conversation, repeating phrases and making good eye contact. **Safety** Always use safety equipment such as gates, reins. Look out for objects that babies might pull onto themselves such as plants and tablecloths.	• Push and pull toys • Large toys that move – e.g. brick trolleys • Baby swings • Simple shape sorters, bricks, stacking rings, beakers

Babies are individuals

In Chapter 4 (pages 74–6) we saw that children develop at different rates. The same is true of babies. The chart above shows us the general pattern of babies' growth and development but it is extremely important to recognise that they develop at different rates. Some babies smile within the first six weeks while others might be able to grasp objects. Some people think that all babies are the same, but every parent and primary carer finds that their baby has its own personality!

Portfolio activity

Ask your supervisor if you can observe a baby in your workplace. Find out its age in weeks and months.

1 *Observe the baby when it is awake and alert.*
2 *Write down a list of the things that the baby is able to do.*
3 *Compare this list to the chart.*
4 *Does the baby seem to be following the same pattern of development?*
5 *Try to observe the same baby two weeks or more later. What differences can you see?*

Babies need to play

In their first year of life, babies need to play. Play is important because it helps them socialise with their carers and explore their environment. Fine and gross motor skills are developed, as babies tend to repeat actions in their play – for example, they might press a button to keep hearing a sound. This repetitive type of play is often called **mastery play** as they repeat movements so they can master and control these movements. During this year, babies are playing by themselves (solitary play) and can be so absorbed in their play that they are almost in their own world.

Knowledge into Action

Ask your supervisor if you can observe a baby between three and nine months old playing with a new rattle or appropriate toy.

1 *How does the baby play with it?*
2 *For how long does the baby play with it?*

Babies play and learn in their first year by relying on their senses – especially taste, touch and smell. Researchers have discovered that within a few days babies

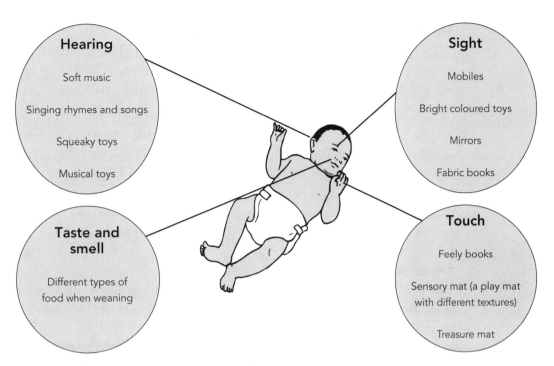

Using a baby's senses

can recognise the smell of their primary carer. After a few weeks, rattles, beakers and other toys are taken to the mouth.

Babies use their senses to learn about their environment. We can help babies by providing equipment and experiences that stimulate the senses.

From birth onwards   From 12 months onwards

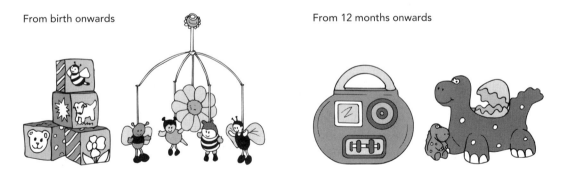

Good practice – providing toys and equipment for babies

✔ Adults looking after babies must be extremely careful that babies are not given anything that they could choke on – e.g. toys with small parts.

✔ Toys and equipment need to be correct for the age of the baby.

✔ Manufacturers' instructions must be followed.

✔ Toys should have a safety mark on them.

Finding a balance

Although babies need some stimulation and times to play, they also need times to explore at their own pace. We need to remember that in this first year of life, they are taking in a lot of information about the world around them. This can be tiring for them.

Young babies may just lie still and look at a mobile. Adults caring for babies need to learn how much stimulation each baby needs. Too much stimulation can mean they become overtired and show this by crying and becoming frustrated. Too little stimulation means that babies can become bored or are slower in their development. The line between enough play and stimulation is a fine one and as adults work with a baby they become quick to read the signs that a baby has had enough.

Encouraging physical development

During the first year babies gradually master the skills of sitting up, crawling or shuffling and standing. It is important that they do these things at their own pace, as these physical milestones can only be achieved when the baby has enough strength and co-ordination. Our role in helping babies is to make sure that we encourage them by making eye contact and talking to them.

Walking. At the end of the end of their first year some babies may be starting to walk, while others will only just be starting to pull themselves up to a standing position. Adults can encourage development by:

- praising them

- supporting them with two fingers

- providing them with toys that they can push along.

When babies are starting to become mobile, we need to make sure that they have enough space and that any potentially dangerous objects are removed. Babies need space to explore safely and many accidents occur when they are first standing and walking, as they may hold onto unstable objects which then fall on them.

Portfolio activity

Ask your supervisor if you can play with a baby. Decide what toys to use.

1 *Write about the toys and equipment that you used to play with the baby.*
2 *How did the baby react to the toys?*
3 *How long was the baby able to play for?*
4 *Write down what you learnt from carrying out this activity.*

Communicating with babies

Communicating with babies is one of the most important roles of the early years worker. In the first year of life, babies learn to communicate their needs even if they are not able to speak. They do this by crying and then gradually, they find other ways of communicating with us. They may smile or point at things or use their faces to show when they are not happy.

Communication is a two-way process. Babies need to feel that we want to communicate with them. We can show this by making good eye contact with them and by using our faces to show our delight when they try to make sounds and by communicating with our bodies – for example, hugging and cuddling.

To promote babies' language, early years workers must chat and talk to them even though they are not able to answer back. As the months go by, the baby will try to add more to the one-way conversations!

Think about it

Adult: Let's sort you out with a clean nappy shall we?
        (Makes eye contact with baby who then smiles)
Adult: Does that little smile mean that you've got a surprise in there for me, you little chipmunk?
        (Tickles baby's tummy. Baby laughs and babbles)
Adult : You have, haven't you!
Baby: Blows bubbles and laughs
Adult: There's no getting out of it, you little sweetie, this nappy is going to be done!

It is essential that in any dialogue the baby feels included and part of what is happening.

1 *How has the adult in this conversation made the baby feel part of what is happening?*
2 *How does the adult acknowledge the baby's attempts to communicate?*
3 *How has the adult shown that they love and care for the baby?*
4 *Would it matter if the adult just picked up the baby and changed the nappy without talking?*

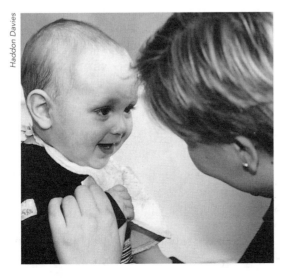

Haddon Davies

Some adults feel embarrassed about chatting and singing to babies, but anyone wishing to work with babies must learn to talk and chat to them. Babies who do not have this type of stimulation are in danger of developing speech problems.

Using our voices when working with babies. In the first few weeks, babies learn to recognise voices. Then gradually, babies try to imitate the sounds that they have heard. Our voices are soothing for babies, they give them reassurance and from the tone of our voices babies are quickly able to sense our love for them.

Babies enjoy listening to songs. Singing has been a traditional way of communicating with babies for centuries. Nearly every language has nursery rhymes and lullabies for babies. The rhythm and repetition of these songs encourage babies to make their own sounds.

As babies get older, they enjoy nursery rhymes that have actions – for example 'This little piggy went to market' or 'This is the way the farmer rides.' Babies show their delight by smiling or laughing. This is a signal that we should repeat the rhyme. Nursery rhymes and songs are so powerful, that even as adults we can still remember parts of those we learnt when we were very young.

Knowledge into Action

Early years workers looking after babies need to know some nursery rhymes.

1 *Make a list of 15 nursery rhymes.*
2 *Divide the list into sections – e.g. counting rhymes, lullabies.*
3 *Choose two or three rhymes to learn and try them out in your workplace.*
4 *Which worked well, and why?*

Creating a positive environment for babies

In Chapters 2 and 3 (pages 22–45 and 47–54) we looked at creating suitable environments for children. In many ways the principles are the same for babies. Babies also need to be in a safe, hygienic and stimulating environment. The main difference between babies and young children is the need for babies to be in contact with the same carer. A key worker system is essential when babies are cared for in large group settings. This means that, most of the time, babies are handled by the same person so that they can build a stable relationship with them. This is considered an important principle when caring for babies. The 1989 Children Act suggested that the staffing ratio for babies should be smaller than for older children in recognition of their need for adult attention.

Caring for babies also means adapting to their changing needs. Every baby has its own routine and it is good practice for babies in large settings to keep to their own routine rather than be made to fit in with others. Parents also need to be given information about their baby at the end of the session. It is important for them to know how many sleeps and feeds their child has had.

Variations in routines. No baby sticks rigidly to the same routine – for example, one day they might sleep for an hour, but the next day they might need an hour

```
 8.00 am  Arrive
 8.30 am  Breakfast
 9.00 am  Nappy change/play
 9.30 am  Garden time — if fine
10.00 am  Snack: beaker or bottle
          and rusk
10.30 am  Water play
11.00 am  Nappy change/sleep
12.00 am  Lunch
 1.00 pm  Nappy change
 1.30 pm  Walk in pushchair
 3.00 pm  Snack/nappy change
 4.30 pm  Tea
 5.00 pm  Play until collected
```

Routine for a 10-month-old baby in a day nursery

and a half. This means that, although it is sensible to have an idea of a baby's routine, it is always best to adopt a flexible approach allowing the baby to set the pattern of the day. Any significant changes to a routine – for example, a baby missing out a feed – should be passed on to the supervisor or in a home environment, to the parents.

Knowledge into Action

Record the daily routine of a baby in your workplace

Include nappy changes, sleeps and feeds.

1 *Look at the routine on another day.*
2 *Does the baby still have the same routine?*
3 *If it has changed, how and why?*

Pressures on families

Early years workers need to understand that, although parents love and enjoy their babies, the responsibility of having babies and children is enormous. Many parents find themselves under pressure for many reasons – these which might include:

■ **Tiredness.** Lack of sleep due to nightfeeds and sleeping problems can cause strain especially if parents have to go to work.

■ **Financial.** Many parents find looking after a baby expensive. Most parents find they have less money to spend as either they cannot work so many hours or they are paying for childcare.

■ **Time.** Caring for babies is time-consuming. Many parents find they do not have any time for themselves either to relax or to see friends.

■ **Responsibility.** Parents can find the responsibility of keeping another little person alive and well overwhelming. Many of their decisions have to revolve around the care of the baby.

Case Study

Dawn is married and has two children aged 9 and 15. She was surprised when she found that she was expecting twins. The twins are now eight months old and are starting to crawl. Dawn's husband is rarely at home as he works a shift system and tries to do as much overtime as possible to boost the family's income. The two-bedroomed house is now cramped and they cannot afford to buy anything larger. Dawn had to give up her part-time job after she had the twins, as finding someone to look after both of them and collect the nine-year-old from school was going to cost her more than she could earn.

Most of the time Dawn and her husband are exhausted. The twins are sharing the bedroom with them and they never get a moment alone together.

Other expenses such as buying safety gates, pushchairs and keeping the house warm are starting to push them into debt. They feel they are always saying no to the 15-year-old when he wants to have new clothes and go out with his friends.

Questions
1 *What other expenses are they likely to have in the coming months?*
2 *Why is it more difficult for parents on a low income with twins?*
3 *As the home is small, where else could Dawn take the twins in the day?*

A healthy and safe environment

Caring for babies is a particularly responsible job. Part of this job is to recognise when they are not feeling well. Babies are particularly vulnerable to infections and as they are unable to say when they are feel unwell, we must be alert to any signs of illness.

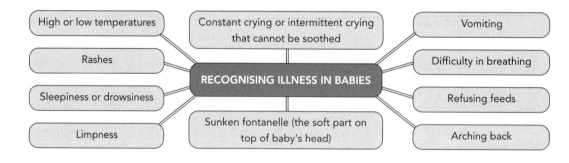

As young babies' illnesses can rapidly worsen, it is essential that medical assistance is sought straight away. Recognising that babies are unwell and getting help can save a life! You must always have the name of the family's doctor and an emergency contact number in case of an accident or medical emergency, even if you are only babysitting for an hour or so.

In Chapter 6 (pages 118–19) we looked at different types of common illnesses and their signs and symptoms. If you are going to care for babies it is essential that you can remember these. Try out the quick quiz below.

Think about it

1   *What are the signs of meningitis in babies?*
2   *What are the signs of whooping cough?*
3   *What might red spots with raised centres be a sign of?*

Sudden Infant Death Syndrome (SIDS)

Every year 500 babies die unexpectedly in their sleep. This is often called cot death or Sudden Infant Death Syndrome. Recent research has meant that parents and early years workers are now issued with the following advice when putting babies to sleep.

- Lie babies on their sides or backs, not on their fronts.

- Make sure that babies are not overheated with too many clothes or blankets.

- Do not put pillows in cots.

- Avoid exposing babies to smoky environments.

The causes of SIDS are not fully understood although research is ongoing. The current advice seems to be effective as the numbers of babies dying from cot death has decreased sharply.

Preventing the spread of infections

Hand-washing	Hands need to be washed	
	before	**after**
	• preparing babies feeds and food	• using the toilet
	• changing nappies	• blowing noses
Disposing of nappies and other waste materials	Nappies should be wrapped up and never flushed down the toilet. Other waste materials – e.g. baby wipes and cotton wool should be disposed of carefully. In large settings disposable gloves should also be worn and then thrown away.	
Items for personal hygiene	Items such as towels, flannels and toothbrushes need to be kept clean and separate from others. In large settings they could be named to avoid confusion. In family settings, it is important that good hygiene procedures are also observed although the early years worker must agree these with the parents.	

As a professional early years worker in any setting, we must always be alert to the risk of cross infection. This happens when bacteria or viruses are passed on from one person to another. In order to protect ourselves from infection as well as babies and young children – who are particularly vulnerable to infections – it is important that the following precautions are always taken.

Care of skin, hair and teeth

Our skin is a protective layer that acts as a barrier to infection as well as helping to control our temperature. This means that to keep babies healthy, their skin needs to be cared for.

The skin-cleaning routine will depend on the parents' wishes and should respect cultural traditions. For example, Muslims bathe under running water. Some babies may need lotions or other skin products as they might have skin conditions such as eczema.

Topping and tailing. This expression means washing and drying babies' faces and bottoms! The idea of topping and tailing is to keep babies clean and fresh either instead of or between baths.

Hair. Some babies are born with no hair while others have masses of it! Caring for babies' hair is relatively simple. It needs to be gently brushed with a soft brush or a wide-toothed comb and washed as part of the bathing routine. Where babies' hair is styled – e.g. some Afro-Caribbean babies may have small plaits – it is important to ask parents what they would like you to do when brushing or washing it.

Teeth. At around six months babies start getting their first teeth. It is important that these are cared for, as they help guide the more permanent teeth into position. Gentle brushing with a small-headed, soft-bristle brush should start once the first teeth appear. Sugary drinks and foods need to be avoided to prevent dental decay. Fruit juices and sugary drinks in bottles are not recommended.

Bathing babies

As well as being important in the routine of caring for babies, bathtime is often great fun for babies. Most babies love being in the bath and gain many benefits from playing in the water.

Helping babies to enjoy bathtime. We need to allow the baby plenty of time to explore the water. As babies get older we can provide some simple toys for them to grasp and use. Some babies are afraid of water and so we may have to reassure them by talking or singing to them.

Making sure that bathtime is safe. Although bathtimes can be fun, they can also be dangerous. Every year some babies drown or are scalded at bathtime. The following safety advice must always be followed when bathing babies and young children.

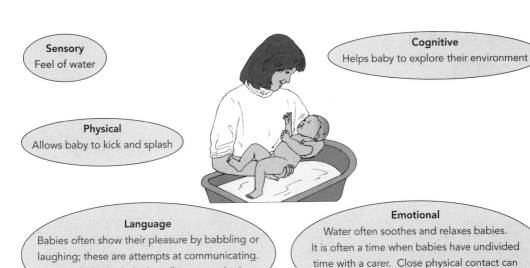

Sensory
Feel of water

Cognitive
Helps baby to explore their environment

Physical
Allows baby to kick and splash

Language
Babies often show their pleasure by babbling or laughing; these are attempts at communicating. We can help the baby by talking as we bathe.

Emotional
Water often soothes and relaxes babies. It is often a time when babies have undivided time with a carer. Close physical contact can also make the baby feel more secure.

Bathing babies can be fun and beneficial

Bathtime accessories

- Never leave babies or young children alone near or in water.

- Always check the temperature of water. It should be around 38°C – warm, but *never* hot.

- Make sure that any toys for the bath are suitable for the age of the baby.

Good preparation and organisation are essential when bathing a baby. Everything should be laid out before starting to undress the baby. The room needs to be warm – 20°C – as babies chill quickly. Adults also need to check they are not wearing anything that might scratch babies' skin – for example, a watch or jewellery. An apron is often useful, as babies tend to splash!

Essential checklist	Optional checklist
• Clean nappy • Clean clothes including vest • Cotton wool or baby wipes • Bag or bucket for waste materials such as dirty nappy and wipes • Towels • Shampoo	• Thermometer to check temperature of water • Barrier cream to prevent nappy rash • Soap • Bubble bath • Talcum powder (The optional skin products should only be used after checking with parents as babies may have skin allergies.)

Topping and tailing

1. Take off outer clothing. Wash each eye with a separate piece of moist cotton wool. Use warm water.

2. Wash each ear gently with a clean piece of moist cotton wool.

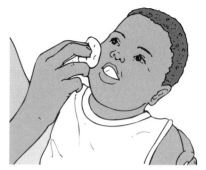

3. Wash the rest of the face and finally the mouth.

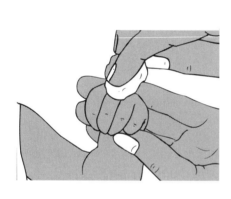

4. Wash the baby's hands.

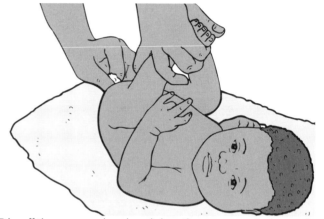

5. Take off the nappy and wash and clean the nappy area in the usual way.

Bathing older babies. As babies get older they are able to sit up in baths and we can wash their hair by gently pouring water over their heads.

It is a good idea to use a flannel to top and tail before they get into the bath so that if they drink any of the water, it is likely to be clean.

Changing nappies and dressing a baby

One of the less pleasant aspects of caring for babies and young children is nappy-changing. It is, nonetheless, an absolutely essential part of the job. Frequently changing nappies prevents the skin in this area from becoming sore and prevents infections. Never leave a baby in a dirty or wet nappy.

Safety. To change nappies quickly and safely, you must be well prepared and have everything that you need to hand. Babies must never be left alone as they could put their hands into a dirty nappy or roll off a surface. Some early years workers prefer to change nappies on the floor to prevent any possible accidents.

There are two types of nappies – disposable and terry towelling. Plastic pants and safety pins are needed when using terry-towelling nappies. To avoid chills babies should be changed in warm rooms – about 20°C – that are free from draughts.

Bathing a baby

Prepare all the equipment and fill the baby bath with warm water.

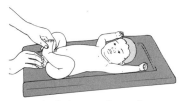

1. Put the baby on a flat surface, undress him/her and take off the nappy. Clean the nappy area.

2. Wrap the baby gently but securely in a towel, so that the arms are tucked in. Wash the face with moist cotton wool.

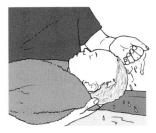

3. Hold the baby over the bath and wash the head and hair.

4. Take off the towel. Holding the baby securely under the head and round the arm, lift him/her into the water.

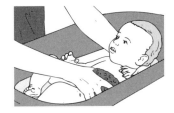

5. Use your spare hand to wash the baby.

6. Lift the baby out of the bath supporting under the bottom, and quickly wrap him/her in a warm towel.

Checklist	Step by step
<ul><li>Changing mat</li><li>Disposable gloves</li><li>Clean nappies</li><li>Nappy pin and plastic pants if using terry nappies</li><li>Cotton wool or wipes</li><li>Bucket or bag to dispose of soiled nappies and waste products</li><li>Spare clothing</li><li>Barrier cream (to prevent nappy rash)</li></ul>	This a simple guide to changing nappies. Nothing beats practice or being shown by a supervisor. 1 Wash your hands; put on disposable gloves. 2 Undress the baby as needed and lie on mat. 3 Undo nappy – if removing a terry-towelling nappy, close pin and put somewhere safe. 4 Gently lift up baby's legs by ankles. 5 Wipe off faeces using cotton wool or baby wipes. 6 Remove soiled nappy and waste materials. 7 Thoroughly clean the genital area. 8 Make sure that the skin in the nappy area is dry. 9 Put on clean nappy.

Good Practice – nappy changing

✔ Always wipe girls from front to back to avoid infection.

✔ Do not pull foreskin back on baby boys.

✔ Always wash hands before and after changing nappies.

✔ Wipe down changing mats using disinfectant.

Talk to babies during the nappy-changing process so that they feel reassured. It is also a good idea to give them rattles or simple toys to distract them as they get older. As boys often urinate during the nappy change, it is sensible to wear an apron to avoid the fountain!

Choice of nappies

Parents choose between types of nappies for many reasons and there are advantages and disadvantages to both types. Some parents may use both.

Disposable. There is a large choice of disposable nappies. At present 80 per cent of parents use disposable nappies. Disposable nappies come in different sizes according to the weight of babies and children. Some brands also sell separate types for boys and girls. Cheaper nappies are made of wood pulp and the more expensive 'Ultra' nappies contain granules that turn into gel when the nappy becomes wet.

Terry towelling. Some parents prefer to use terry-towelling nappies because they feel they are more environmentally friendly or because they are cheaper. Terry-towelling nappies need to be thoroughly disinfected and rinsed through. To avoid this, some parents use laundry services that deliver clean folded nappies and take away the soiled ones. In the last few years different types of terry-towelling nappies have become available including shaped nappies with Velcro fastenings.

Nappy rash

Nappy rash is common in babies. It is sore and painful and so early years workers must do everything they can to prevent babies from developing it.

Reasons why nappy rash may occur	How to prevent nappy rash
• Reaction to washing powder or bath product • Diarrhoea • Poor nappy-changing technique • Nappies left on for too long • Teething (although some doctors disagree with this)	• Change nappy frequently • Make sure that skin in the nappy area is dry before putting on new nappy • Leave nappy off for a few minutes each day • Use barrier cream to stop urine and faeces directly touching the skin

Differences in bowel and bladder actions

Young babies can produce interesting bowel movements or stools in their nappies! Regular bowel movements show that the digestive system is working well and they can be very frequent in young babies. This is quite normal.

Signs of normal bowel movement There is a difference between the stools of breast-fed and bottle-fed babies.

Breast-fed babies	Bottle-fed babies
Orange, yellow mustard, often watery	Pale brown, solid and smelly (not unpleasant smell)

It is important for early years workers to note down any significant changes of bowel action such as a baby not passing any stools in the day or stools becoming hard. Any changes in the colour, frequency or softness of stools must be reported immediately to supervisors or parents as it may be a sign of an infection or illness. It is also important for the early years worker to be sure that babies are passing urine frequently, as this means that the kidneys are working properly. If you think that babies are not passing enough urine, you must pass on this information to supervisors or parents.

When to seek help

- Any sign of blood
- Small green stool over a period of days (may indicate underfeeding)
- Stools are very watery and have unpleasant smell
- Babies cry when passing a motion

Knowledge into Action

You are babysitting for a few hours and when you change the baby's nappy you notice that the skin around the genital area is beginning to look red.

1 *What steps can you take to prevent the nappy rash from spreading?*
2 *Why is it important that you report the nappy rash to the parents when they return?*
3 *Why is it important to tell them what steps you have already taken?*

Toilet training

Not all cultures and countries use nappies. For example, some families choose to put their babies on a pot before and after feeds. This encourages babies to empty their bowels as a reflex. Towels may be put under the babies at other times. If we work with a family where this is the case, we must respect this decision, although in large settings, babies need to wear nappies to avoid cross infection.

In most settings parents decide to start toilet training when children have more control over their bodies, at around 18–36 months. If you wish to read more about toilet training look at Chapter 4 (pages 89–90).

Knowledge into Action

1 *Using catalogues and local shops, find out the range of nappies available and their costs.*
2 *Design a questionnaire to find out what types of nappy parents prefer and why they use them.*
3 *Use the questionnaire with at least five parents and present the information as a simple typewritten report.*

This exercise can be done in pairs or small groups.

Equipment for babies

Babies need different types of equipment during the first year of their lives. Most baby equipment is linked to the weight rather than the age of child – for example, a first car seat may take a baby up to 10kg.

It is quite a surprise to new parents to see how much equipment is needed when babies are so small!

These are some of the factors involved in choosing equipment.

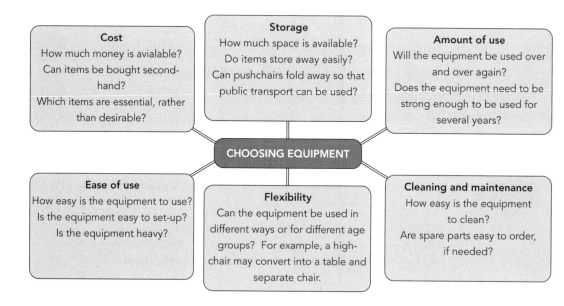

Cost
How much money is avialable?
Can items be bought second-hand?
Which items are essential, rather than desirable?

Storage
How much space is available?
Do items store away easily?
Can pushchairs fold away so that public transport can be used?

Amount of use
Will the equipment be used over and over again?
Does the equipment need to be strong enough to be used for several years?

CHOOSING EQUIPMENT

Ease of use
How easy is the equipment to use?
Is the equipment easy to set-up?
Is the equipment heavy?

Flexibility
Can the equipment be used in different ways or for different age groups? For example, a high-chair may convert into a table and separate chair.

Cleaning and maintenance
How easy is the equipment to clean?
Are spare parts easy to order, if needed?

Buying second-hand equipment

Equipment can be expensive, so many parents choose to buy some of it second hand. Care must be taken when buying any second-hand equipment.

- Equipment should be checked for signs of wear.
- Older cots should be avoided as safety regulations have changed. Cot bars need to be no further than 7.6cm apart to prevent babies' heads from becoming stuck.
- Toys and equipment need to be thoroughly cleaned.
- Old car seats should be avoided as they may not be safe.
- Second-hand cot mattresses have been linked to cot death or SIDS.

Buying new equipment

- New equipment should always carry safety marks.
- Manufacturers' instructions and guidelines must be followed and kept for reference.

Knowledge into Action

1   *Make a list of the equipment that your workplace uses to care for children.*

    Divide your list into the following headings:

    Safety   Sleeping   Feeding   Transport

2   *Choosing an age over three months, work out the cost of providing the equipment that would be needed for this age of baby. You might use a baby catalogue or visit a store.*

This activity could be done in pairs.

Maintaining and cleaning equipment

It is the early years worker's role to make sure that any equipment used with babies is safe and hygienic.

Large equipment such as pushchairs, playpens and highchairs can all wear out. This means that they must be checked each week for safety.

Checks might include looking at:

- reins and harnesses

- moving parts – e.g. hinges, wheels, brakes

- stability of legs and feet

- plastic parts that might split or crack – e.g. seats in highchairs.

Cleaning and sterilising equipment

Every item that is in contact with babies is a potential source of infection. If babies are being cared for in large settings, it is particularly essential that sterilisation and other cleaning procedures are carried out often. This may mean that rattles and other toys are sterilised at the end of each session. Equipment that is used for feeding – for example, highchairs – need to be cleaned every time they are used.

Good practice – points to remember when cleaning equipment

✔ Use the right cloths, sponges and other materials kept for the purpose.

✔ Follow manufacturers' guidelines when cleaning equipment.

✔ Make up sterilising fluid and disinfectant according to the instructions on the bottle.

✔ Make sure that any equipment that goes into babies mouths is sterilised and rinsed thoroughly.

✔ Do not put damp equipment away – the moisture encourages bacteria to grow.

Clothing and footwear

Babies grow very quickly and often need several changes of clothes in a day. This is one area where parents can save money by buying items second hand. By law all garments have to show washing instructions and fabric content. Most baby clothes are made with cotton as this fabric is easy to care for and does not irritate the skin.

Babies' clothes need to be washed with a gentle detergent as their skin is fragile. Non-biological detergent is suggested and all items need rinsing thoroughly. Babies with eczema may need special detergents that are particularly gentle.

Checklist when buying clothes

▪ **Are they easy to put on?** Small babies may need to be changed several times in the day because of being sick or because a nappy leaked. Older babies who are crawling may not want to lie still while having their nappies changed which means that clothes must be easy to put on and remove.

▪ **Do they allow for growth and movement?** This is especially important when babies start to crawl. Dresses are harder to crawl in than dungarees!

▪ **Are they easy to wash?** Most baby clothes can be machine-washed. Manufacturers' washing instructions should always be followed.

Footwear

Young babies do not need shoes until they start walking. Babies' feet can be kept warm using socks or padders. Any footwear must be checked for size and should not restrict the feet. Babies' feet can be damaged by socks and other items of clothing that are too small – for example, check the amount of foot space in bodysuits.

Think about it

You are working as a mother's help and you have been asked to pack a bag so that the four-month-old baby can spend an autumn weekend with the grandmother. The grandmother has a cot, sheets and blankets, but no other items such as nappies and clothes.

In pairs, make a list of the items that would need to go into this bag. You may need to go back over this chapter to remind yourselves about the needs of this age of baby!

2 Feeding babies

Early years workers caring for babies may need to prepare feeds for them. This is a major responsibility as feeding equipment needs to be sterilised and feeds have to be made up correctly.

Nutritional needs

In the first year of life, most babies treble their birth weight. This means that they need to feed well to allow this growth to take place.

In the first four to six months, babies gain all the nutrients (see Chapter 5, page 101, for details of nutrients) they need from either formula or breast milk. After six months, babies need other sources of food, especially those that contain iron.

The choice of whether to breast- or bottle-feed lies with the mother. Some mothers start by breast-feeding and then decide to use a bottle. It is important that mothers are not made to feel guilty about their choice as babies thrive on both types of feeding. The process of starting solid foods is called 'weaning' although milk still remains an important part of a baby's diet.

Breast-feeding

Breast milk is recognised as being the best type of milk for babies – after all, it was designed for human babies! The milk contains not just the nutrients that are needed to promote growth, but also the antibodies from the mother which help fight against infections. Breast milk also changes according to the needs of the baby. In the first few days the milk is thin and yellow – this is called 'colostrum'. This is particularly good for babies as it contains antibodies. After the third day, the milk changes and is lighter in colour.

For women who cannot always be with their baby, but who wish to breast-feed, it is possible to 'express' milk (this means squeezing it out of the breast) and put it into a bottle or freeze it.

The advantages of breast-feeding include the following.

- It provides antibodies.

- There is close contact between mother and baby that makes it a pleasant experience for both.

- Feeding is instant because there is no waiting for bottles to cool and no sterilisation to be done.

- It is also free, which may be important for families on low incomes but who do not qualify for state benefits.

- It helps the womb to contract more quickly.

To produce enough milk for a baby, it is important that the mother eats well and drinks enough fluid.

Bottle-feeding

Some parents decide to bottle-feed using formula milk. There are many different reasons why a woman may decide to bottle-feed. She may feel that she cannot cope if she has a multiple birth, or she may wish to return to work. In some cases doctors advise some women not to breast-feed – for example, if a woman is on strong medication some of the drugs will be passed onto the baby through the milk. The main advantage of bottle-feeding is that anyone can take over from the mother, although where possible it should be the same people feeding the baby. The disadvantages of bottle-feeding are that all items need sterilising and great care must be taken in making up the feeds.

Think about it

1 *Were you a breast-fed or bottle-fed baby?*
2 *Why do you think that some women prefer to bottle-feed?*

Sterilising equipment

Babies are very vulnerable to infection, which means that in early years settings, we must be careful to prevent bacteria from spreading. The risk of infection can be reduced if the following steps are followed.

- Always wash hands when handling feeding equipment as bacteria on the hands can be passed on.
- Always store made up bottles in the fridge to prevent bacteria from multiplying.
- Never give a bottle over 24 hours old to a baby.
- Make sure that feeding equipment is properly cleaned and sterilised.

The three main ways in which items can be sterilised are by boiling, steaming or using a chemical solution.

Equipment

- Teats
- Bottles
- Covers
- Lids and discs.

Step-by-step guide to sterilisation

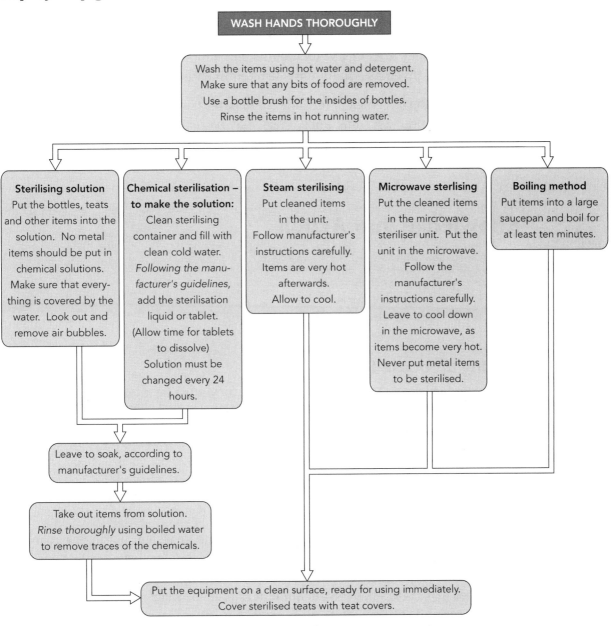

WASH HANDS THOROUGHLY

Wash the items using hot water and detergent.
Make sure that any bits of food are removed.
Use a bottle brush for the insides of bottles.
Rinse the items in hot running water.

Sterilising solution
Put the bottles, teats and other items into the solution. No metal items should be put in chemical solutions. Make sure that everything is covered by the water. Look out and remove air bubbles.

Chemical sterilisation – to make the solution:
Clean sterilising container and fill with clean cold water. *Following the manufacturer's guidelines,* add the sterilisation liquid or tablet. (Allow time for tablets to dissolve) Solution must be changed every 24 hours.

Steam sterilising
Put cleaned items in the unit. Follow manufacturer's instructions carefully. Items are very hot afterwards. Allow to cool.

Microwave sterlising
Put the cleaned items in the mircrowave steriliser unit. Put the unit in the microwave. Follow the manufacturer's instructions carefully. Leave to cool down in the microwave, as items become very hot. Never put metal items to be sterilised.

Boiling method
Put items into a large saucepan and boil for at least ten minutes.

Leave to soak, according to manufacturer's guidelines.

Take out items from solution. *Rinse thoroughly* using boiled water to remove traces of the chemicals.

Put the equipment on a clean surface, ready for using immediately. Cover sterilised teats with teat covers.

Portfolio activity

Ask your supervisor if you can sterilise some feeding equipment.

Write about how you did this.

1 *Which items did you sterilise?*
2 *What were the steps in sterilising?*
3 *What did you learn from doing this activity?*

Types of milk

Bottle-fed babies are given formula milk. This comes in several forms, derived from cow's milk, goat's milk or soya beans. Ordinary cow's milk cannot be given to babies until they are at least six months old, although the current advice is that it should not be given as a main milk drink until babies are a year old.

As there are different types of formula milk, parents must be asked which type of milk should be used as, sometimes, there may be religious or cultural preferences. For example, some babies have milk made from soya because they are allergic to other types of milk or because their parents are vegans.

Knowledge into Action

Find out about how babies are fed in your workplace.

1   *Write down what types of milk are used.*
2   *How is feeding equipment sterilised?*

Making up bottle feeds

Making up feeds is a major responsibility, as they must be made up accurately and hygienically. It is essential that the manufacturers' instructions are followed.

Putting too much powder in a feed can mean that babies develop problems with their kidneys.

Putting too little powder in a feed can mean that babies lose weight or show poor weight gain and become constipated and distressed.

The amount of milk that babies need depends on their weight not their age. New-born babies need less milk than older, heavier babies. They will usually need several small feeds – for example, 8 feeds in 24 hours. It is extremely important that babies are offered the correct amount of milk for their weight. Always check with parents and supervisors to make sure that you understand how much milk should be offered at a time as this can vary from baby to baby.

Knowledge into Action

1   *Record the feeding routine of a baby in your workplace.*
2   *Note the times that they feed and how much they take.*
3   *Find out the exact age of the baby.*
4   *In your group, compare your notes with other people's.*
5   *Are babies of similar ages feeding in the same way?*

Step-by-step guide to making up a feed

1. Read the manufacturer's instructions on the tin.

2. Fill a kettle and let it boil. Allow the water to cool down.

3. Wash hands thoroughly.

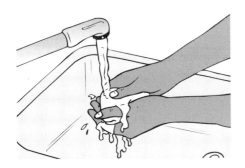

4. Using a sterilised bottle, put in the boiled water to the required level.

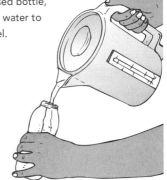

5. Using the scoop measure the exact amount of powder. Level off with a knife. Add the powder to the sterilised bottle.

6. Screw the ring and disc on the bottle (but not the teat) and shake well.

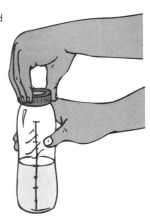

7. Allow the bottle to cool down before giving to the baby.

8. If making up several bottles, cool immediately and store in the fridge. Bottles must be used within 24 hours.

```
┌─────────────────────────────────────────┐
│            FEEDING RECORD                │
│  Name  David E.                          │
│                                          │
│  Date   8/6/98                           │
│  ┌─────────┬──────────────┬───────────┐  │
│  │ Time    │ Food/Drink   │ Comments  │  │
│  ├─────────┼──────────────┼───────────┤  │
│  │ 8.30    │ Breakfast    │           │  │
│  │         │ fruit purée  │ Enjoyed the banana │
│  │         │ and 3oz milk │ and pear mixture. │
│  │ 10.30 am│ Bottle 8oz   │ David managed all │
│  │         │              │ his bottle today. │
│  │ 1.00 pm │ Vegetable    │ Carrot and potato │
│  │         │ purée and    │ purée was taken │
│  │         │ 6oz boiled   │ slowly, but enjoyed. │
│  │         │ water        │           │
│  │ 4.30 pm │ Bottle 7oz   │ 8oz was offered, │
│  │         │              │ but David only │
│  │         │              │ wanted 7oz. │
│  └─────────┴──────────────┴───────────┘  │
│  Signature of keyworker ................  │
└─────────────────────────────────────────┘
```

Feeding a baby

Unless you are caring for a very young baby, you will probably find that the baby has established a feeding routine. This does not mean that each day they will take exactly the same amount of milk as some days they may feel hungrier than others. Parents should always be told when their baby has refused feeds or has not taken as much milk as they normally do. This can be a sign that the baby is feeling unwell. It is good practice to keep a record of the time a feed is given and how much milk was taken.

Early years workers have to be organised if they are caring for babies. Babies who are crying with hunger want to be fed immediately! It is important that feeds are ready for them. This means keeping an eye on the time and getting feeds ready beforehand. Most settings make up several bottles as part of the daily routine.

Bottles that have been made up in advance need time to heat up or reach room temperature. Bottles that are made just before a feed need time to cool down.

Never use a microwave to heat up bottles. There is a risk of scalding a baby's mouth because the milk can be unevenly heated and have 'hot spots'.

This should be a special time for the baby and you. There is more to feeding a baby than just giving the milk. Eye contact, cuddles and talking gently to the baby means that this is a pleasant experience, giving the baby reassurance and security. Try to choose a quiet place to feed where there are no interruptions to spoil this special time.

By about four months babies try to hold their bottles. You should still support the bottle to make sure that no air is taken in while they are feeding.

Good practice – feeding babies

✔ Never leave a baby propped up with a bottle (they may choke or drown).

✔ Always wash your hands thoroughly before preparing or giving a feed.

✔ Always use sterilised equipment.

✔ Always check the temperature of the feed.

Feeding babies

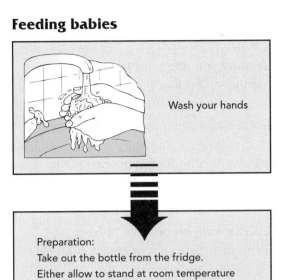

Wash your hands

Preparation:
Take out the bottle from the fridge.
Either allow to stand at room temperature for 30 minutes or stand in a jug of hot water to heat up. Do not leave for more than 40 minutes or make up the bottle and allow to cool.

Collect together everything that you need during the feed, such as cloths, bibs and tissues.
(Babies often dribble or are sick after a feed and these items are needed.)

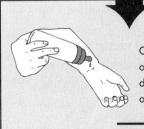

Check the temperature of the bottle by dripping some milk onto your wrist.

Check the flow. If it is coming out too fast the baby may choke, if it is too slow the baby may become fustrated.

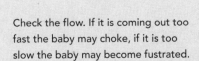

Always throw away unfinished milk.

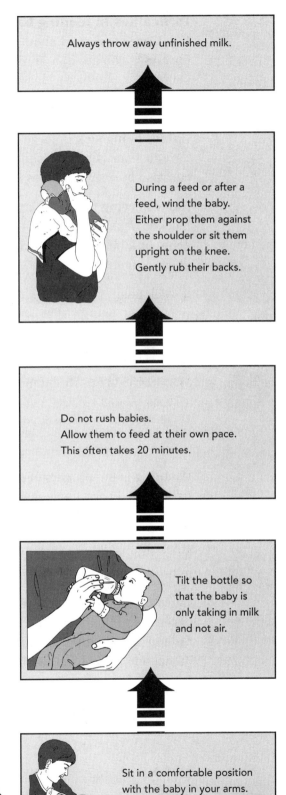

During a feed or after a feed, wind the baby. Either prop them against the shoulder or sit them upright on the knee. Gently rub their backs.

Do not rush babies.
Allow them to feed at their own pace.
This often takes 20 minutes.

Tilt the bottle so that the baby is only taking in milk and not air.

Sit in a comfortable position with the baby in your arms. Gently rub the teat over the lips to let her know that the milk is there.

Difficulties in feeding babies

If you are concerned about how a baby is feeding you must immediately tell the parents if you are in a home environment or the supervisor if you are in a group setting.

Common difficulties include:

Babies being sick in large quantities during or after the feed. This can mean that too much air is being swallowed and the baby needs to be winded more often. It can also be a sign of illness.

Babies crying but not taking the bottle. This can happen because the teat is blocked or the milk is flowing too slowly. It can also be a sign of colic (stomach ache) or a baby not being able to suck.

There are many reasons why babies may have difficulties, but your role is always to seek help.

Portfolio activity

Ask your supervisor if you can prepare a feed and/or bottle-feed a baby.

1 *Write down how you did this task.*
2 *What did you learn from doing it?*

Weaning is the process of getting babies used to taking solid food. By six months babies need solid food, as they cannot get all the nutrients they need from milk alone – for example, they need iron in their diets. The process of weaning also helps babies to become part of the family and they learn to socialise through having the same food as others. Learning how to chew food develops the muscles in the mouth that are also used for speech.

The decision about when to start the weaning process should come from the parents and the baby! The baby may show signs of needing extra food from around four months. Starting the weaning process before this age can cause damage to babies' kidneys and may create allergies later on.

Common signs that babies are ready to wean include:

- beginning to wake in the night for another feed

- finishing all feeds and still seeming hungry

- being restless

- poor weight gain.

It is important to work with parents when babies are ready to be weaned so that early years workers can make sure that any dietary preferences or restrictions are understood. For example, vegetarian parents may prefer their child not to have any meat-based products. See the chart in Chapter 5 (page 113) which outlines dietary restrictions associated with different religions.

Weaning is often divided into three stages. By the end of their first year, most children are getting used to eating solid food and are trying to feed themselves.

Weaning

Stage	Age	Preparation	Types of food
1	4–6 months	Purée or liquidise food so that it is easy to swallow.	Baby rice Vegetable purées (potato, yam, carrot) Fruit purées (plantain, banana, apple, pear etc.) Introduce tastes one at a time. **Once spoon feeding is established:** Vegetable and meat or fish purées, yoghurt, a wider range of vegetables
2	6–9 months	Mash foods so that they are slightly thicker, but still easy to swallow.	Fish, meat, poultry and a wide range of vegetables and fruit. Anything that can be mashed. Babies can share in family meals, if the food is mashed for them. **Highchairs can be used but babies must not be left alone in them.**
3	9+ months	Introduce foods that can be eaten with fingers as well as with a spoon.	Add in foods that babies can handle – e.g. pitta bread, chappattis, fish fingers, pieces of banana etc. **Stay near the baby in case of choking.**

Stage 1 (puréed food)

Starting weaning requires patience, as the baby needs to learn how to take food off a spoon and what to do with the food! If parents have asked you to start this process, it is best if you choose a time when the baby is not too hungry or tired. After a nap and part way through a milk-feed is often a good time. A sterilised plastic spoon and bowl is needed along with a bib or cloth to wipe the baby's mouth.

Early morning	Milk
Breakfast	Milk, 1 tbspn cereal, fruit
Lunch	Lunch – puréed food – e.g. meat and vegetables, drink of boiled water
Late afternoon	Milk – 1 tbspn puréed fruit
Evening	Milk

Example of a feeding pattern for a five-month-old baby

Baby rice is often given as a first food as it is not dissimilar in taste to milk, although different types of cereals can be used as a first food. A small quantity – enough for three to four teaspoons – should be mixed with formula or breast milk. The spoon is put gently onto the baby's lips. At first babies tend to suck the food off. Many babies spit out the food at first, as they are not used to the texture. Over a period of a few days,

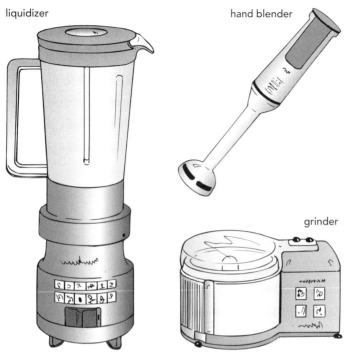

liquidizer

hand blender

grinder

babies gradually learn to take from the spoon.

Once the baby is used to the spoon, new tastes can gradually be added, although it is a good idea to introduce new foods one at a time. This means that if a baby is allergic to any food, it is easier to identify.

As babies take more and more solid food, they will need less milk, although it should remain an important part of their diet until they are at least two years old. From now on babies must be offered drinks so that they do not dehydrate. Cooled boiled water is considered to be the best and babies can be introduced to the use of beakers.

The amount of solid food taken depends on each baby. Some babies take a tablespoon at a time, other may only take a teaspoonful. It is important to make sure that the baby is not hungry.

Early morning	Milk
Breakfast	Cereal, puréed fruit, milk
Lunch	Mashed main meal, pudding, water
Late afternoon	Cheese sandwich, yoghurt, milk
Evening	Milk (if baby wakes)

Example of a feeding pattern of a seven-month-old baby (Note that milk feeds are being dropped)

Early morning	Water or very diluted juice
Breakfast	Cereal, fruit, milk in a cup
Mid morning	Fruit and water
Lunch	Mashed main meal, pudding, water
Late afternoon	Finger foods, fruit or yoghurt, milk from a cup

An example of an 11-month-old baby

Stage 2

In this stage, babies are learning to chew a little before swallowing. Food can be mashed rather than puréed. At this stage, babies also begin to want to feed themselves and show this by trying to hold the spoon. It is important that we encourage babies to feed themselves and we can do this by praising the baby and letting them

have a spoon of their own. From around six months, most babies are sitting in highchairs and can be at the table with other children or their families. Harnesses need to be used and babies must not be left alone in a highchair. Babies will be dropping a milk feed, but will still need a drink. Cooled boiled water is considered to be the best drink.

Stage 3

Babies are now starting to feed themselves and can chew their foods. Finger foods such as bread, toast and bananas are eaten independently. This is also a messy stage, as babies are using their senses to explore their food. They may squeeze food and drop it and many times they may take it towards their mouths, only to miss! A good supply of flannels, bibs and cloths are needed as early years workers must encourage babies to feed themselves.

Knowledge into Action

Ask your supervisor if you can record the feeding pattern of a baby in your workplace.

1   *Note at what times feeds and solid foods are offered.*
2   *In pairs, compare different babies' feeding patterns.*
3   *Why is it important to learn about individual babies' feeding patterns?*

Advice about foods

As professional early years workers, we need to listen carefully to any health advice about foods and change our practices accordingly.

Present guidelines about weaning and food for babies include the following.

■   Weaning should not start until four months.

■   Sugar and salt should not be added to foods.

■   Uncooked or soft-boiled eggs should not be given to babies or young children.

■   No wheat products should be given until babies are over six months.

■   Liver should not be given to babies and young children.

■   Cow's milk should not be given before six months and preferably not until after the first year.

■   Unpasteurised cheeses should not be given to babies.

> **Before food preparation**
> Wear an apron, tie hair back.
> Always wash hands before any food preparation.
> Check and clean if necessary any surfaces.

⬇

> **During food preparation**
> Always sterilise feeding equipment for babies, up until at least
> 6 months in home settings and longer in large work settings (often
> 15 months).
> Keep cooked foods and uncooked foods separately.
> Wash hands after touching raw meat or uncooked foods.
> Wash hands after sneezing, coughing or blowing nose.

⬇

> **Storing foods**
> Always throw away unfinished foods.
> Throw away foods that are past their 'sell-by' date.
> Cool down cooked foods quickly, wrap them and store them
> in the fridge.
> Do not keep uncooked foods near cooked foods in the fridge.
> Make sure the fridge is at the correct temperature.

⬇

> **Re-heating foods**
> Re-heat foods at high temperature for several minutes
> to kill bacteria.
> Do not reheat foods more than once.
> Frozen foods must be thawed thoroughly before re-heating.
> Follow manufacturer's instructions carefully when
> re-heating shop-bought foods.

Vitamin and other food supplements

Some babies may need vitamin drops in their food or drink if there are concerns about their general diet and health. The addition of any extra vitamin or food supplements – for example, calcium – to a baby's food is normally done on medical advice. If you are asked to add vitamin or food supplements it is important that you read the instructions on the packet or container carefully and make sure that you give the correct dosage. It is generally thought that food supplements and vitamins are not necessary if babies and young children are eating a balanced diet.

Preparing and storing foods

A good level of hygiene is essential when preparing food, especially for babies and young children. The main rules are quite simple. More information about food hygiene is in Chapter 5 (pages 107–9).

Food allergies and special diets

Some babies may be put on special diets if they have food allergies. Always find out from parents what foods should be avoided. In large settings, always check with your supervisor if you are unsure about a baby's diet.

Gluten-free diet. Babies who have coeliac disease must avoid gluten. This is commonly found in bread, biscuits, cakes, pastry, breakfast cereals and other foods made with wheat and other cereals such as rye.

Dairy-free diet. Babies who have allergies such as eczema and milk intolerance need to avoid dairy products such as cheese, milk and butter. Products made from soya beans are often given instead, including soya milk.

If you have any concerns over the way babies are feeding, it is important they are passed on to the parents or the supervisor, depending on your workplace. You can learn more about weaning, allergies and other issues concerning food by contacting a local health visitor, family practice or health promotion unit. In addition, the Health Education Authority publishes many leaflets about this aspect of health. The address is:

Health Education Authority
Hamilton House
Mabledon Place
London
WC1H 9TX

Unit test

Quick quiz

1   By what age are most babies able to sit up easily without support?
    a   1–2 months
    b   2–3 months
    c   4–5 months
    d   6–7 months.

2   A suitable temperature for a baby's room is:
    a   15°C
    b   18°C
    c   22°C
    d   24°C.

3   When putting a young baby to sleep, an adult should make sure:
    a   that the baby is on their back or side
    b   that the room is not too hot
    c   that the baby is well wrapped up
    d   that there are no pillows in the cot.

4   When bathing babies the temperature of the bath water should be:
    a   38°C
    b   40°C
    c   42°C
    d   44°C.

5   Which of these foods must not be given to babies who are on solids?
    a   rusks
    b   soft-boiled eggs
    c   bananas
    d   potatoes.

Short answer questions

1   Name a type of milk that is commonly given to bottle-fed babies who have allergies.

2   Name three ways of sterilising bottles.

3   At what age can babies first be given solid foods?

4   Give two reasons why some parents prefer to use terry-towelling nappies.

5   When can babies first be fitted with shoes?

Skills for Employment

There are many work opportunities for trained early years workers. For example, you might find work in a nursery, as a nanny or even in a crèche at a holiday resort. To benefit from these job opportunities, it is essential that you understand what an employer is looking for in an employee. This chapter is split into two sections:

Section 1 outlines your role when working for others. It includes how to be a good team member as well as your own rights and responsibilities as an employee.

Section 2 outlines the principles in using technical equipment and setting out learning materials for others.

1 Working for others

What is meant by the term organisation?

The types of early years settings where early years workers may be employed are so different that in this chapter we will be using the word organisation to describe early years settings where there is more than one employee.

Structures of organisations

Every organisation, no matter how small, has a staffing structure. The aim of a structure is to make sure that employees' time is used effectively and that all necessary tasks are allocated to someone. Most organisations have a hierarchical structure, which means that the people at the top take the most important decisions and have the most responsibility. They will also be more highly paid.

Look at this diagram of the structure of Jigsaw Day Nursery.

Manager. Emma has overall responsibility for running the nursery. This includes managing the budget, employing staff, making sure that the nursery meets all the legal requirements of being a daycare setting and an employer. She works out working rotas for staff and deals with any concerns that parents have.

Deputy Manager. Chris' job includes being responsible for developing the nursery curriculum and for managing the practical side of the nursery. He orders equipment and works with the cleaner and caretakers to make sure that the nursery is kept clean and well maintained. He deals with most of the day-to-day running problems. He also stands in for Emma when she is on holiday

Team leaders. Fatima and Anne Marie are responsible for the smooth running of their areas. They run meetings with their teams to plan activities and to discuss the needs of individual children. If they had concerns over children or a member of their team, they would report to Chris. When a new child comes into the nursery, they allocate a keyworker for that child. They meet at least once a week with Chris and Emma.

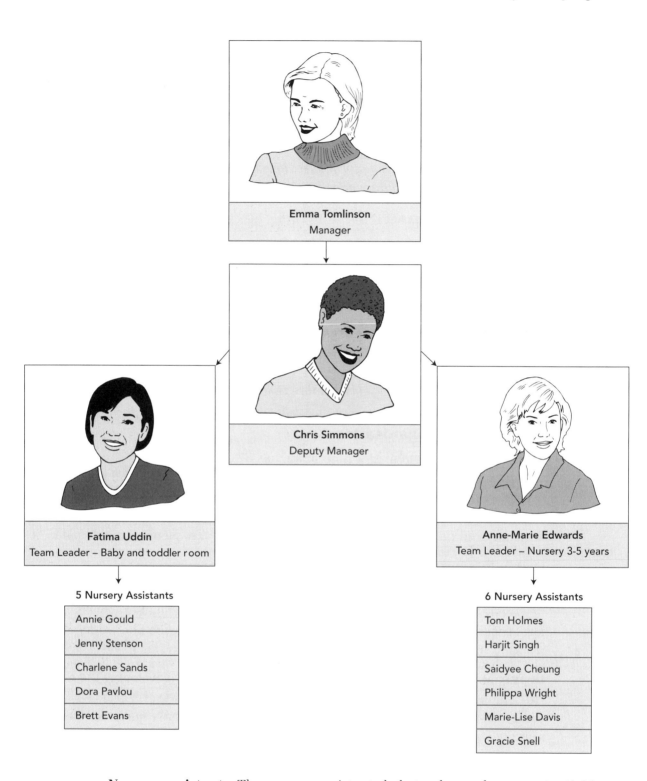

Emma Tomlinson
Manager

Chris Simmons
Deputy Manager

Fatima Uddin
Team Leader – Baby and toddler room

Anne-Marie Edwards
Team Leader – Nursery 3-5 years

5 Nursery Assistants

| Annie Gould |
| Jenny Stenson |
| Charlene Sands |
| Dora Pavlou |
| Brett Evans |

6 Nursery Assistants

| Tom Holmes |
| Harjit Singh |
| Saidyee Cheung |
| Philippa Wright |
| Marie-Lise Davis |
| Gracie Snell |

Nursery assistants. The nursery assistants help to plan and carry out activities. Some of their duties are rota-based, such as being responsible for making snacks and drinks, so that no one feels they are always doing the same jobs. As keyworkers they share information with parents about the children for whom they are directly responsible, although if necessary they would refer them on to their team leader.

Think about it

Think about the work that the nursery assistants carry out in a workplace that you know of or work in.

1 *Write a list of their duties.*
2 *In pairs, compare your lists.*
3 *Are your lists the same?*

Most organisations need a system to make sure that tasks are being carried out. This can be done by making some employees responsible for teams or for particular tasks. These people are called **line managers**. For example, in Jigsaw Nursery, nursery assistants have a team leader as their line manager.

Organisations also need a structure to allow information to be passed on and for employees to know whom they can talk to about any problems that may arise. It is important for any new employee to find out who there line manager is, as this is the person to whom they are responsible.

Portfolio activity

As an employee or as a student, it is important for you to find out about the structure of your workplace.

1 *Draw a flow diagram, similar to the one above, that shows the structure of your workplace.*
2 *To whom are you responsible?*
3 *If a member of staff needed some time off work, who would they see?*
4 *How are the themes and activities chosen?*

Aims and routines of organisations

Every workplace 'feels' different. This is partly because every staff team is different, but also because the aims of organisations vary. An organisation that is privately owned will differ from an organisation that is run by volunteers. The aims of the organisation affect its practice. For example, a crèche in a shopping centre will charge a set fee, regardless of parents' ability to pay the fee. It has to do this because it is a business. This is different from a playgroup, which may have some free places for parents who cannot afford the fees.

In the same way routines will vary according to the aims of the organisation. For example, if the organisation aims to provide childcare for working parents, it may have longer opening hours and the employees may work a shift system.

Knowledge into Action

1 *What are the aims of your workplace?*
2 *Write down the routine of your workplace.*
3 *How does this routine fit in with the aims of the workplace?*

Good practice in organisations

Throughout this book we have looked at areas of good practice in childcare. When you work for an organisation, you will need to learn about their practices and ways of doing things. For example, hometime may be managed in different ways. In one early years setting, children might stand at the door to be collected, whereas in another parents might come in to collect them and be responsible for putting on their coats.

It is extremely important to understand that there is no single way of running an early years setting and that employees who arrive in an organisation and immediately start criticising it become very unpopular very quickly!

Understanding the roles of other employees

To work effectively, you will need to understand the roles of the people you work with. This is especially important when you first start in an organisation, as it is easy to do a task which is someone else's responsibility or to exceed your authority.

Case Study

Lisa has recently joined a nursery as a nursery assistant. This is her first job.

Jamie's mother asks her if it would be all right for him to stay on at the nursery for two hours longer. Lisa says that there would be no problem as she is going to be around.

Later on she mentions in passing to her team leader that Jamie is going to stay for an extra two hours. The team leader is quite cross with Lisa because:

a   he is meant to know what is going on at all times

b   Jamie's key worker has not been asked

c   the nursery happens to be extra busy in the afternoons and there will not be enough staff to meet the staff-child ratio.

d   the nursery has a policy that parents should write to the manager to ask for extra hours so that proper accounts can be kept.

This is an example of how an inexperienced nursery assistant exceeded her authority, thinking that she was helping out a parent. This shows how important it is that you understand not only your own role, but also the roles of others in the organisation. The idea of being part of a team is to support each other, but not to do other people's jobs for them! A good team spirit is created when employees carry out their work well and consult other people when they are not sure how to handle a situation.

Health and safety at work. Employers have to follow the 1974 Health and Safety at Work Act, which makes them responsible for ensuring a healthy and safe work place not only for their employees, but also for members of the public on the premises. To carry out this duty, organisations have health and safety policies that relate to their workplace. For example, an organisation that uses nappies will have a policy on how to dispose of them safely.

As an employee, you are required by law to co-operate with your employer by following their policy. The law also requires you to take reasonable care of your own health and safety and that of others who may be affected by your actions or failure to carry out procedures. For more detailed information on this topic please turn to Chapter 3, page 47.

Think about it

In pairs discuss how your workplace:

1 *deals with waste materials such as nappies and tissues*
2 *keeps First Aid boxes.*

Are the same procedures used?

Equal opportunities policies. In Chapter 1 (page 10) we looked at the importance of equal opportunities policies. Many organisations ask employees to sign a statement to say that they have read and will follow the policies of the workplace. This means that as a new employee, you will need to read the document and find out how the equal opportunity policy of the organisation is put into practice.

Understanding your role as a member of a team

Most early years and educational settings have managers and team leaders, but rely on people working together as teams. A team is a group of people who are working together towards the same goal or aim. The team members might not do the same jobs or have the same responsibilities but by working together they can achieve the aims of the organisation. Most employers are looking not only for excellent childcare practice but also the ability to be a good team member.

Teams. As teams are made up of people and every person is different, it is possible you will not share the opinions or attitudes of the other members in your team. It is important to remember that everyone has different strengths and weaknesses and this makes for a balanced team. In business circles it is sometimes thought that having a team that always agrees can be bad – if team members have different views, this leads to debate and through the process of debate the team think through what they are doing.

Your role in working with other team members is to establish good working relationships. This is not the same as being friends, although many people do find friends at work.

Building a good working relationship means being able to listen to and respect other people's points of view. It also means putting aside any personal feelings that you may have, in order to put the needs of the team and ultimately the children first.

Good practice – how to be a good team member

✔ Make sure that you carry out your duties well.

✔ Be cheerful.

Haddon Davies

✔ Be considerate of other people in your team.

✔ Do not gossip.

✔ Contribute to team meetings.

✔ Follow instructions carefully.

✔ Understand that your supervisor or team leader is the first person you should be talking to if you have any problems.

✔ Acknowledge other people's ideas and support.

Think about it

Louise and Sarah work as nursery assistants in the same nursery. Louise finds out that Sarah is now going out with her former boyfriend and she suspects that this boyfriend may have dumped her so he could go out with Sarah.

Louise and Sarah have been asked to work together to produce a list of equipment for the outdoor play area. Louise does not feel that she can work with Sarah.

In pairs, discuss how Louise should handle this situation

Team meetings

The aim of meetings is to allow team members to get together and share concerns and ideas. As an employee, you may find that attending team meetings out of your normal working hours is part of your written contract. Meetings can be held for different reasons – for example, a meeting may be organised to discuss fund-raising events or to plan the next term's work. How often meetings are held and who is responsible for them depends on the organisation's needs. There is a standard pattern to the way most meetings are held and run.

Before the meeting

- An agenda is drawn up and team members are invited to forward items for discussion.

- The agenda is sent out or displayed in a central location.

At the meeting

- One person leads the meeting – the chairperson. Notes are taken during the meeting – these are called minutes. Whoever is recording the minutes is known as the secretary.

- The chairperson starts the meeting and the secretary notes who is present.

> **BARNABY'S NURSERY TEAM MEETING**
>
> *8/6/98*
>
> *Agenda*
>
> *1. Apologies*
>
> *2. Matters Arising*
>
> *3. Ideas for new books (MAC)*
>
> *4. New parents evening (CA)*
>
> *5. Concerns about individual children*
>
> *6. Stock requests (JH)*

- Items on the agenda are discussed one by one.

- In formal meetings, people should normally ask for permission to speak, but in most meetings people just wait for others to finish and then make their comments.

- A good chairperson makes sure that everyone's views are heard and prevents people from wasting time in talking about side issues. Sometimes, if no clear decision can be made, a vote is taken.

- The date for the next meeting is set at the end of the meeting.

After the meeting

- The minutes from the meeting are typed or written up neatly.

- The chairperson signs the minutes to say that they are a true record of what was discussed.

- Copies of the minutes are sent out to people who attended or who were invited but could not attend.

Your role in a meeting

- Always read the agenda before the meeting.

- Make sure that you are on time.

- If you cannot attend a meeting you should let the chairperson know. This is called sending your apologies.

- Take a diary and a pen and paper with you.

- Make sure that you have any documents or papers that you might need.

- Remember that meetings are your chance to have your say. There is no point in keeping quiet if you feel strongly about a subject and it is not professional to say nothing but complain later.

- Listen carefully to what is being said to avoid asking a question that has already been covered.

A multidisciplinary conference attended by father, educational pyschologist, teacher, speech therapist and social worker

Multidisciplinary meetings

There are times when people from several organisations need to come together for a meeting. An example of this is a case conference. Case conferences are held to discuss individual children's needs, sometimes because there is a child protection issue to discuss, or to review a child's learning. In order for the child's needs to be fully met, many different people involved with the family need to contribute. This may include the parents or their representative, a social worker, educational psychologist, the family's doctor, health visitor or school nurse.

If you are asked to attend a multidisciplinary meeting, it is a good idea to find out the roles of the people who will be attending. Apart from that you should prepare yourself in the same way as for any other meeting. All matters discussed should be regarded as confidential and you have a duty to respect this.

Knowledge into Action

You have been asked to evaluate your course so far. Arrange a meeting of your group.

1 *Choose one member of the group to be the chairperson and another to be the secretary.*
2 *Draw up an agenda that covers all the issues that your group wishes to raise.*
3 *Hold the meeting and distribute the minutes afterwards.*

Understanding your role as a provider of a service

In the past few years, attitudes among early years and educational workers have changed. There is a growing understanding that we must see ourselves as service providers and that the needs of children must always come first. This means that many organisations have started to listen more to what parents and children are saying. Some primary schools have started school councils so that children can raise issues with the staff. Private sector nurseries, crèches and other child care providers are often in competition with one another. This means that if parents do not feel their child is being well cared for, they will take their child (and their money) to another organisation.

Confidentiality

Confidentiality is about trust and loyalty. During the course of your work, you will learn personal information about children and their families, as well as business matters affecting the organisation. Parents and employers trust you not to break confidentiality rules by gossiping about what you have found out.

All information that you learn during the course of your work is confidential and you must be careful not to discuss it outside of the workplace or with anyone who does not have direct involvement. Breaking confidentiality is always serious and in many organisations it is a disciplinary matter that may lead to dismissal.

Respecting parents and children

Since parents and children are their clients, it is important that early years workers show respect when working with them. Early years workers must listen to their wishes. As professional workers, our own prejudices and personal feelings cannot be allowed to influence the way we work. Professional early years workers do not have favourite children, or parents they treat more favourably than others. It would be a little like a supermarket giving food away to some people and charging high prices to others! You have to learn to establish effective working relationships with other members of your team, and the same is true with parents and children.

Understanding accountability and responsibility

When you are offered a job in an organisation, you should be given a job description. This outlines your duties and responsibilities. It is essential that you read it and make sure you understand what you are required to do.

Most job descriptions tell you who your line manager is.

As an employee, you are responsible for carrying out the work in the job description, to the best of your ability. A good employee accepts this responsibility and does not try to make excuses for their mistakes. If you have any problems in carrying out the work, it is essential that you ask for help or clarification.

Case Study

Anne-Marie is responsible for keeping the paper cupboard tidy and for ordering paper and other equipment. After a month in the job, her line manager asks to see her to find out why the cupboard is in such a mess. Anne-Marie says that because one of the shelves is broken, the paper keeps falling out. She has had one go at tidying the paper, but until the shelf is fixed there is nothing that she can do.

Questions

1 Is Anne-Marie responsible for the cupboard being in a mess?
2 Why might other employees feel cross with Anne Marie?
3 Why is it important for areas such as the paper cupboard to be kept tidy?

CLAVERHAM DAY NURSERY
JOB DESCRIPTION

POST: Part time Nursery Assistant at Claverham Day Nursery
Hours 2.00–8.00 p.m. daily

GRADE: Day Grade 1: Scale Points 6–11: £8,721–£10,499 p.a. (pro-rata)

RESPONSIBLE TO: Nursery Manager

RESPONSIBLE FOR: Helping to ensure that a safe, secure, stimulating environment is provided in the Nursery, and providing a high standard of care for children 0–5 years.

Main Duties

1. To ensure that the aims and objectives of East Sussex County Council's Early Years childcare programme are met within the Nursery.

2. To have an awareness of the 1988 Children Act and to implement the standards of care set out in the Act.

3. To provide stimulating activities for the children, based on:-

   i) Emotional security and personal growth.
   ii) Social development and behaviour based on self-respect and respect for other children and adults.
   iii) Development of language and other means of self expression e.g. music, arts and crafts, etc.

Continued . . .

   iv) Physical activities which encourage co-ordination and independence with a proper regard to safety.
   v) Educational activities which encourage co-ordination and independence with a proper regard to safety.
   vi) Education activities based on guided pay with a wide range of materials.
   vii) Outings which include appropriate training in road safety.
   viii) Providing a warm, happy and safe environment.
   ix) Ensuring children with special needs are catered for.
   x) Making sure that Equal Opportunities Policy is complied with.
   xi) Liaising with parents and guardians.
   xii) Attending meetings as required.
   xiii) Supervision of meals and snacks.
   xiv) Making sure books and play equipment are maintained in good condition.
   xv) Keeping the nursery clean and tidy.
   xvi) Supervising students on placements, under the guidance of the Deputy Nursery Manager.

4. Such other duties as might reasonably be requested by the Principal.

This job description sets out the duties of the post at the time when it was drawn up. Such duties may vary from time to time without changing the general character of the duties or the level of responsibility entailed. Such variation are a common occurrence and cannot of themselves justify a reconsideration of the grading of the post.

In many organisations there is a system of staff appraisal. This means that employees have an opportunity to talk about their work and that employers are able to give feedback about the employees' performance. Most employees are appraised by their line managers. Sometimes an action plan is drawn up so that areas of weakness can be improved. This may mean that an employee is offered training to improve their performance. An appraisal can also be an opportunity for employees to draw to their line manager's attention a skill that they feel is not being used. For example, an employee might say that they would like to carry out more musical activities with the children.

In some organisations, staff appraisal is linked to pay and a line manager will use the job description to decide whether the staff member has been carrying out duties fully.

Loyalty and group accountability. Once you become an employee of an organisation, you become a small part of it. If the organisation has a good reputation, you share in its success. Being part of an organisation or team means that you need to think about what is best for that organisation or team as you share responsibility for its actions.

Case Study

Karen has had a long day at the crèche. She has put her coat on and is ready to leave when a parent comes in saying that her daughter left her coat behind yesterday. Karen explains that yesterday was her day off, so she does not know if the coat has been put away. She smiles and, seeing that the others in the team are busy, goes and looks in the lost property cupboard, finds the coat and signs it out in the book. She is now leaving 20 minutes late.

Questions
1 *Why did Karen feel that she had to sort this situation out?*
2 *Do you think that Karen should get overtime for staying on longer?*

Following instructions

Good employees understand that one of their duties is to follow instructions. Sometimes they may disagree with the instructions or may not like the task they have been given but as long as it is a fair and reasonable request, they will do it willingly. Employees who moan and try to get out of tasks will quickly find they are not considered for promotion. They will also find that other team members become irritated with them, especially if they have left a task unfinished.

When you are given a task, make sure that you understand exactly what you need to do and when the task needs to be completed. If you are unsure about whether you are capable of carrying it out, you should voice your concerns straight away.

Time management

In many jobs, people have more than one thing to do. They may have routine tasks to do as well as longer-term tasks such as ordering equipment or planning activities. A skill that new employees need to learn is how to use their time effectively. It is easy to fall into the trap of blaming lack of time for tasks not being completed.

When you have several tasks to do, it is often a good idea to consider which ones are absolutely essential and concentrate on those. Many employees write lists so that when they have some free time they can do one of the tasks. It is also a good way of making sure that you focus on the time that you have. Ten minutes is not a long time, but may be enough to complete a small task such as addressing letters to be sent home.

Some people set themselves goals – for example, 'By the end of today I will have finished the display and written three reports.' Goal setting can be useful because it divides the work into manageable tasks. Employees who find it difficult to use their time effectively are often wasting time by thinking 'There's no point in starting this, as I won't be able to finish it.'

Good practice – time management

✔ Make a list of tasks that need completing.

✔ Prioritise these tasks according to importance.

✔ Use small blocks of time to complete tasks that can be stopped and started easily.

✔ Do not put off jobs that you dislike – give yourself a target for when they should be completed.

Communicating with other employees

Most stress and conflict in teams is caused by differing views and poor communication. Learning how to work with other people is an important skill. We have looked at the role of team meetings as a way of sharing concerns and ideas, but it is also important to look at how people communicate on a day-to-day basis. In a team, everyone needs to pull together and support each other. If a team cannot do this, the quality of its work and subsequently the quality of care suffers. It is the role of the team leader to try to motivate a team, but unless people in the team can communicate well together, morale will be low.

Day-to-day communication is an important skill. There are three elements to communicating:

1 Courtesy and politeness
2 Recognition
3 Explanation.

1 Courtesy and politeness acts as the oil in day-to-day situations. Always remember to say please and thank you, even if you are in a rush. Small things such as holding doors open and offering to carry things if someone is overloaded make the working environment more pleasant.

2 Recognition of what other people think or do is also essential. No one in a team can manage alone and recognising other people's contributions and expertise helps build good relationships. You should thank a

Excuse me I'm busy!

member of the team who has helped you and you should listen to other people's points of view and respect them, even if you cannot share them.

3 **Explaining** your actions or your thoughts also helps day-to-day communications. You will get more help from your colleagues if you explain why you need equipment or if you explain why you disagree with an idea. Employees who do not take the time to explain tend to be thought of as arrogant or abrupt, although quite often this is not the case.

Think about it

Look at these two conversations.

Nursery Assistant: I need a copy of this letter for Mrs Smith.
Secretary: I don't know when I'll have the time to do it, I'm still finishing sorting out the wages.
Nursery Assistant: I'll just leave it here then and come back at lunchtime.

Nursery Assistant: Hello! You look like you're up to your eyes in it this morning.
Secretary: Yes, I'm sorting out the wages.
Nursery Assistant: I know this is a bad moment, but I need a copy of this letter for Mrs Smith. What shall I do with it?
Secretary: If you'd just like to leave it here, I'll do my best to get it done for breaktime.
Nursery Assistant: Thank you, I'm really grateful. I hope the morning improves.

1   *Why is the secretary in the second conversation more likely to copy the letter?*
2   *What has the nursery assistant in the first conversation done wrong?*

Planning and recording

Nearly all organisations plan and record. As an employee you will have to find out what types of planning and recording are expected of you. You may find that you have to plan the activities that you are going to carry out with children, showing the benefits; or you may find that this is done with other team members at team meetings. Some organisations plan for several weeks at a time, whereas others plan week by week.

Portfolio activity

Ask your workplace supervisor if you can see the types of planning and recording that happen in your workplace.

1   *Write about the planning and record keeping in your workplace.*
2   *Who is responsible for completing the plans and records?*
3   *Who checks that the work is done?*
4   *Are there special forms to fill in?*
5   *Is planning done in work hours?*

Find out from others in your group how their workplaces make plans and records.

In early years organisations, records are kept of children's attendance as well as ongoing records that allow staff to look at their progress.

Self-awareness means understanding and recognising your strengths and weaknesses. Try out this quiz!

Think about it

Are you a good employee?

Look at these statements and give yourself a score out of five.

0 = extremely poor   5 = excellent

1   *I am always on time.*
2   *I listen to what other people say.*
3   *I ask questions when I do not understand.*
4   *I enjoy meeting parents.*
5   *I never gossip.*
6   *I take a pride in my work.*
7   *I am good at working with other people.*
8   *I can follow instructions.*
9   *I enjoy learning new skills.*
10 *My personal problems never interfere with my work.*
11 *I do not mind staying late if necessary.*
12 *I can take the initiative.*
13 *I can see the funny side of things.*
14 *I am patient and understanding.*
15 *I never lose my temper.*

Show your scores for each of these questions to a friend or someone who knows you well. (If you are feeling brave, you could ask your tutor or a workplace supervisor.)

Do they agree with your scorings?

Further training

It is a mistake to think that once you have qualified there is nothing left to learn. Ideas about early years practice do change and finding out more keeps you fresh and enthusiastic.

To gain promotion and to develop a career, it is important that you keep studying and learning. For example, you may need to learn more about computers and information technology if your organisation is starting to use them more with children. You may decide that, to be able to take on more responsibility, you need to learn more about the business side of running an organisation. There are many long and short courses on offer and through further training, you may meet people who are also doing the same work as yourself.

It is always worth asking your local college about courses and looking at evening-class prospectuses.

You can contact CACHE, the examining board for child care qualifications, at:

8 Chequer Street, St Albans, Herts AL1 3XZ

Knowledge into Action

1 *Find out what further training in childcare your local college offers.*
2 *Find out where you can take a First Aid course.*
3 *Where would you go, if you needed further career advice?*

The rights and responsibilities of employers

TERMS AND CONDITIONS OF EMPLOYMENT

1) This statement dated .... sets out certain particulars
   of the terms and conditions on which

2) The Gables Day Nursery

3) Employs ....

4) Your employment with The Gables Day Nursery began on ....

5) You are employed as ....

6) You will be paid £ .... per annum on a monthly basis. Your
   salary will be reviewed annually.

7) Normal hours of work are Monday to Friday, between the hours of
   .... and ....

8) Your entitlement to holidays will include all public holidays and four weeks,
   one of which is to be taken between Christmas and The New Year.

9) Notification of absence from work due to illness or any other cause should
   be made on the first day that you will be absent from work to the
   appropriate member of staff. If you are absent for more than a working
   week, a doctor's certificate should be obtained. Statutory pay will operate
   where appropriate.

10) Maternity leave and pay is statutory.

11) The amount of notice of termination to be given is four weeks notice in
    writing. The Nursery will give four weeks notice to an employee who has
    been employed for less than two years and then one complete week
    for each complete year thereafter.

12) If you are dissatisfied with any disciplinary decision which affects you,
    you should raise the matter, in writing, with the Nursery Manager. The
    disciplinary rules which apply to you in your employment are attached.

13) Under the Health and Safety at Work Act 1974 it is the duty of all
    employees to confirm to policy and safety codes of practice and to
    accept and carry out their responsibilities.

14) You must be aware of, and promote all Nursery policies at all times.

.... Employee's signature to acknowledge receipt

of this statement .... date.

Once you have been offered a job that is for more than 16 hours per week, you should be offered a contract. A contract is a legal document that sets out what is expected of you and what you can expect of your employer. This is known as the terms and conditions of employment. It is important that you have a written contract, although some families who employ nannies do not use them. Under the 1978 Employment Protection Act and the Employment Acts of 1980 and 1982, employers must draw up a contract with any employee who works more than 16 hours a week.

The contract must contain:

▨ names of employee and employer

▨ title of post

▨ date of commencement

▨ scale or rate of pay

▨ hours of work

▨ entitlement to holidays

▨ provision for sick pay

- pension arrangements

- notice of termination of employment

- details of any disciplinary procedures.

It is important to read a contract carefully before signing as it is a legal document. If you find that you do not understand any part of it, you should always say so before signing. When you sign a contract, you are agreeing to follow the conditions of employment, which means that if you break them, you can lose your job.

When you are offered a job, it is important to find out when you will be paid. Most employers pay monthly or weekly. You will also need to give your employer your National Insurance number so that Income Tax and National Insurance contributions can be deducted from your wages.

In law, an employee has several duties to the employer which include:

To work – employees must turn up for work and work to a reasonable standard.

To obey orders – employees must obey lawful orders. But they cannot be asked to do anything dangerous or outside their contract of employment.

To take reasonable care – employees can be sued by their employer if they make mistakes and are not shown to have taken reasonable care.

Knowledge into Action

Ask your supervisor if you can be shown a contract of employment for your workplace.

1 *Do you understand it?*
2 *How many days holiday are employees entitled to?*
3 *How many hours of work a week are expected of a full-time employee?*

Trade Unions and professional organisations aim to improve working conditions for their members. They also provide advice and training for members.

The trade union movement began at the end of the 19th century when employees had no rights and workers realised that if they united, they would be able to stand up to the employers and obtain better working conditions.

The trade union movement today is well established and quite often employers and trade union officials have good working relationships.

All employees have the right to join an independent trade union and if employers prevent employees from doing so, they have to pay compensation. This does not mean that you have to join a trade union or a professional organisation.

Many people join trade union and professional organisations so that if they ever had a problem at work – for example, being treated unfairly or dismissed – they would be able to get support and advice. It is also possible to get independent advice from a local solicitor or Citizen's Advice Bureau. Below are the addresses of two unions often used by nursery nurses.

Professional Association of Nursery Nurses
St James Court
Friar Gate
Derby DE1 1BT
01332 343029

UNISON
1 Mabledon Place
London
WC1 H 9AJ
0171 388 2366

Working in the public sector

There are many opportunities for early years workers to work for health authorities, education authorities and services provided by local government. Below is a chart that outlines some of the work available. Types of work vary from area to area.

Employer	Types of jobs	Where to look
Health Authority	Assistants to health visitors Play workers in hospitals Nursery assistants in workplace nurseries	Write to the Health Authority Local newspapers Job Centres
Education Authority	Nursery assistants in state nurseries Classroom assistants Classroom assistants supporting children with special needs Midday supervisors	Write to the Education department and ask for a job vacancy list Contact schools directly Local newspapers
Local government services	Nursery assistant in family centres Nursery assistant in children's homes Play worker in the community	Most work is funded by the social services department Write to the headquarters of local government asking for a job vacancy list Local newspapers

There are advantages and disadvantages to working in the public sector. Pay and conditions are likely to be better than in the private sector, but jobs can be harder to find, especially with Health Authorities.

Recently, new employees in the public sector have found they are offered short-term contracts. This is happening because many of the services that are provided are funded on a yearly basis. Cutbacks to the public sector budgets often mean that services are reduced – for example, classroom assistants may have their hours cut or playworkers may find their contracts are not renewed.

Working in the voluntary and private sectors

There are many opportunities for early years workers in the voluntary and private sectors. Voluntary-sector employment is paid, but the organisations are not aiming to make a profit. For example, a charity such as NCH will employ nursery assistants and playworkers. Private-sector employment is ranges from families employing nannies to large holiday companies employing nursery assistants for their holiday clubs.

Employer	Types of work	Where to look
Voluntary sector (Charities and not-for-profit organisations)	Playworkers Nursery assistants After-school club assistants Playscheme and holiday club workers	Local newspapers Phone or write a letter to a local project Your local TEC will have details of after-school projects
Private sector Nursery schools Day nurseries Crèches Holiday clubs Play centres Leisure centres Crèche on cruise ship	Nursery assistants Play leaders for clubs Birthday party organisers	Local newspapers National newspapers Job centre Phone or write in directly to a business.
Families	Mother's help (help with children and housework) Nanny Au pair	Nanny agencies Local newspapers Nursery World magazine The Lady magazine Job centre

Voluntary sector work can be varied and interesting, although some types of work are not permanent or secure. Many charities and voluntary groups receive grants to fund their projects. Contracts cannot always be renewed once the grant has finished. It is a good idea, if you are taking a job that is funded by a grant, to find out how long the grant will last for.

Working in the private sector. There are a wide range of opportunities and in some businesses there is a career structure. Some types of employment such as working on a cruise ship or in a holiday club tend to be very competitive.

Working for a family. There are many 'nannying' horror stories. Working for a family is not always easy and many nannies are not aware that it can be lonely and hard work. On the other hand there are many happy families with happy nannies! The secret of being successful as a nanny is to find out exactly what is expected of you and to make sure that there is a written agreement between you and your employer. It is also important never to forget that you are working for an employer, not a friend, and so your work standards must be as high as if you were working in a nursery. Confusion about the relationship between nanny and employer can lead to both parties feeling hurt if things do not work out.

Knowledge into Action

Preparing for an interview can help in getting a job.

Working in pairs:

1   *Think about the types of childcare work that you might be interested in.*
2   *Prepare answers to the following 'classic' interview questions.*
3   *Ask each other the questions as if you were in a real interview situation.*
    *   *Tell me about yourself.*
    *   *What type of training have you done so far?*
    *   *What do you feel are your strengths?*
    *   *What do you feel are your weaknesses?*
    *   *What do you feel you can bring to this organisation/work/ family?*
4   *Give each other honest feedback – for example:*
    *   *Did your partner speak clearly?*
    *   *Did your partner look confident?*

2 Technical equipment and learning materials

Administrative and technical support

Most organisations today use a range of equipment such as computers, photocopying machines and faxes. We live in a world where technology is advancing and better, easier-to-use machines are continually introduced. This means that the learning environment for children is changing. As part of your role as an employee, you might be asked to use equipment or prepare learning materials for others. This section outlines the principles in using equipment and setting out learning materials to support others.

Types of equipment in early years settings

In many nurseries and classrooms you will see that a wide range of equipment is used to promote children's learning. This includes:

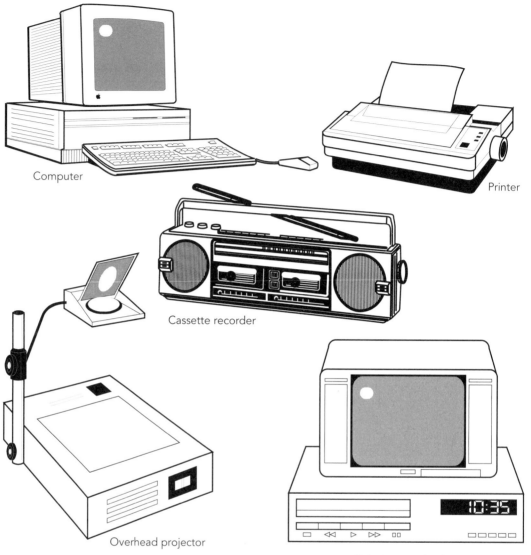

Computer

Printer

Cassette recorder

Overhead projector

Television and video

1 audio equipment (tape recorders and hi-fi equipment)

2 televisions and video recorders

3 overhead projectors and slide projectors

4 scientific equipment

5 computers and printers

6 photocopiers

7 fax machines.

Every type of equipment has its own uses, but there are some general principles when setting up equipment.

Safety

Equipment that uses electricity is a potential hazard to children and therefore the following safety guidelines should be used.

- Make sure that wire flexes are not damaged.

- Check that the wires going into the plug are not loose.

- Do not leave batteries lying around.

- Dispose of 'dead' batteries away from children.

- Do not leave equipment in reach of very young children.

- Tape down flexes where there is a risk of children or other adults falling over them.

- Remove equipment after use and store it carefully.

Manufacturers' instructions

Damage to equipment is often caused by people not taking time to read the instructions carefully. Every model and make of equipment is likely to work in a slightly different way, even if the principles are the same.

Instruction booklets should be carefully stored either with the equipment or in a central area.

What to do if the equipment is not working

There is nothing as frustrating as finding that a piece of equipment is not working. If you are setting up equipment for other people, you must leave it so that it is ready for use. This means that you need to allow enough time to check it after you have set it up. If equipment fails to work, remember the following.

Keep calm and think:
Is it plugged in?
Is it switched on?
Are the batteries flat?
Is there a loose flex?
Are all the parts present?

Read the manufacturer's instructions
Is there a fault-finding section?
Is there a helpline number?

Never start taking a machine to pieces!
You could invalidate the warranty and you may cause further damage.

Report the problem to your supervisor
Never put the equipment away without reporting the fault.
Leave a note on the equipment saying what is wrong with it, so that other people do not waste time trying to use it.

Spare parts

You may be responsible for ordering and keeping a check on spare parts. The idea of having spare parts is that equipment can be repaired and put back in use quickly. Spare parts should be carefully stored according to the manufacturers' instructions. This often means keeping them in a cool, dry place.

If you are ordering spare parts you must make sure that you know the model and make of the equipment. A spare part for one machine is unlikely to fit another make.

Manufacturers recommend that you buy spare parts approved by them.

Common spare parts may include bulbs for overhead projectors, ink cartridges for printers and headphones for cassette players.

1 Audio equipment is often used in early years settings to provide music for children to dance to or to allow children to record their work. It often includes cassette recorders and CD players.

Checklist for setting up audio equipment

- Find a safe place that is convenient for use.
- Check that the equipment is working.
- Have the tape or CD ready in the right place.

2 Televisions and video recorders come in many sizes. Some televisions and videos are in one unit and many use remote controls. Always be careful when lifting televisions and do not attempt to lift a large television. Televisions should be carried with the screen facing you.

Checklist for setting up televisions and video recorders

- Find a safe and stable place to put the equipment.
- Make sure that children will be able to see the screen.
- Check that you have the correct remote controls for these items.
- If using a television alone, check that the aerial is plugged in.
- If the television and video are separate, make sure that you have a connection from the video to the television.
- Find the AV channel on the television.
- Try out the video.
- Wind the video to the correct place.

3 Overhead projectors. An overhead projector allows written materials to be projected onto a board. They are not often used in early years settings, although they may be used in training situations.

A white screen or board is needed.

Checklist for setting up an overhead projector

- Put the overhead projector directly in front of the screen or white board.
- Use a table or the trolley designed for it.

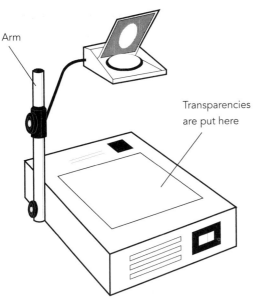

Arm

Transparencies are put here

- Plug it in and turn on the switch on the machine.

- Put on a transparency to check if it can be read easily.

- Move the arm of the projector up or down to improve the focus.

- Turn off the machine at the switch until ready.

4 Scientific equipment may include items such as magnets, thermometers, electrical circuits and mirrors. These tend to be kept in a separate area so that items do not get broken or lost. Some items such as thermometers are potentially hazardous as they are made of glass and some may contain mercury, which is a poison.

Setting up scientific equipment

- Find out exactly what is required from the person you are helping.

- Find out how they intend to do the work – do they want the equipment put into piles ready for different groups?

- Check all the pieces of equipment to see if they are damaged.

- After the activity, check the items again and store carefully.

5 Computers and printers are found in many early years settings. Software is specially designed to enable children to learn.

It is unlikely that you will have to set up a computer as most early years settings keep them on trolleys or on tables. You may be asked to turn on a computer and load a piece of software or to load up the printer with paper. It is important to be shown how to use the computer in your workplace, as there are many variations in doing these tasks.

Basic rules when using a computer

- Never turn off a machine without going through the closing down process – this can damage the machine.

- Learn how to save material on the computer.

- Do not load material from disks without knowing what is on them, or where they have come from. Some disks contain 'viruses' which damage the computer's memory.

6 Photocopying. There are many different types of photocopiers available. Most organisations find that a photocopier is essential. It is worth understanding some of the terms that are often used.

A4	the size of a piece of file paper (210mm × 297mm)
A3	the equivalent of two sheets of A4 put side by side (420mm × 297mm)
Single-sided	only one side of the paper is used
Double-sided	both sides of the paper are used
Enlarged	the photocopy is larger than the original document
Reduced	the photocopy is smaller than the original document

As photocopies can add significantly to an organisation's running costs, it is wise to be careful when photocopying. This means using A3 paper when you need to photocopy a double spread and trying to photocopy on two sides of a piece of paper. The most effective way to minimise costs is to make sure that you are using the machine properly and not making mistakes – for example, by laying the original on the glass plate the wrong way round.

Carrying out photocopying

1 Find out exactly how many copies are needed and in what form – e.g. double-sided or A3.

2 Check that the machine is on and that it has warmed up.

3 Lay the originals on the glass according to the machine's instructions.

4 Lower the lid gently.

5 Key in the number of copies and the size needed.

6 Most organisations have a book or paper to sign so that the amount of photocopying can be recorded.

7 Remove the original and paper-clip it to the top of the copies.

Common problems include having to reload the paper tray and coping with paper jams. To solve both of these problems, you will need to read the instructions or get help.

Newer machines can reduce and enlarge copies as well as collecting sets of them together in order (collating). To find out how to do this, you need someone to show you. It is worth taking a few notes so that you remember for another time.

Copyright restrictions

Copyright laws are designed to prevent people from copying material rather than buying it. This means that most books should not be photocopied. Always check that anything you are copying is not under copyright. Most books state that they are protected by copyright in the first few pages.

Portfolio activity

Ask your supervisor or your tutor if you can photocopy a document.

1 *Write down how copies are recorded.*
2 *Write down how to photocopy single-sided A4 paper.*
3 *Write down how to photocopy double-sided A4.*
4 *Does the machine reduce or enlarge copies?*
5 *Find out what you should do if there is a paper jam.*
6 *Find out what you should do if the machine runs out of paper.*

7 Fax machines. Many early years settings now have a fax so that documents and information can be transferred quickly. As machines can vary, it is important to find out how the one in your workplace works. Sending a fax is a simple procedure, although it is important to make sure that you insert the paper correctly. In some early years settings a record is kept of the faxes that are sent. If you are expecting to receive a fax, always check that there is sufficient paper in the machine.

Preparing materials

One of your roles may be to set out materials for activities in an early years setting. This may include putting out art and craft materials, PE equipment or even preparing a babyroom for a series of nappy changes.

Setting out and preparing materials

▪ Make sure that you know what needs to be put out.

▪ Find out where materials are to be laid out.

▪ Find out when it is required and for how many children.

▪ Allow enough time to find and put out the materials.

▪ If you cannot find the materials or are unsure about how to lay them out you must ask for help.

Art and craft materials. There are many types of material for art and craft which means that it is essential that you know what is required. Here are some examples of the types of materials that you may need to put out.

Paint	Collage materials	Paper	Glue	Crayons and pastels
Card	Brushes	Scissors	Pencils	Chalk

It is particularly important to find out what types of paint are needed: powder-paint, ready-mixed paint, watercolour tablets or poster paints!

Powder-paint needs mixing. Add a little water to the powder and form a paste, then gradually add in the rest of the water.

PE equipment is often put out for groups of children to use. It is important to find out exactly what is required and how it needs to be arranged. Be careful when lifting equipment – heavy equipment should not be lifted alone.

Most activities need to be set up and cleared away quickly – for example, when children are having their lunch or at snack time. This means that you have to work efficiently and know where everything is kept. As a new employee, you will need to spend some time finding out where all the resources are kept.

Portfolio activity

Ask your supervisor if you can set out an activity. Make notes as follows.

1 *What activity did you prepare?*
2 *What equipment and materials did you need?*
3 *How did you prepare them?*
4 *How long did it take you to set out the equipment and materials?*
5 *What did you learn from doing this activity?*

Keeping stock

Many organisations have stock cupboards so that they do not run out of paper or other supplies such as paint and glue. It may be your role to keep an eye on the

levels of stock. This means that you must regularly look to see what is there and what needs to be re-ordered. It is also important to monitor how quickly stock is going down and also to decide whether, at certain times of the year, extra supplies may be needed because of an event or work on a theme which is likely to put a strain on supplies.

When stocks are becoming low, you should inform your line manager so that the ordering process can begin. You should also alert your line manager if stock seems to be vanishing!

If you are in charge of the stock cupboard, you should make sure that everything is accessible, neat and, if possible, clearly labelled. This makes it easier for everyone to keep it tidy and it also means that you can see more clearly what is there.

You should keep rotating some types of supply – for example, glue and paint. New stock should be put at the back so that items are used in order of age. This prevents some items from being wasted because they have dried up or are past their best before date. Always check a new item of stock to see how it should be stored.

Dough, clay and other items for use with children should be stored according to the Health and Safety policy of your workplace. If you are unsure about storing items, you should talk to your line manager.

The 1994 Control of Substances Hazardous to Health regulations state that employers must store and dispose of chemicals and other toxic substances carefully. In early years settings, this means that bleach, disinfectants, oils and other chemicals have to be stored out of reach of children. If this is your responsibility, you should check with your employer's Health and Safety policy.

Knowledge into Action

Find out who is responsible for ordering stock in your placement.

1   *Where is stock kept?*
2   *Is any stock locked away? If so, why?*
3   *Which types of materials are ordered the most?*

Unit test

Quick quiz

1   Which of these jobs is most likely to be in the private sector?
    a   Early years worker in a playgroup
    b   Nursery assistant in a family centre
    c   Classroom assistant in an infant school
    d   Nursery assistant on a cruise ship.

2   A job description:
    a   sets out what the employer must pay you
    b   outlines the roles and responsibilities of your job.
    c   states how well you are doing in your job
    d   is a way of advertising a post.

3   The expression 'minutes of the meeting' means:
    a   how long the meeting lasted
    b   notes on what was said or decided at the meeting
    c   notes on who spoke the longest
    d   notes on how the meeting finished.

4   Under the 1974 Health and Safety at Work Act employees must:
   a   have a yearly medical
   b   have First Aid training
   c   follow the Health and Safety policy of the employer
   d   learn how to use fire equipment.

5   An employer should provide an employee with a written contract if they are working
   a   for more than 10 hours a week
   b   for more than 14 hours a week
   c   for more than 16 hours a week
   d   in an organisation where there are more than five people.

Short answer questions

1   Why should you never load material from disks onto computers, if you do not know where the disk has come from?

2   Name two types of materials that by law need to be stored safely.

3   Which is larger, a sheet of A3 or a sheet of A4?

4   If a book is protected by copyright are you allowed to photocopy it?

5   An electrical appliance does not seem to work. What are the first two things to check?

NVQ Matching Chart

Certificate	NVQ Level 2 Child Care and Education	NVQ Level 2 or 3 Early Years Care and Education
Module	**Core Units**	**Mandatory Units**
2 The Care and Education Environment	E1 Maintain a child orientated environment	E1 Maintain an attractive, stimulating and reassuring environment for children
3 Child Safety	E2 Maintain the safety of children	E2 Maintain the safety and security of children
4 Physical Care of the Developing Child	C2 Care for children's physical needs	C1 Support children's physical development needs C2 Provide for children's physical needs (level 3)
5 Provision of Food and Drinks for Children	C2 Care for children's physical needs	C1 Support children's physical development needs C2 Provide for children's physical needs (level 3)
6 Childhood Illness	C2 Care for children's physical needs	C2 Provide for children's physical needs (level 3)
7 Working with Young Children	C9 Work with young children	C8 Implement planned activities for sensory and intellectual development C9 Implement planned activities for the development of language and communication skills
8 Play and the Young Child	C8 Set out and clear away play activities	C8 Implement planned activities for sensory and intellectual development C9 Implement planned activities for the development of language and communication skills
9 Emotional and Social Development	C4 Support children's social and emotional development	C4 Support children's social and emotional development
10 Parents and Carers	P2 Establish and maintain relationships with parents of young children	P1 Relate to parents P2 Establish and maintain relationships with parents (level 3)
11 Understanding Children's Behaviour	C6 Contribute to the management of children's behaviour	C4 Support children's social and emotional development

Certificate	NVQ Level 2 Child Care and Education	NVQ Level 2 or 3 Early Years Care and Education
Module	Core Units	Mandatory Units
Option – Endorsements (2 units each) **A – Work with Babies**		
1a Caring for Babies 6 weeks–1year	C13 Care for babies	C13 Provide for babies' physical development needs
1b Feeding Babies 6 weeks–1 year	C12 Feed babies	C12 Feed babies
B – Work in Support of Others		
2a Working for Others	M3 Contribute to the achievement of organisational requirements	
2b Administrative and Technical Support	M1 Give administrative and technical support on request	M1 Monitor, store and prepare materials and equipment

Answers to Quick Quizzes

Chapter 1
1c/2b/3c/4b/5a/6c/7c/8b/9a/10d

Chapter 2
1b/2c/3d/4c/5b/6b/7a/8c/9a/10d

Chapter 3
1b/2c/3d/4c/5a

Chapter 4
1a/2c/3d/4b/5d

Chapter 5
1b/2a/3c/4a/5d

Chapter 6
1c/2a/3c/4d/5b

Chapter 7
1c/2b/3d/4b/5c

Chapter 8
1d/2a/3b/4d/5b

Chapter 9
1c/2b/3a/4d/5b

Chapter 10
1c/2a/3b/4b/5d

Chapter 11
1c/2b/3b/4c/5c

Chapter 12
1a/2b/3c/4b/5d

Chapter 13
1d/2b/3a/4a/5b

Chapter 14
1d/2b/3b/4c/5c

Index